New Meanings for Ancient Texts

New Meanings for Ancient Texts

Recent Approaches to Biblical Criticisms and Their Applications

EDITED BY
STEVEN L. MCKENZIE
JOHN KALTNER

© 2013 Westminster John Knox Press

First edition
Published by Westminster John Knox Press
Louisville, Kentucky

13 14 15 16 17 18 19 20 21 22—10 9 8 7 6 5 4 3 2 1

All rights reserved. No part of this book may be reproduced or transmitted in any form or by any means, electronic or mechanical, including photocopying, recording, or by any information storage or retrieval system, without permission in writing from the publisher. For information, address Westminster John Knox Press, 100 Witherspoon Street, Louisville, Kentucky 40202-1396. Or contact us online at www.wjkbooks.com.

Scripture quotations, unless otherwise indicated, are from the New Revised Standard Version of the Bible, copyright © 1989 by the Division of Christian Education of the National Council of the Churches of Christ in the U.S.A., and used by permission. Scripture quotations marked RSV are from the Revised Standard Version of the Bible, copyright © 1946, 1952, 1971, and 1973 by the Division of Christian Education of the National Council of the Churches of Christ in the U.S.A., and are used by permission.

Excerpts from Norman Habel, "Introducing Ecological Hermeneutics," in *Exploring Ecological Hermeneutics*, ed. Norman Habel and Peter L. Trudinger (Atlanta: SBL, 2008) are used by permission. All rights remain. Portions of chapter 4 have appeared in a previous work by the author, *The New Historicism* (Minneapolis: Augsburg Fortress, 2002) and are used with permission of the publisher. An earlier edition of the interpretative study on Genesis 18:1–15 in chapter 4 has appeared in a previous work by the author, "Why Did Sarah Laugh?" in *Distant Voices Drawing Near*, ed. Holly Hearon (Collegeville, MN: Liturgical Press, 2004), 57–67, and is used here by permission of the publisher. A fuller version of the discussion in "Jesus Reads the Scriptures" in chapter 7 was published in a previous work by the author, "Jesus Reads the Scriptures," in *Those Outside: Noncanonical Readings of the Canonical Gospels*, ed. George Aichele and Richard Walsh (London, T. & T. Clark, 2005), 1–16, and is used here by permission of the publisher.

Book design by Sharon Adams
Cover design by Dilu Nicholas
Cover illustration: Elegant red background layout with parchment © Attitude/shutterstock.com

Library of Congress Cataloging-in-Publication Data

New meanings for ancient texts : recent approaches to biblical criticisms and their applications / Steven L. McKenzie, John Kaltner, Editors. — First edition.
  pages cm
Includes bibliographical references and index.
ISBN 978-0-664-23816-2 (alk. paper)
1. Bible—Criticism, interpretation, etc. I. McKenzie, Steven L., 1953– II. Kaltner, John, 1954–
BS511.3.N49 2013
220.601—dc23

2013003065

∞ The paper used in this publication meets the minimum requirements
of the American National Standard for Information Sciences—
Permanence of Paper for Printed Library Materials, ANSI Z39.48-1992.

Most Westminster John Knox Press books are available at special
quantity discounts when purchased in bulk by corporations,
organizations, and special-interest groups. For more information,
please e-mail SpecialSales@wjkbooks.com.

To our colleagues in the Department of Religious Studies at Rhodes College

Contents

List of Contributors ... ix

Preface ... xi

1. Cultural-Historical Criticism of Bible
   Timothy Beal ... 1
2. Disability Studies and the Bible
   Nyasha Junior and Jeremy Schipper ... 21
3. Ecological Criticism
   Norman C. Habel ... 39
4. New Historicism
   Gina Hens-Piazza ... 59
5. The Bible and Popular Culture
   Linda S. Schearing and Valarie H. Ziegler ... 77
6. Postcolonial Biblical Criticism
   Warren Carter ... 97
7. Postmodernism
   Hugh S. Pyper ... 117
8. Psychological Biblical Criticism
   D. Andrew Kille ... 137
9. Queer Criticism
   Ken Stone ... 155

Index ... 177

Contributors

TIMOTHY BEAL
Florence Harkness Professor of Religion
Case Western Reserve University
Cleveland, Ohio
Cultural Criticism of the Bible

WARREN CARTER
Professor of New Testament
Brite Divinity School
Fort Worth, Texas
Postcolonial Biblical Criticism

NORMAN C. HABEL
Professorial Fellow
Flinders University
Bellevue Heights, Australia
Ecological Criticism

GINA HENS-PIAZZA
Professor of Biblical Studies
Jesuit School of Theology at Berkeley
Berkeley, California
New Historicism

NYASHA JUNIOR
Assistant Professor of Hebrew Bible and Old Testament
Howard University School of Divinity
Washington, DC
Disability Studies and the Bible

D. ANDREW KILLE
Editor of BibleWorkbench
Psychological Biblical Criticism

HUGH S. PYPER
Professor of Biblical Interpretation
University of Sheffield
Sheffield, UK
Postmodernism

LINDA S. SCHEARING
Professor of Hebrew Scriptures
Gonzaga University
Spokane, Washington
The Bible and Popular Culture

JEREMY SCHIPPER
Associate Professor of Hebrew Bible
Temple University
Philadelphia, Pennsylvania
Disability Studies and the Bible

KEN STONE
Professor of Bible, Culture and Hermeneutics
Chicago Theological Seminary
Chicago, Illinois
Queer Criticism

VALARIE H. ZIEGLER
Chair and Walter E. Bundy Distinguished Professor of Religious Studies
DePauw University
Greencastle, Indiana
The Bible and Popular Culture

Preface

This book has been conceived as a sequel to an earlier volume also published by Westminster John Knox Press: *To Each Its Own Meaning: An Introduction to Biblical Criticisms and Their Application*, edited by Steve McKenzie and our Rhodes College colleague, Stephen R. Haynes. That work, which was published in 1993 and followed by a revision in 1999, was designed as a textbook to serve a need that the editors saw for a single-volume introduction of major methods and approaches to study of the Bible for nonspecialists. Twenty years later it continues to serve this purpose and to be widely used in seminaries, colleges, and universities, largely because there is nothing else quite like it available.

Since the appearance of that first volume, the field of biblical studies has evolved and changed considerably, especially where methodological matters are concerned. "The Current Shape of Biblical Studies" in the introduction of *To Each Its Own Meaning* explains that the essays within the book represent several types of methods: traditional, historically oriented criticisms (historical, source, tradition-historical, form, and redaction); newer, literary-oriented ones (structural, narrative, reader-response, poststructuralist, and ideological); and some others that do not fit under either of those categories (social-scientific, canonical, and rhetorical). Six years later, the second edition added another example of ideological criticism that focused on socioeconomic reading in addition to the original article illustrating a feminist approach. The two articles testified to a growing movement in the field toward explicitly ideological and reader-oriented perspectives. Taken together, the various approaches treated in the book gave a good sense of the range of methods for study of the Bible that were prevalent at the time it was written.

What a difference twenty years make! While *To Each Its Own Meaning* remains a useful and reliable introduction to the methods it discusses, it does not adequately reflect the diversity of approaches that presently constitute the field of biblical studies. Scholars now regularly employ ways of studying the Bible that were either unheard of or in their infancy in the early 1990s. This becomes apparent if the most recent program book of the annual meeting of the Society of Biblical Literature, the largest organization of Bible scholars in the world, is compared to the one from 1993 when *To Each Its Own Meaning* was first published. There are now about twice as many program units—more than 160 now, and about 80 then—and many of them embrace new methods that have been widely accepted by scholars.

As these newer approaches become more established and influential, it is essential that students and other serious readers of the Bible be exposed to them and become familiar with them. That is the main impetus behind the present volume, which is offered as a textbook for those who wish to go further than the approaches covered in *To Each Its Own Meaning* by exploring more recent or experimental ways of reading. Of the approaches discussed here only one—psychology and biblical interpretation—had its own program unit in the 1993 Society of Biblical Literature meeting, and it was only in its third year of existence. Several others, like queer criticism and postcolonial criticism, were employed in individual papers that were read at that meeting, but they did not yet have a permanent "home" with their own program units as they do today. Still others treated in this volume, like those informed by ecological criticism and disability studies, are virtually absent from the 1993 program.

As diverse as the approaches treated here are from one another, we notice certain similarities in comparison with the 1993 collection that hint at further changes in biblical studies. For instance, all of the methods in 1993 were presented as criticisms, most with particular methodologies. However, such is not the case for the present assemblage. While most still sport the title "criticism," the authors, almost to a person, point out that their topics do not represent methods that can be delineated through a series of steps but are rather approaches or perspectives—ways of looking at the Bible. They are lenses, if you will, or angles for addressing its literature. This may be due in part to an interest on the part of practitioners in 1993 to counter charges of subjectivity and arbitrariness and to present their approaches as academically sophisticated and critical. Perhaps now there is less sense of defensiveness and more candor about the subjectivity of any interpretation, less call to pose as a programmatic *method* for getting at the meaning of the Bible and more recognition that we all read it from different, albeit sometimes shared, vantage points, be they ideologies, orientations, or, as in the case of psychology, the platform of insights from an adjacent discipline.

The format for this volume and our modus operandi as editors are very similar to those adopted for *To Each Its Own Meaning*. We have sought out leading pioneers of the approaches chosen here, and we have asked each of them to define and describe their approach as clearly as possible for nonspecialist readers and to relate it to other ways of reading. We also asked them to illustrate the approach "in action" with reference to a particular text or set of texts in either the Pentateuch or the Gospels. Finally, we asked them to explain and respond to any criticisms that have been leveled at the approach. As a further aid to readers, they have assembled a list of key terms and definitions relating to the approach and a set of bibliographic entries for further reading.

We wish to express our deep gratitude to the contributors for their collaboration in this project—for their enthusiastic willingness to take on the assignment, for the clarity with which they have written and presented their approaches, and for their promptness in sending their essays to us. We also wish to acknowledge our debt to our colleague, Steve Haynes, without whom *To Each Its Own Meaning* would never have come to be, and to our other colleagues in the Department of Religious Studies at Rhodes College, to whom this book is dedicated.

Working on this volume has led us to ponder the future of biblical studies as an academic discipline. What will a book of this nature look like in another twenty years? The vibrancy of the field and the pace of change make it impossible for us to predict, but we find it an exciting topic for speculation, and we hope that this book contributes in some small way to attract and engage future scholars in our discipline who will help to answer such questions.

Chapter 1

Cultural-Historical Criticism of Bible

TIMOTHY BEAL

Cultural-historical criticism of the Bible explores how biblical words, images, things, and even ideas of "the Bible" take particular meaningful forms in particular cultural contexts. It seeks not to interpret biblical texts but to interpret interpretations as productions of cultural meanings of the biblical, with the larger goal of elucidating and historicizing the biblical cultures in which these cultural productions live and move and have their being. Its aim, in other words, is not to understand the Bible but to understand the cultures in which the Bible takes on particular meanings and how those meanings are produced, reproduced, and transformed over time.

CULTURAL HISTORY

In academic discourse, cultural history refers generally to historical research that explores the ways meaning takes form within culture, often but not exclusively popular culture. Often drawing on anthropological approaches (some cultural historians prefer to be called historical anthropologists), it presumes that meaning is a matter of cultural production; it is produced and reproduced through our words, our actions, the things we make and use, and the media technologies by which we extend ourselves into our world. These words, actions, things, and media technologies are the ways a society expresses itself, revealing its more or less conscious desires, anxieties, sensations, memories, and so on. The cultural historian therefore treats these data as, to borrow Marjorie Garber's phrase, "symptoms of culture."[1] A symptom is a phenomenon that indicates a condition of some kind, a form of evidence, a sign. The cultural historian examines various cultural phenomena, be they "high" or "low," as symptoms by which she may diagnose cultural meanings, which are not always, indeed not often, explicit.

Cultural history has emerged over the past few decades out of, and sometimes over against, previously dominant Marxist base-superstructure approaches (e.g., the French *Annales* school and British and American social history), which understood a society's economic mode of production as the base, or cause, of all other aspects of social organization and culture.[2] Such social-historical approaches therefore treated cultural meanings as superstructural effects of the base economic system. Cultural history, on the other hand, takes such phenomena more seriously, on their own terms, as means of exploring how human beings, as cultural subjects, are both produced by culture and produce it.

The theoretical and methodological influences on recent cultural history are many and diverse. Several of the most influential anthropological approaches, moreover, are familiar to students of religion, including Mary Douglas's study of purity, pollution, and taboo in Leviticus; Edward Evans-Pritchard's work on magic and witchcraft; and Clifford Geertz's work on religion as a cultural system. Beyond these, two non-religionist scholars are particularly helpful in developing a cultural-historical approach to Bible: Raymond Williams on culture and the structure of feeling and Michel Foucault on discursive practices and the archeology of knowledge.[3]

Rejecting the elitist idea of culture as "high culture," the special possession of "cultivated people," Raymond Williams developed a theory of culture that incorporated two key aspects: on the one hand, the ordinary, that is, the commonly held meanings of a society's "whole way of life;" and on the other hand, the individual, innovative meanings that derive from arts and learning, and that can challenge the common and ordinary aspects of a culture.[4] Whereas the former aspect of culture is what makes it common and familiar, the latter is what explains individual difference and allows for cultural transformation.

Another key concept in Williams's understanding of culture that proves especially provocative vis-à-vis religion and biblical studies is what he calls the "structure of feeling," by which he refers to the specific character and quality of common cultural sense and lived experience. This lived experience involves

> . . . the interaction between "official" culture—laws, religious doctrine, and other formal aspects of culture—and the way that people live in their cultural context. The structure of feeling is what imbues a people with a specific "sense of life" and experience of community. It comprises the set of particular cultural commonalities shared by a culture despite the indi-

vidual differences within it. Cultural analysis of structure of feeling aims at uncovering how these shared feelings and values operate to help people make sense of their lives and the different situations in which the structure of feeling arises.[5]

Of course, all people in a given context do not share such feelings; these are, rather, the common feelings of the dominant culture. This fact points to a central theme in Williams's work: cultural struggle and resistance. How do power and dominance work within culture, and what dynamic relations make change and even revolution possible? Williams identifies three aspects, or dynamics, of any historical period within a culture: (1) *dominant* aspects of a culture, that is, the structures of feeling and common meaning that try to dictate and authorize certain behaviors and thoughts while discouraging or punishing others; (2) *residual* aspects, that is, older values and meanings from previously dominant cultural formations that have survived into new cultural contexts; and (3) *emergent* aspects, that is, new values and meanings that put pressure on dominant aspects of culture and indicate potential cultural shifts and changes. Culture, then, is never a monolithic whole but a system of dynamic relations in which different kinds of individual and collective power and knowledge are forming and re-forming.

The French philosopher and historian Michel Foucault has been especially influential in drawing attention to how such formations and re-formations of knowledge and power take place within a culture. He was especially interested in how our particular, individual thoughts, beliefs, and behaviors—indeed, our very selves and worlds—are constructed, largely unawares, by what he called discourses or discursive practices, that is, systems or "grids" of thought and meaning composed of shared worldviews, beliefs, values, ideas, and morals. This process of *subjection* to discourse is, paradoxically, the way we become thinking, acting *subjects* within society. Put simply, the ways we think and the truths we hold to be self-evident are cultural constructions, produced and perpetuated within discursive practices that are as familiar to us as the air we breathe.

The task of the cultural historian, then, is what Foucault describes as a kind of archeology of knowledge: to uncover these discursive practices, determine the structures and rules embedded within them that make them functional, and, in the process, to bring to light the fact that the various ideas, values, and practices that a culture takes for granted as self-evident and timeless have been produced and concretized through the "long baking process of history."[6] The things we take for granted as common sense—things we say we know, from medicine and madness to the state and religion—are not historical givens but are, rather, "discursive objects" that take form within the systems or grids of thought and meaning within which we exist. They are "truth-effects" produced within those systems through concrete, everyday human practices.

But how, then, does change happen? Where do new ideas and courses of action come from? What are the mechanisms by which the thinkable within a culture might alter and shift? How are new truth-effects produced? What particular, individual, concrete practices effectively disrupt currently operative grids of knowledge and power and produce new ways of thinking and acting? To address these questions calls for an approach that biblical scholars might describe as *exegetical*: eschewing generalizations and universal claims, one must attend very closely to the specific details of particular texts, objects, and practices within a cultural archive, treating them as individual discursive practices that produce or reproduce unique forms of knowledge within particular cultural-historical contexts.

CULTURAL HISTORY OF BIBLE

Recall our initial definition of cultural history in general from the beginning of the last section: it explores the ways meaning takes form within culture. The cultural history of Bible, then, explores the ways the meanings of biblical texts, images, and "the Bible" itself take form within culture. It, too, presumes that such meanings are matters of cultural production; they are produced and reproduced not only through spoken or written words but also through popular media, material objects, and embodied actions. These words, things, actions, and media technologies are the ways a culture expresses its conceptions of the Bible and the biblical. The cultural historian of Bible, therefore, treats these data as meaning-bearing signs, "symptoms" of biblical culture.

The absence of a definite article, "the," in "cultural history of Bible" is not a typo. The proper focus of cultural-historical criticism in biblical studies is not *the* Bible, but Bible. We omit the definite article because "Bible" is, from the perspective of cultural history, indefinite. It is not a singular thing or a self-evident object of our intellectual analysis; it is not eternal; it has never been fixed or unchangeable; its form, content, and meaning change within different cultural networks of knowledge and power. Particular concepts of "the Bible" are produced through particular cultural practices, including collective and individual ritual, education, publishing, media technology, and so on. Such practices generate a sense of "Bibleness," a discursive formation of the Bible and the biblical that is both an ideological object and, as Williams might put it, a structure of feeling.

A cultural-historical approach to Bible, therefore, presupposes that Bible is not a thing but an idea that is culturally produced and reproduced. What Foucault said of other subjects of historical research, such as medicine and the state, may also be said of the Bible and the biblical: they are not given or self-evident intellectual objects to be particularized or incarnated in various interpretations through time; they are, rather, formulations of discourse, constantly changing as they are made and remade in different cultural productions of meaning. "The Bible" that predominates American evangelical culture today, for example, is the product of a network of loosely related cultural products and practices, from teaching and preaching in churches, to group Bible studies for adults and youth, to personal devotionals, to Bibles and biblical curricula produced and marketed by large evangelical publishing houses, to name a few. All these, moreover, are embedded within larger cultural networks of power and knowledge, and all are susceptible to larger processes of cultural transformation. How, for example, will the current media revolution affect "the Bible" as discursive formulation in evangelical Christian culture? To what extent is its general concept of the biblical tied to print culture, especially to the idea of the print book, and how might it change vis-à-vis the rise of digital network media culture?

It follows, then, that a cultural-historical approach in biblical studies does not separate literary content from material form. There is no such thing as a disembodied Bible or biblical text. Bible is always material as well as symbolic, sensual as well as semantic. The cultural history of Bible is about things as much as ideas, forms as much as contents, performances as much as interpretations, media as much as message. One cannot separate contents, words, or message from material form and media technology. The first verse of Genesis in a handwritten Hebrew Torah scroll sung by a cantor in a Shabbat service is not the same as the first verse of Genesis in a contemporary English version "Biblezine" read alone during quiet time at a Baptist Bible camp retreat is not the same as a production of *Jesus Christ Superstar* at the local public high school.

The main precursor to cultural history of Bible is biblical reception history, which explores the history of the reception of biblical texts, images, stories, and characters through the centuries in the form of citation, interpretation, reading, revision, adaptation, and influence.[7] Rooted in literary theorist Hans Robert Jauss's "aesthetics of reception" and, behind Jauss, the philosophical hermeneutics of Hans-Georg Gadamer, biblical reception history finds the meaning of a text neither in the text itself nor in the experience of the reader, but in the relationship between the two.[8] With Jauss, biblical reception history insists that biblical texts do not exist independent of the history of their reception by readers; their meaning is, rather, a dynamic, historically situated *relationship* between production and reception—in Gadamer's terms, a "fusion of horizons" of the text and reader(s).[9] As such, biblical reception history moves beyond earlier research into the history of biblical interpretation, insofar as it embraces a much broader definition of "interpretation," including not only academic and theological readings but also biblical appearances in visual art, literature, music, politics, and other cultural works.

Yet, whereas reception history focuses on the impact or influence of biblical texts, the cultural history of Bible focuses more sharply on the cultural meaning of them, as well as of "the biblical" and "the Bible" itself, insofar as those too are cultural constructs whose meaning and value are culturally contextual. Indeed, a cultural-historical approach begins with the fact that there is no singular, fixed, original "the Bible" or "the biblical" to be received across history; rather, there are multiple, often competing, symbolic and material productions of them that are generated and generative in different scriptural cultures. In this light, the cultural history of Bible inverts traditional biblical interpretation, including reception history: it is less about interpreting the Bible via culture than it is about interpreting culture via Bible.

CULTURAL HISTORY OF BIBLE IN PRACTICE

The cultural history of Bible is a field, not a method. There is no single prescribed disciplinary procedure, but rather a range of approaches, drawing on different disciplines, all aimed at understanding how meanings of biblical texts, images, and values in particular, as well as meanings of the Bible and the biblical in general, are generated within particular cultural contexts through particular discursive practices. Within this range of cultural-historical biblical research and analysis, we may identify three general approaches. What follows are examples of each.

1. Ethnographic Approaches

First, there are anthropological approaches that analyze particular biblical practices, such as group Bible studies, worship services, and individual devotionals. These approaches usually involve extensive ethnographic fieldwork, including close observation of such practices and interviews with participants. An excellent model is anthropologist James S. Bielo's book, *Words upon the Word: An Ethnography of Evangelical Group Bible Study*.[10] Bielo observed 324 Bible study meetings of nineteen groups over more than a year and a half. In the course of his research, he became interested in the ways these groups managed disagreements and tensions among different readings of particular biblical passages and how these differences often related to different understandings of the Bible more generally. He observed that successful group facilitators were able to foster certain "textual practices" *with* the Bible—how to read, cite, and interpret particular passages, for example—and "textual ideologies" *about* the Bible, especially ways of asserting the idea of the Bible as the only absolute, infallible authority for faith and life. Insofar as leaders were able to inculcate these practices and ideologies within the group, they were able to downplay differences among participants. At the same time, that sense of unity among members served to keep out any potential participants who could not conform. While studying Proverbs 11–12, for example, a participant in one group questioned the text's proclamations that the righteous always prosper while the wicked suffer—"when I see faithful people take it on the neck. How do you square that?" Without dismissing or directly challenging the question, the facilitator steered the discussion back to the group's agreed presupposition of biblical authority. "I don't have all the answers. All I'm saying is that this is a book of promises from beginning to end.... We have life, and a better life, by claiming all the promises in this book as ours."[11] Although the man's experience may appear to contradict scriptural authority in that moment, the leader suggests, continuing to claim it as such will in the long term be a blessing—not only to the individual but to the group as a whole. That man, Bielo later notes, quietly quit attending the group. Here and in other cases, Bielo reveals how the often subtle governing of "words upon the Word" within Bible study culture works to downplay hermeneutical and theological differences and tensions that could otherwise fragment not only the group but also the very Word that is believed to be its foundation.[12]

Another example of the ethnographic approach to the cultural history of Bible is Dorina Miller Parmenter's analysis of the public display among American evangelicals of heavily worn Bibles and the phenomenon of "duct-tape Bibles," including not only Bibles whose worn-out covers and binders were repaired with duct tape, but also brand-new duct tape Bibles sold by large evangelical publishers who understand that there is sacred capital in that well-used look.[13] Parmenter's interest is in "how status and authority is generated not only through semantic meaning, but also through material and embodied actions." These seemingly mundane, everyday biblical practices around the proud display of worn-out, taped-up Bibles contributes to the cultural production of the Bible as icon within evangelical Christianity, even as it identifies the carrier of such a Bible as a certain kind of "Bible believer" who lives so thoroughly "in the Word" that she or he literally, lovingly wears its material form out, like a biblical version of *The Velveteen Rabbit*.

2. Analysis of Biblical Products

A second approach to cultural history of Bible focuses on close reading and analysis of particular biblical media, that is, particular Bibles and related products, which may be studied either as a whole or with regard to their presentations of particular biblical texts, images, or stories. Understanding that the medium is the message, such an approach attends not only to the translation of the text but also to material form, the media technologies employed, the visual appearance and layout of the text, as well as the value-adding, (and often *values*-adding), supplemental notes and commentary.[14] Consider, by way of brief example, the presentation of Leviticus 18 and 20 and the issue of homosexuality in Zondervan's *NIV Teen Study Bible*, which has sold over 2.5 million copies and is the best-selling Bible among twelve- to fifteen-year-olds.[15]

Hebrew Scriptures and the New Testament do not clearly address contemporary debates among Christians about homosexuality. In fact, Hebrew Scriptures have very little explicitly to offer by way of moral teaching or legislation on matters of sexuality in general, let alone homosexuality. Two passages in the legal corpus of Leviticus (18:22 and 20:13) prohibit a man from lying with another man "as he lies with a woman." This prohibition appears along with prohibitions against bestiality; adultery; sex with a menstruating woman; and marrying a divorced woman, a former prostitute, or a brother's widow (a practice that is in fact required elsewhere, in Deut. 25:5; cf. Gen. 38:8). Neither text prohibits homosexuality per se. They do not address lesbianism or even sexual orientation. All they do is prohibit male-male intercourse. In fact, as Danna Nolan Fewell and David Gunn have argued, a close analysis of the Hebrew text of this prohibition in context makes clear that the chief concern here is not sexual behavior per se but the wasting of male seed by putting it where it cannot bear fruit.[16] Nor is Leviticus typically considered a go-to text for Christian ethics and morality. It also prohibits eating shellfish and pork, wearing mixed-fiber clothing, and planting different plants in the same garden. It also requires ritual sacrifices and condones slavery.

Jesus in the New Testament has nothing to say about homosexuality and very little to say about sexuality in general. Paul's letters do indeed disparage some specific male-male sexual practices common in the larger Greco-Roman society (e.g., pederasty, or sexual "mentoring" of young men by older men, and soliciting young male prostitutes), but they do not explicitly condemn consensual same-sex relations between adults. The simple fact is that Christian Scriptures are not clear on this issue. It is a matter of biblical interpretation and ethical reflection in which faithful Christians can and do disagree.

Yet, like many other Bibles marketed to teens, the *NIV Teen Study Bible* incorporates "supplemental" elements that effectively produce what is commonly called the "biblical view" of homosexuality, "what God says" about it, namely, that it is a sinful abomination. On the same page as Leviticus 18:22 in this Bible, there is a "The Bible Says" feature with the bold heading, "Only One Right Choice." Laid out in orange text in a contemporary, sans-serif font and highlighted with a blue swoosh that makes it jump off the page and leave the traditionally biblical looking (serif font) Levitical text in the background, this bold feature decries the idea that homosexuality could be an "alternative lifestyle." According to it, Leviticus 18 clearly states, "It's wrong to have homosexual sex," and "this isn't the only Bible passage that says homosexual sex is a sin. Read also Romans 1:26–27. If someone tells you homosexuality is an alternative lifestyle—meaning that it's OK—don't let those words fool you. It's an alternative all right. A sinful one."

Four pages later, near Leviticus 20:13, there is a full-page image of a sheet of lined stationery with a handwritten note from "Chris in Crystal Springs" addressed to "Dear Sam," the fictional advice columnist who responds to letters like Chris's about teenage concerns throughout this Bible. The lined page looks like a note that's been torn from a notepad and slipped into Chris's Bible at this particular spot. In the note, Chris writes that he doesn't understand how he can follow Jesus' teaching to love everyone, including homosexuals, without accepting their "alternative lifestyle." A response to "Dear Chris," hand-signed by Sam of "Dear Sam Inc." on what looks like a light orange post-it note stuck on top of Chris's letter, gives the answer: love the sinner but hate the sin; understand that the Bible is very clear that homosexuality is a sin. "You can't approve of something evil that God has forbidden."

These "Dear Sam" additions, which visually jump off the page even as the biblical text recedes into the background, generate a familiar, paternal (father-son or pastor-youth) dialogue between an earnest young questioner and an authoritative elder who speaks not only for the Bible but also for God. This dialogue places the reader of the *NIV Teen Study Bible* in the subject position of a youth who moves from honest questioning, based on what he's heard in other dialogues apart from the Bible, to an authoritative answer in the Bible, from worldly problem to biblical resolution. In the process, it overwrites the ambiguity that exists in the texts of Leviticus, thereby leaving no room for the reader to consider other interpretations.[17] The sticky note literally covers the question. All the while strongly asserting, visually and rhetorically, that Sam's answer is in fact the Bible's, and God's, unequivocal answer.

Such features in the *NIV Teen Study Bible* and many others like it purport to "supplement" or "amplify" the biblical text, but they do more than that. Visually and rhetorically, they are the center of attention, a necessary supplement that in fact reproduces a certain conservative evangelical, morality-oriented understanding of biblical values and of the Bible as a source for answers to practical questions, especially about sex.[18] Practically speaking, they become part of the Bible, if not its central and unifying voice. It would be perfectly understandable for a thirteen-year-old with an *NIV Teen Study Bible* to say that the Bible clearly prohibits homosexuality and that it's not an alternative lifestyle. The Bible says so. Or was that "Dear Sam?" Either way, it's what the Bible says. That is to say, the *NIV Teen Study Bible* is not the Bible *plus* a lot of supplemental commentary and "Dear Sam" features; for Chris and readers who identify with him, it is *the Bible*. Put another way, from a cultural-historical perspective, it is a cultural production of the Bible, and as such reifies commonly held biblical values that are part of a larger network of meaning.

3. Analysis of Cultural Interpretations of Bible

A third approach, and the most common in biblical studies, focuses on the critical examination of particular cultural productions in which interpretation or representation of biblical texts, stories, images, or even of the Bible itself figures prominently. Often such an approach focuses on mainstream works of popular culture in which Bible is a prominent dimension. Consider, for example, studies of movies or television shows that tell biblical stories, such as the Gospel narrative of Mel Gibson's 2004 film, *The Passion of the Christ*, or of Pier Paolo Pasolini's 1964 film, *Il vangelo secondo Matteo* (*The Gospel According to Matthew*), or the Joban tale of the *South Park* episode, "Cartmanland," in which Kyle believes he is reliving the biblical story of Job, asking why the wicked prosper and questioning God's justice, when he is smitten with the ultimate hemorrhoid after Cartman inherits $1 million and opens a lucrative amusement park.[19]

Others, however, focus on marginal or "outsider" cultural productions of the Bible and the biblical. One especially disturbing and fascinating example is the "Phineas Priesthood" phenomenon within radical white supremacist movements, inspired by a story in Numbers 25 about divinely sanctioned violence for the sake of ethnic and religious purity.[20] In the 1990s, the "Phineas Priesthood" emerged within Christian white supremacist culture as the privileged title for those who rise up to enact militant racist terror in the name of God. Here are a few examples:

> After being convicted of murdering an interracial couple at a Greyhound bus station in Spokane, Washington, a skinhead named Chris Alan Lindholm referred newspaper reporter Bill Morlin to the story of Phineas in Numbers 25 as his justification. "I wasn't mad at them or anything. I just knew they should die for what they had done. I think he put his arm around her or something."[21]
>
> Members of the Aryan Republican Army, a militantly anti-Jewish organization that robbed twenty-two banks during 1994 and 1995, identified themselves with the "Phineas Priesthood."[22]
>
> In April of 1996, cars parked at a Unitarian-Universalist fellowship in Idaho Falls were leafleted with anti-gay tracts signed by "The Phineas Priesthood" declaring those who transgress biblical law to be "walking death sentences." They described the 1986 murder and bombing at an adult bookstore in North Carolina as actions of "Phineas Priests" who carried out divine judgment against transgressors of biblical law, and warned, "In cities and towns all over America, names and addresses of law violators are being compiled. Six-man teams are forming across the nation. Soon, the fog that comes from Heaven will be accompanied by a destroying wind of a righteous God."[23]
>
> White supremacist Buford O'Neal Furrow, who went on a shooting spree at a Los Angeles area Jewish community center in August 1999, called himself a "Phineas Priest."

The biblical inspiration for these self-ordained Phineas Priests is the story of Phineas in Numbers 25. In that story, the Israelites are suffering from a deadly plague the narrative presents as the result of their intermixing with Moabites, signifying a transgression of religious-devotional purity and integrity. That is, the significance of Israelites marrying the daughters of Moab is that they are adopting their religious practices (25:2), to the extent that "Israel joined himself unto Baal-peor; and the anger of the LORD was kindled against Israel" (25:3). In a jealous rage, God tells Moses to hang all the leaders of the people so that his rage may abate. As Moses orders his judges to slay everyone who has been "joined to Baal-peor" (25:4–5), an Israelite man named Zimri and a Midianite woman named Cozbi come into the presence of Moses and the weeping congregation. Seeing this apparently brazen couple, a priest named Phineas (Aaron's grandson) leaves the congregation, follows the couple into their tent, and runs them both through their bellies on the same spear (25:7–8). In immediate response to this zealous double murder, God stays the plague against the Israelites and blesses Phineas, giving him and his descendants "my covenant of peace . . . even the covenant of an everlasting priesthood; because he was zealous for his God, and made atonement for the children of Israel" (25:11–13).

Phineas is also mentioned in Psalm 106, in a recollection of Israel's wilderness wanderings. The psalm praises Phineas for taking a stand and executing judgment in response to the religious unfaithfulness of the Israelites, declaring that his zeal was "counted unto him as righteousness," exactly as Abraham's faith was "counted unto him as righteousness" in Genesis 15:6.

The relationship between these two biblical representations of Phineas and militant white racist appropriations of the title "Phineas Priest" is not entirely self-evident. Throughout most of the history of biblical interpretation in Judaism and Christianity, readings of the Phineas story in Numbers 25 and Psalm 106 have emphasized the sin of *religious* intermixing rather than familial intermixing as the reason for God's and Phineas's righteous indignation. Psalms, after all, mentions no specific sin, and although Numbers 25 does initially mention that the Israelites were joining themselves to the daughters of their enemies (25:1), the narrative emphasizes the religious consequences of these new familial bonds, namely, that the Israelites were joining themselves to other gods. How, then, did this biblical story come to play such a central role in the formation of radical white racist identity?

The missing link is white supremacist theologian and financial advisor Richard Kelly Hoskins's 1990 book, *Vigilantes of Christendom: The Story of the Phineas Priesthood*, which presents a glorified postbiblical lineage of "Phineas Priests" who have committed acts of violent racial and moral purification out of righteous jealousy for God's Law, and which summons a new generation of white Christian zealots to similar action: "There are those who obey God's Law and those who don't. Those who obey are the Lawful. Those who disobey are outlawed by God. God has specified the outlaw's punishment. The Phineas Priests administer the judgment, and God rewards them with a covenant of an everlasting priesthood."[24]

Hoskins's book presents what he describes, echoing Numbers 25, as the story of an everlasting lineage of Phineas Priests who fought to the death in defense of God's laws, enforcing racial purity and Christian identity, and biblical prohibitions against usury, among other things. Beginning with the biblical story of Phineas, Hoskins's lineage includes legends like Saint George and Robin Hood, heroes in the "war of northern aggression" like the Confederate general Nathan Bedford Forrest and Lincoln's assassin, John Wilkes Booth, and the vigilante executioners responsible for thousands of post–Civil War lynchings, among many others.

Biblical passages are interwoven throughout Hoskins revisionist history. These passages are often inserted into the text, indented in a bold or italic font, without any explanation. In many cases, moreover, Hoskins drastically abbreviates the passages he quotes with ellipses, as in this example from the last pages of the book:

> How long can one expect it to be before six men at a time gather at brass altars with drawn weapons?
>
> > 'Cause them that have charge . . . to draw near, even every man with his destroying weapon . . . six men came . . . and one man . . . with a writer's inkhorn at his side: and they went in and stood beside the brazen altar . . . And to the others he said . . . Go ye . . . and smite: . . . and begin at my sanctuary. Then they began at the ancient men (elders) which were before the house' (Ezek. 9.1–6).
>
> Does one actually expect an impoverished Saxon [equated by Hoskins with Israelite] to pass by and look over the iron fence at Goliath living unpunished in his mansion, one who is known to have committed capital crimes against God, and yet securely lives on Saxon land and feasts on Saxon wealth?[25]

So Hoskins continues, riffing on the David and Goliath story with nary another mention of Ezekiel 9. Of course, this passage provides inspiration, albeit somewhat obliquely detailed inspiration, for the ensuing battle of the righteous against the powers that be. Does it also suggest a role for Hoskins himself as the writer whose destroying weapon is the inkhorn of self-publishing? Hoskins leaves that to the reader to determine. On the one hand, the rhetorical effect of quoting biblical passages in this way, setting them off from the rest of the text with little or no explanation, is that they *appear* to have authority to speak for themselves. They need no interpretation. On the other hand, the multiple ellipses that Hoskins uses to abbreviate and streamline the passages he quotes undermine this implicit assertion of the autonomous authority of Scripture. Thus Hoskins's method of biblical quotation—inserting highly truncated passages into his text with little or no prose explanation—allows him to interpret the text without appearing to do so. His interpretation is located in the placement and streamlining of the quotations.

This rhetorical strategy is very clear in Hoskins's presentation of the biblical story of Phineas. Although it is the foundation for his entire revisionist history, his presentation of this story occupies less than a page of text, including quotations. It begins with a highly abbreviated quotation of Numbers 25:6–13, indented and in italics:

> One of the children of Israel came and brought . . . a Midianitish woman . . . and when Phineas . . . saw it, he rose up from among the congregation and took a javelin in his hand; . . . and thrust both of them through . . . and the Lord spoke . . . saying Phineas . . . hath turned my wrath away from the children of Israel, . . . that I consumed not the children of Israel . . . Behold I give unto him my covenant of peace: . . . and his seed after him, even the covenant of an everlasting priesthood: because he was zealous for his God, and made an atonement for the children of Israel (Num. 25.6–13).[26]

This abbreviated rendition of the story in Numbers 25 zeros in on Phineas's action and God's reward. Note, moreover, that Hoskins elides those details in the biblical text that emphasize concern about *religious* intermixing, thereby implying that the transgression was that of ethnic (for Hoskins, racial) intermixing.

After this quotation from Numbers 25, and without further interpretive commentary on that text, he moves immediately to Psalm 106:29–31, which thereby serves as a means of explaining the lesson of the longer story in Numbers, namely, that "plague results from violating God's instructions." The effect of laying the two texts out together, with one immediately following the other, is that Numbers 25 tells the story and Psalm 106 gives its lesson. Remember, moreover, that Hoskins's abbreviated version of the Numbers story makes it into a story about racial rather than religious intermixing. Thus the logic of Hoskins's interpretation goes as follows: (a) God brought a plague on Israel because they were practicing racial intermarriage, which is against God's law; (b) by killing a racial intermixer, Zimri, Phineas executed judgment against Israel on behalf of God's law; (c) in response to this action on behalf of the law of racial purity, God lifted the plague and blessed Phineas on account of his zealous action, which was reckoned to him as righteousness. Thus Hoskins renders the biblical story of Phineas as a story that ordains racial violence as a primary defense of divine law, reckoning as righteous those who zealously carry out such violence. Yet the rhetorical effect of his presentation gives the impression that he is not imposing a racist interpretation on these texts, but rather is simply presenting the Bible as it stands and letting it speak for itself.

Indeed, Hoskins's interpretation represents a dramatic shift in focus, concerned as it is with a certain modern idea of *racial* purity as much as it is with religious purity. This shift involves highlighting some aspects of the story that traditionally have been overlooked, especially the scandal of ethnic or tribal intermixing. Whereas Christian and Jewish traditions have focused on religious intermixing in the story, Hoskins focuses on the ethnic intermixing intermarriage of Israelites with non-Israelites. Hoskins pushes this reading further, moreover, by importing a modern idea of race, however foreign to ancient Near Eastern cultures, and thereby suggesting that the unlawful intermarrying in the story is interracial rather than simply inter-ethnic or inter-familial. Indeed, like many other white supremacists steeped in the theology of Christian Identity, Hoskins sees the Israelites, God's holy people, as "white" and the Midianites as ungodly "blacks," and history as the racial holy war of the "Christian separatist God" and his people against the diabolical threat of miscegenation.[27] For Hoskins, religious identity is racial identity.

For Hoskins, then, the crime of Zimri and his fellow Israelites was miscegenation of holy whites with unholy blacks. Phineas's zealous act of murder rose from the desire to maintain the holy purity of the image of God within Israel, which is the central aim of all biblical law. This is why the four self-proclaimed Phineas Priests affiliated with white supremacist religious organizations mentioned above bombed both Planned Parenthood (for murder) and local banks (for usury).[28] This is also why Aryan Nations and other organizations call people who are homosexual "walking death sentences" (for sexual transgressions of the biblical law). These activities are taken as transgressions of God's Law, and as such they threaten to brown the whiteness of the law-abiding "Adamic Man," who for Hoskins is the very image of God.

Hoskins's idea of the Phineas Priesthood is, of course, an easy target for criticism, rife as it is with deep ironies. From an academic perspective, for example, it is certainly ironic that the biblical law to which Hoskins vows devotion, and which Phineas and his modern-day, anti-Jewish white heirs struggle to defend, is probably rooted in postexilic Judean "Priestly" traditions. Not to mention the irony within the biblical narrative itself that Moses, like Zimri, married a Midianite. But the sense of irony has never been strong among the religiously racist right.

Ironies notwithstanding, the fact is that the idea of the Phineas Priesthood, set within its larger racist biblical interpretive framework, works to produce a certain concept of the Bible and biblical values, as well as certain biblical practices. It does so by ordaining further militant racist action—"Phineas acts"—as divine commission, reckoned as righteousness, and placing the modern-day Phineas Priests who carry out those acts within a larger biblical narrative of racial holy war, a great cloud of witnesses stretching back to the biblical Phineas and forward to ultimate divine victory. In short, they become part of the Bible's grand narrative. In the process, moreover, the Phineas ideal provides a biblically based set of unifying terms for an otherwise extremely disparate and centerless movement, thereby lending a sense of collective religious identity and social coherence out of a smattering of isolated, more or less underground, organizations and individuals—from neo-Nazis to Christian Identity parishioners to phantom cell militias. Indeed, although seldom recognized as such, radical white supremacist culture in the United States is in many respects a *biblical* culture. Historically rooted in the Christian Identity movement, a key means of growth and development continues to be biblical preaching in the context of worship, informal Bible study, and prison ministry. Its primary text is the Christian Bible, accompanied by a vast apocrypha of sermon transcripts and recordings, biblical commentaries, Bible study aids, and hagiographies, all of which are widely circulated in churches, at conventions and rallies, at Bible studies, in prisons, on the Internet, and through small publishing houses. Cultural works like Hoskins's *Vigilantes of Christendom* help produce and reproduce the discursive network of meaning that generates a specific understanding of Bible and biblical values and motivates radical militant social identity and action.

CONCLUSION

As these three methods indicate, there is a diverse range of disciplines and approaches within the emerging field of biblical cultural history. Yet all share certain interests and priorities that distinguish them from other approaches in biblical studies.

First and foremost, they all assume that the Bible and the biblical are not self-evident things, handed down through religious history in the same essential form with the same essential contents; rather, they are cultural concepts. What Foucault said about medicine and the state are equally true about the Bible. It is a discursive object that is produced, reproduced, and deconstructed within particular cultural contexts.

The second commonality follows logically from the first. If the Bible and the biblical are not changeless things that are received and interpreted within different cultural contexts but are discursive objects that are produced in different biblical cultures, then the aim of the cultural historian of Bible is understanding those particular biblical cultures, past and present, as systems of meaning that produce particular, historically contingent conceptions of the Bible, biblical values, and biblical practices. The cultural historian of Bible therefore must pay close, almost exegetical, attention to the ways particular biblical practices and things (a Bible study, duct tape Bible lore, a teen study Bible, a white supremacist interpretation of Numbers) produce, reproduce, or undermine those meanings. In any case, the goal is not to evaluate the validity or truth-value of a particular biblical culture as a right or wrong, good or bad interpretation, but rather to understand how the meaning it produces works, how it makes sense, for those who are part of that culture.

Third, these different approaches to the cultural history of Bible are all centrally concerned with the intimate relationship between knowledge and power, how power produces knowledge and knowledge produces power. When we talk about one, we are talking about the other—power/knowledge. One becomes a thinking, speaking, acting subject within a cultural system in the process of becoming subjected to it. Subjectivity and subjection go hand in hand, and therefore so do knowledge and power. That is the paradox of subjection: one gains power as a subject in the process of being subjected to the system in which one's power is realized. Power cannot be completely consolidated or controlled by any one position within culture. Within any network of power/knowledge, there are forces of discipline and oppression as well as forces of resistance and change. Power does not simply come down from on high; it circulates through the entire social body.

Clearly, cultural-historical approaches to Bible do not replace other, more familiar approaches and methods in biblical studies, especially those that focus on close textual analysis of biblical texts, including textual criticism, form and source criticism, redaction criticism, rhetorical criticism, structural and poststructural approaches, and other literary-critical approaches. Such approaches, which are staples of traditional theological studies curricula, are centrally concerned with either the historical reconstruction of the early literary and religious history of the text or with the structures, meanings, and dynamics within the texts themselves. The central concern of biblical cultural history, by contrast, is to understand the cultures that produce the meanings of those biblical stories and texts, as well as of the Bible itself. As such this approach is perhaps less at home in the field of biblical theology within a seminary or divinity school and more at home in the field of academic religious studies in a college or university. Indeed, although cultural histories of Bible "won't preach" in most cases, we may recognize in them new and exciting potential contributions that biblical scholars can offer in academic religious studies and in the academic humanities and social sciences more generally.[29]

KEY TERMS

archaeology of knowledge. A phrase coined by Michel Foucault to describe historical analysis that seeks to discover the systems or networks of thought that operate within culture and how these systems come to be known within a culture as natural and self-evident—in other words, how knowledge comes to be taken as knowledge, even as other ways of knowing are excluded.

cultural history. Sometimes described in shorthand simply as "the history of meaning," cultural history explores how meaning takes form within culture, often but not exclusively popular culture. Its methods are diverse, including ethnography, literary criticism, film and television history, music history, and discourse analysis. (*see also* culture)

culture. Drawing from the field of anthropology (especially structuralist or semiotic approaches), cultural history sees culture as a network or web of meaning that both produces us and is produced by us. As Clifford Geertz put it, "Believing, with Max Weber, man is an animal suspended in webs of significance he himself has spun, I take culture to be those webs, and the analysis of it to be therefore not an experimental science in search of law but an interpretative one in search of meaning."[30] The cultural historian, then, like the anthropologist, attempts to understand culture through "thick description" and interpretation of different cultural products and practices within it. As Williams, Foucault, and others make clear, moreover, a culture is never monolithic, never a perfectly integrated whole in which all the strands are woven seamlessly together.

discourse/discursive practice. Terms used for collective ways of talking, writing, acting, and thinking that give expression to larger systems of thought within a culture. Foucault and others argue collective discourses, rather than individual writers, are the proper subject of historical research, whose aim is the archaeology of cultural knowledge.

medium (pl. media). Often misunderstood as simply the conveyer of a particular message or communication, medium is in fact inseparable from message, as Marshall McLuhan famously declared in 1964. He defined *medium* provocatively as any extension of oneself into the world. The *message*, then, is not only the meaning of something (e.g., content communicated through printed words in a book or spoken words in a speech) but its total social and personal effect. "The medium," he wrote, "is *socially* the message."[31] In this light, the cultural historian of Bible would never isolate a particular Bible's message from its medium; they are inseparable. There is no Bible in general, only particular Bibles, each of which is both medium and message. The scholar's aim is to understand not only a Bible's literary meaning but also its larger personal and social effect.

reception history. A field of biblical studies that moves beyond traditional scholarship on the history of interpretation to explore the broader history of the reception of biblical texts, images, stories, and characters through the centuries in the form of citation, interpretation, reading, revision, adaptation, and influence.

structure of feeling. Raymond Williams's term for the specific character and quality of common cultural sense and lived experience, which involves an interaction between "official" culture and the ways people live their everyday lives in their cultural context.

NOTES

1. Marjorie Garber, *Symptoms of Culture* (New York: Routledge, 1998). Garber writes, "I do not propose to diagnose culture as if it were an illness of which it could be cured, but to read culture as if it were structured like a dream, a *network of representations that encodes wishes and fears, projections and identifications, all of whose elements are overdetermined and contingent*" (9; italics added).
2. For accounts of the shift from social history to cultural history in all its diversity over the past several decades, see the lead essay by Lynn Hunt in her edited *The New Cultural History* (Ithaca, NY: Cornell University Press, 1989); William H. Sewell, "The Concept(s) of Culture," in Victoria E. Bonnell and Lynn Hunt, eds., *Beyond the Cultural Turn* (Berkeley: University of California Press, 1999); and chapters 2 and 3 of Geoff Eley, *A Crooked Line: From Cultural History to the History of Society* (Ann Arbor: University of Michigan Press, 2005).
3. These figures are introduced in William E. Deal and Timothy Beal, *Theory for Religious Studies* (New York: Routledge, 2004), from which my briefer discussions here, vis-à-vis cultural history, draw extensively; also Peter Burke, *What Is Cultural History?* 2nd ed. (Cambridge, MA: Polity Press, 2008), esp. 55–59.
4. Raymond Williams, "Culture Is Ordinary," in John Higgins, ed., *The Raymond Williams Reader* (Oxford: Blackwell, 2001) 10–13. This essay was first published in 1958.
5. Deal and Beal, 161.
6. Michel Foucault, "Nietzsche, Genealogy, History," in Donald F. Bourchard, ed., *Language, Counter-memory, Practice: Selected Essays and Interviews* (Ithaca, NY: Cornell University Press, 1977), 144.
7. John F. A. Sawyer, who has been a leading influence on the development of biblical reception history over the past two decades, defines it simply as "the history of how a text has influenced communities and cultures down the centuries," in *Sacred Language and Sacred Texts* (London: Routledge, 1999), 2.
8. See esp. Hans Robert Jauss, "Literary History as a Challenge to Literary Theory," *New Literary History* 1 (1970) 7–37, which is a translation of chapters 5–12 of *Literaturgeschichte als Provokation der Literaturwissenschaft* (Konstanz,

1967). It is included, along with other related essays, in *Toward an Aesthetic of Reception*, trans. Timothy Bahti, vol. 2 of the Theory and History of Literature series (Minneapolis: University of Minnesota Press, 1982).
9. Hans-Georg Gadamer, *Truth and Method*, trans. Joel Weinsheimer and Donald G. Marshall (New York: Continuum, 1989); first published in German as *Warheit und Methode* (Tübingen, 1960); the principle of *Wirkungsgeschichte* and the concept of the fusion of horizons is summarized in Deal and Beal, *Theory for Religious Studies*, 77–78, and, most helpfully, in Ulrich Luz, "The Contribution of Reception History to a Theology of the New Testament," in Christopher Rowland, Christopher Mark Tuckett, Robert Morgan, eds., *The Nature of New Testament Theology: Essays in Honour of Robert Morgan* (Oxford: Blackwell, 2006), 124–25.
10. James S. Bielo, *Words upon the Word: An Ethnography of Evangelical Group Bible Study* (New York: New York University Press, 2009).
11. Ibid., 57.
12. Another outstanding example of this approach is Brian Malley, *How the Bible Works: An Anthropological Study of Evangelical Biblicism* (Walnut Creek, CA: AltaMira Press, 2004). Malley argues that, among many evangelicals, calling oneself a "literalist" is less about making a specific argument about the biblical text than it is about identifying with conservative evangelical Christianity over against "liberal" or "mainstream" forms. What "literalist" means has less to do with any doctrine of biblical inerrancy or infallibility and more to do with religious social identity as conservative.
13. Dorina Miller Parmenter, "Iconic Books from Below: The Christian Bible and the Discourse of Duct Tape," *Postscripts* 6.1/2/3 (2010): 185–200.
14. The finest book-length study that takes this approach is David Dault, *The Accessorized Bible* (New Haven, CT: Yale University Press, forthcoming), which delves deeply into the theological interests and diversions of many popular evangelical Bibles on the market today.
15. *The NIV Teen Study Bible* (Grand Rapids: Zondervan, 2004). What follows is an abbreviated version of my analysis of this Bible and others like it in the chapter on "Biblical Values" in Timothy Beal, *The Rise and Fall of the Bible: The Unexpected History of an Accidental Book* (New York: Houghton Mifflin Harcourt, 2011), 52–59.
16. Danna Nolan Fewell and David M. Gunn, *Gender, Power, and Promise: The Subject of the Bible's First Story* (Nashville: Abingdon, 1993), 106–8.
17. Still other translations go so far as to remove that ambiguity from the biblical text as well. The New Living Translation, for example, which is used in the best-selling *Life Application Study Bible* and many other Bibles published by Tyndale House, renders Lev. 18:22 as, "Do not practice homosexuality; it is a detestable sin."
18. Nearly all Americans are familiar with the idea of the Bible as God's book of answers and morality textbook. Indeed, most endorse it. According to the Pew Forum on Religion and Public Life, 78 percent of all Americans say that the Bible is the "word of God," and almost half of those believe that, as such, "it is to be taken literally, word for word" (Pew Forum 2006). Polling data from the Barna Group indicate that nearly half of all Americans agree that "the Bible is totally accurate in all of its teachings" (88 percent of all "born-again" Christians believe the same), and the Gallup Poll finds that 65 percent of all Americans believe that the Bible "answers all or most of the basic questions of life" (Gallup and Simmons 2000). See Beal, *Rise and Fall*, 4–5, 201–2.
19. On *The Passion of the Christ*, see, e.g., Timothy K. Beal and Tod Linafelt, eds., *Mel Gibson's Bible: Religion, Popular Culture, and* The Passion of the Christ (Chicago: University of Chicago Press, 2006).

20. The following brief discussion is based on my fuller analysis in Timothy K. Beal, "The Phineas Priesthood and the White Supremacist Bible," in Jonneke Bekkenkamp and Yvonne Sherwood, eds., *Sanctified Aggression: Legacies of Biblical and Post-Biblical Vocabularies of Violence* (Sheffield: Continuum, 2004). Biblical quotations are from the King James Version because that is the version most commonly quoted by Hoskins (see below) and other white supremacist and Christian identity adherents.
21. Morlin's interview with Lindholm is described in David A. Niewert, *In God's Country: The Patriot Movement and the Pacific Northwest* (Pullman: Washington State University Press, 1999), 126.
22. Ibid., 124–25.
23. Gene Fadness, "Phineas Priests May Be Responsible for Racist Leaflets," *Idaho Falls Post Register* (18 April 1996), A1.
24. Richard Kelly Hoskins, *Vigilantes of Christendom: The History of the Phineas Priesthood* (Lynchburg: Virginia Publishing Company, 1990), 213.
25. Ibid., 417. Earlier, in a discussion of the tragic downfall of Robert Matthews's militant group The Order, Hoskins quotes the same passage as the biblical basis for keeping membership in Phineas groups to six (the seventh member being God).
26. Ibid., 25.
27. For more on the religious dimensions of racial identity and Anglo-Israelism in Hoskins's ideology, see Beal, "The Phineas Priesthood," 125–28.
28. Likewise, months before the pastor Paul Hill murdered Dr. David Gunn as he was at an abortion clinic in Pensacola, Florida, on 10 March 1993, he wrote "Should We Defend Born and Unborn Children with Force?" http://theroadtoemmaus.org/RdLb/21PbAr/LifHlth/Abrt/PaulHl.htm, which used Numbers 25 as the primary biblical justification for violence against abortion workers.
29. See, e.g., Qur'anic scholar Wilfred Cantwell Smith, "The Study of Religion and the Study of the Bible," *Journal of the American Academy of Religion* 39 (1971): 131–40, who foresaw such approaches to biblical studies emerging in religion departments in nonreligious colleges of the humanities and social sciences since the 1960s. In his 1971 presidential address to the American Academy of Religion, Smith suggested that these new academic contexts require a shift from teaching religion to studying it as a human phenomenon. In that context, he called for a course of study focused on "the Bible as scripture," with Scripture as a "generic phenomenon," allowing comparison of the concepts and roles of "scripture as a religious form" in different traditions and communities throughout history (132–33). For more discussion of this address and its aftermath, see Timothy Beal, "Reception History and Beyond: Toward a Cultural History of Scriptures," *Biblical Interpretation* 19 (2011): 357–72.
30. Clifford Geertz, *The Interpretation of Cultures* (New York: Basic, 1977), 5.
31. Marshall McLuhan, *Understanding Media: The Extensions of Man* (Cambridge, MA: MIT Press, 1994), 10; first published in 1964.

FOR FURTHER READING

Beal, Timothy. "Reception History and Beyond: Toward a Cultural History of Scriptures," *Biblical Interpretation* 19 (2011): 357–72.

Bielo, James S. *Words upon the Word: An Ethnography of Evangelical Group Bible Study*. New York: New York University Press, 2009.

Bonnell, Victoria E. and Lynn Hunt, eds. *Beyond the Cultural Turn*. Berkeley: University of California Press, 1999.
Burke, Peter. *What Is Cultural History?* 2nd ed. Cambridge, MA: Polity Press, 2008.
Dault, David. *The Accessorized Bible*. New Haven, CT: Yale University Press, forthcoming.
Deal, William E. and Timothy K. Beal. "Michel Foucault" and "Raymond Williams." In *Theory for Religious Studies*. New York: Routledge, 2004.
Foucault, Michel. *The Archaeology of Knowledge*. Trans. A. M. Sheridan-Smith. London: Tavistock, 1974.
———. *Religion and Culture*. Edited by Jeremy R. Carrette. London: Routledge, 1999.
Hunt, Lynn. *The New Cultural History*. Ithaca, NY: Cornell University Press, 1989.
Malley, Brian. *How the Bible Works: An Anthropological Study of Evangelical Biblicism*. Walnut Creek, CA: AltaMira Press, 2004.
McLuhan, Marshall. *Understanding Media: The Extensions of Man*. Cambridge, MA: MIT Press, 1994.
Parmenter, Dorina Miller. "Iconic Books from Below: The Christian Bible and the Discourse of Duct Tape," *Postscripts* 6.1/2/3 (2010): 185–200.
Williams, Raymond. "Culture Is Ordinary." In *The Raymond Williams Reader*, edited by John Higgins. Oxford: Blackwell, 2001.

Chapter 2

Disability Studies and the Bible

NYASHA JUNIOR AND JEREMY SCHIPPER

Images of disability fill the pages of the Bible. Yet, only in the last decade or so have biblical scholars shown a sustained interest in critically examining disability within biblical literature. This chapter introduces some of the standard issues involved in the critical analysis of disability in biblical literature with a focus on examples from the Hebrew Bible. First, we provide an overview of three different models for studying disability. Second, we examine how the use of disability studies within biblical scholarship relates to the use of other critical methods within biblical studies. Third, we discuss how biblical representations of disability relate to the historical reality of people with disabilities in ancient Israel. Fourth, we provide an example of a disability studies approach to a biblical text by analyzing the role of disability in Genesis 39 as well as some scholarly interpretations of this text. Fifth, we discuss some potential drawbacks or misconceptions regarding the critical study of disability in the Bible.

THE DEVELOPMENT OF DISABILITY STUDIES

When it comes to interdisciplinary scholarship, biblical scholars tend to be academic latecomers. Usually, the literature and perspectives in other disciplines (including new historicism, post-structuralism, postcolonialism, and several of the other approaches discussed in this volume) become incorporated into biblical scholarship well after they are established in other disciplines within the social sciences and humanities. It is no different with disability studies. As an academic field, disability studies first emerged in British social sciences in the late 1970s and early 1980s. It grew out of larger American and European political and social advocacy movements such as the Disability Rights Movement and the Independent Living Movement.[1] Disability rights advocates include nondisabled persons as well as persons with disabilities who support and take action that promotes the legal, political, social, and economic rights of those with disabilities.

Disability studies, however, is not the same as the Disability Rights Movement. We should not assume that scholars who study disability share commitments similar to those of disability rights advocates, just as we would not assume that a political theorist who studies Marxism votes for or supports Marxist politicians. Furthermore, we should not assume that all scholars studying disability identify themselves as people with disabilities just as one would not assume that all political theorists studying Marxism identify themselves as Marxists.

In the early stages of disability studies, scholars sought to provide a corrective to what they referred to as the *medical model of disability*. The medical model approaches disability as an individual medical or healthcare issue that must be corrected or cured through treatment by healthcare professionals or lifestyle changes by the person with disabilities. This model locates the so-called "problem" of disability in the body of the individual.

Seeking a more comprehensive approach than the medical model, some scholars began to use the *social model of disability*. Unlike the medical model, this approach interprets disability as a social issue rather than an individualized medical condition. The social model distinguishes the term *impairment* from the term *disability*. "Impairment" refers to a biological anomaly that inhibits the body from functioning normatively. By this definition, a damaged limb or organ that makes activities such as walking or seeing difficult qualifies as an impairment. In contrast, "disability" refers to the social and structural discrimination that people with impairments face. For example, a person who uses a wheelchair may have difficulty navigating certain buildings, parks, or public spaces. Such difficulty is not simply due to a biological impairment. Rather, a lack of curb cuts on street corners or access ramps into buildings or other architectural barriers may limit the mobility of a person who uses a wheelchair. The social model of disability rejects the medical model's focus on the individual body. The social model of disability relocates the so-called "problem" of living with a disability from the individual body with impairments to the social and political structures that prevent people with impairments from full access to and participation in our social and political structures.

As disability studies developed, however, the social model received criticism for defining disability as socially constructed discrimination comparable to racism, sexism, or homophobia. Critics observed that disability is not just a matter of discrimination since the bodies and minds of people with impairments do not function like the minds and bodies of the nondisabled. Even if social and structural discrimination against people with impairments did not exist, persons with impairments would continue to navigate their environment differently than the nondisabled because of the biological realities of their minds or bodies. Furthermore, some critics observed difficulties in pinpointing where impairment ends and disability begins when using the social model. For example, the social model might not help us to determine if an eating disorder qualifies as an impairment or a disability.

Since the 1990s, some disability theorists have preferred to use the *cultural model of disability* rather than the social model. The cultural model is popular among scholars in North America working in the humanities rather than the social sciences. According to the cultural model, we cannot define disability by just one factor such as the medical condition of an individual body (medical model) or social discrimination against people with impairments (social model). Unlike the social model, the cultural model does not differentiate impairments from disabilities in a way that might artificially distance the social experiences of people with disabilities from their biological realities. Instead, disability is made up of a complex variety of cultural factors, which might include medical issues and social discrimination, but it is not limited to these factors.

The cultural model does not provide one precise definition of disability. Instead, it examines how notions about disability and *nondisability* (or "able-bodiedness") operate within a given culture. When a literary or artistic work from a given culture includes an image of disability, the image usually represents more than just an objective description or diagnosis of a biological condition. For example, in the United States, many of our books, films, or other forms of artistic expression include representations of disability, such as disability imagery or characters with disabilities. Often, these literary or artistic representations of disability do not seek to provide an accurate portrayal of the everyday experiences of persons with disabilities. Instead, they serve an instrumental role in conveying particular ideals or values that shape our culture such as hope, sin, inspiration, or courage. Such ideals or values may be unrelated to the concrete ways in which many people with disabilities in the United States experience their everyday lives. The cultural model of disability analyzes how a culture's representations and discussions of disability and nondisability help to articulate a range of values, ideals, or expectations that are important to that culture's organization and identity.

The cultural model shows the influence of gender studies and critical race theory in its use of the term nondisability. Although we may associate gender studies with females or critical race theory with racial minorities, such fields demonstrate that "male" is a gender and "white" is a race although white males are often assumed to be the default "norm" from which females and racial minorities deviate. Similarly, "nondisabled" does not serve simply as a term for a universally recognized normal state of human existence. When we consider the mental or physical capabilities associated with childhood or advanced age, the term "nondisabled" does not describe the condition of most people for a large portion of a "normal" lifespan today. Thus, nondisabled may not describe an objective biological difference from persons with disabilities. Rather, the use of the term "nondisabled" may reflect cultural expectations for how frequently we might encounter a particular trait in a person of a particular age. For instance, if a twenty-year-old uses a hearing aid, we consider her or him to be a person with a disability. Yet, if a twenty-year-old uses prescription eyeglasses, we treat her or him as nondisabled. Furthermore, if an eighty-year-old uses a hearing aid, we might consider the use of the hearing aid not as a disability but as related to "normal" advanced age. According to the cultural model, the term "nondisability" is not an objective description of normalcy. Instead, cultural notions of nondisability and disability work together to shape and reinforce cultural understandings of normalcy.

Of the three models reviewed, the cultural model has had the most influence on biblical scholarship. The medical model is not suitable for use in biblical studies since most of the discussions and representations of disability in the Hebrew Bible are unrelated to medicine or healthcare. At first, this may seem like an odd claim because many of us may associate disability with topics such as healthcare, medicine, or a specific diagnosis of an unusual physical, cognitive, or emotional trait isolated in the individual body. Until recently, diagnosis has been a central preoccupation of biblical scholars when they comment on biblical representations of disability.[2] Yet the Hebrew Bible rarely, if ever, approaches disability as a purely diagnostic issue. Instead, its representations of disability help to express a range of ideas or values important to cultural organization and identity in ancient Israel (cf. Lev. 21:16–23). Medical diagnoses or specific healthcare practices are not a central concern in most, if not all, of the biblical texts that use disability imagery.

Furthermore, use of the medical model blurs the line between the study of disability in the Hebrew Bible and the study of medicine or healthcare in ancient Israel. While the study of disability may relate to medicine or healthcare, it is not the same as the study of medicine or healthcare or even a subset of these subjects. The study of disability focuses on how cultural notions of disability operate in biblical texts. By contrast, the study of medicine or healthcare may examine the same imagery to help reconstruct medical and diagnostic practices or healthcare systems in ancient Israel. It is easy to confuse these two different subjects if one uses a medical model approach.

Likewise, use of the social model is not feasible in biblical studies. The social model relies on a separation of impairment from disability. Yet the descriptions of impairments in ancient literature are often too vague to permit identification of the biological condition that is described in these texts. Moreover, we have a very limited understanding of the social norms and values of the ancient cultures that produced this literature. Thus it becomes nearly impossible to separate descriptions of the impairment from descriptions of the discrimination against the impairment in discussions of the body in ancient literature.

The cultural model has proved to be most useful in biblical studies due to timing, location, and suitability. The critical study of disability in the Bible as a subject in its own right gained momentum only within the last decade or so. The cultural model was well established within other humanities-based disciplines by the time biblical scholars joined the conversation. Moreover, most of the biblical scholars studying disability work in North American, humanities-based contexts, where the cultural model had gained the most ground in academia. Aside from timing and location, the cultural model is also a good fit for biblical scholars. Instead of assuming a universal meaning behind disability or nondisability across all cultures, a cultural model may help biblical scholars to: (1) focus on the cultural values associated with disability and nondisability in the Hebrew Bible and the ancient Israelite societies that produced this literature; (2) become more aware of the contemporary cultural values that a scholar assumes in her or his interpretation of these biblical representations of disability; and (3) determine whether scholarly interpretations of how disability operates in a given passage find sufficient support in the biblical text.

DISABILITY STUDIES AND OTHER CRITICAL APPROACHES TO BIBLICAL LITERATURE

Biblical scholars have learned a great deal about biblical literature and the societies that produced it through careful analysis of certain recurring subjects in the Bible, such as ancient Israelite kingship or the regulations for sacrifices. In order to study such subjects, scholars may use source criticism, form criticism, redaction criticism, narrative criticism, rhetorical criticism, and other critical methods commonplace within biblical scholarship. Yet, while a scholar may say that she or he uses source, form, or rhetorical criticism, a scholar would not say that she or he uses "kingship criticism" or "sacrificial regulation criticism" simply because her or his research focuses on these subjects. Although kingship and regulations for sacrifices are common subjects within biblical scholarship, they are not methods of biblical scholarship. Similarly, critical examinations of disability have not introduced a specifically new method of biblical criticism in order to engage this subject. We have used the term "disability studies" rather than "disability criticism" in the title of this chapter in order to emphasize this point. Biblical scholarship has not approached the study of disability as requiring a new type of critical method.

Since disability is a subject within biblical scholarship rather than a new type of biblical scholarship, there is no single method for studying disability in the Bible. How a biblical scholar analyzes disability depends on her or his preferred critical method(s) and training. One could use source criticism, form criticism, or rhetorical criticism in order to analyze disability imagery in the Bible. The scholar studying disability must decide which method or methods will best suit her or his particular questions.

For example, source criticism may help us to understand more clearly what disability represents in different biblical texts rather than treating disability as if it operates in a singular and consistent fashion across the entire Bible. Form and rhetorical criticisms may help us analyze how disability imagery contributes to the message(s) of a particular prophetic text. A postcolonial approach to disability could examine the ways in which characters with disabilities are imagined as "other" in biblical texts as well as how biblical scholarship allows the nondisabled to masquerade as "normal." In short, a scholar can use any number of critical methods or criticisms to study disability as a subject within biblical scholarship.

Nevertheless, the method(s) that a scholar uses to study disability should follow the accepted scholarly conventions for using that particular method or methods. For example, if a scholar uses source criticism to analyze various representations of disability, her or his arguments and conclusions should be ones that any competent source critic could make regardless of her or his personal experience or attitudes concerning people with disabilities. Personal experiences may raise a scholar's awareness of a particular issue, and that awareness may prompt her or him to consider a particular subject in a new way. Yet this experience and awareness alone cannot be used as evidence to support her or his interpretation. Instead, as with any responsible scholarship, the evidence to support one's critical analysis of disability should come from a close reading of the text, a responsible application of critical method(s), and careful engagement with secondary scholarship.

DISABILITY IN ANCIENT ISRAELITE LITERATURE AND HISTORY

Despite the methodological freedom that biblical scholars have in studying disability, they face some limitations when confronted with the limited data on persons with disabilities in the ancient Near East. We are unable to gain access to the lived experiences of these persons for various reasons. We do not have interviews or autobiographies of ancient persons with disabilities. Nor do we have many undisputable representations of peoples with disabilities in ancient Near Eastern iconography or visual artwork. Also, scholars have identified very few, if any, artifacts that clearly served as support technology for ancient persons with disabilities, such as crutches or access ramps. Thus, scholars are unable to develop a thorough historical reconstruction of the lives of ancient persons with disabilities.

Despite a lack of first-hand accounts, visual images, or physical evidence, biblical scholars have numerous representations of disability within biblical and other ancient Near Eastern literature. Some laws and sayings in the Hebrew Bible suggest that people with disabilities in general faced discriminatory attitudes

(2 Sam. 5:8; Prov. 26:7; cf. Lev. 19:14; Deut. 27:18). The narrative portions of the Hebrew Bible include more specific portrayals of several individual characters with chronic disabilities. Unlike many New Testament texts in which characters with disabilities are healed, characters in the Hebrew Bible tend to live with their disabilities. Nevertheless, the aim of these textual representations is not to provide a clear understanding of the everyday experiences of ancient persons with disabilities. In this sense, we may compare these representations to the portrayals of college life in many Hollywood comedies. Such films do not tell us much about the actual experiences of college students because, in part, a realistic portrayal of the typical college experience does not seem to be the purpose of these films. Although biblical texts include representations of disability, we learn very little about the living conditions of people with disabilities in ancient Israel from these texts.

Furthermore, biblical scholars debate how much historical information about specific individuals we can confidently derive from many of the narratives in the Hebrew Bible. Yet, even if we were to take a less cautious position about the historical accuracy of these narratives, most of the characters with disabilities in these narratives have elite social statuses. For example, Mephibosheth has a chronic disability that he acquires in childhood (2 Sam. 4, 9, 19). Yet, as the grandson of King Saul, he is also a potential heir to the throne and has access to King David and the royal palace. He owns land and has a large number of servants at his disposal. Isaac, Jacob, and Eli acquire disabilities in old age (Gen. 27:1; 48:10; 1 Sam. 3:2; 4:15). Yet, Isaac and Jacob are wealthy heads of households. Similarly, Eli is the head priest at a prominent Israelite shrine. These characters do not represent everyday or typical ancient Israelites. They enjoy access to housing, healthcare, and support technologies to which the majority of ancient Israelites may not have had. For example, while Mephibosheth has servants and a donkey (2 Sam. 19), we cannot assume that most ancient Israelites with mobility impairments had access to such assistance and support technologies. We cannot use narratives involving elite Israelites with disabilities to make generalizations about the lives of most Israelites with disabilities.

Also, while biblical narratives include a handful of characters with disabilities, the Hebrew Bible often uses disability imagery when discussing issues that do not focus directly, if at all, on the lives of ancient Israelites with disabilities. Frequently, the Hebrew Bible uses language and imagery of disability to describe the experiences and struggles of the presumably nondisabled. As Rebecca Raphael observes, "Most of the [disability] imagery is metaphorical and not about actual disabled persons. Quite a lot of Isaiah's blind and deaf people have normal eyes and ears."[3] For example, in Isaiah 56:10, the prophet declares, "Israel's lookouts are blind, All of them do not know; All of them are mute dogs that are not able to bark; dreaming, lying down, loving to be drowsy" (au. trans.). This text does not focus on people with disabilities themselves. Instead, it uses the words "blind" and "mute" to criticize certain parties within Israel's leadership (cf. Deut. 28:28–29; Isa. 29:9; 59:10; Zeph. 1:17). A great deal of the biblical imagery of disability does not describe people with disabilities. In fact, in many cases, the disability imagery actually addresses nondisabled people.

Due to a lack of evidence, biblical scholars are unable to reconstruct what life with a disability was like for most ancient Israelites. Biblical representations of disability do not provide us with a window into that experience. Thus, recent biblical scholarship that engages disability studies has avoided attempts at such historical reconstructions. Instead, it has analyzed how cultural notions of disability operate in biblical texts and the scholarship on these texts.

AN ANALYSIS OF SCHOLARSHIP AND DISABILITY IMAGERY IN GENESIS 39

This section illustrates how one might conduct a critical analysis of disability imagery through a brief study of Genesis 39. Influenced by the cultural model of disability, we will pay particular attention to how notions of disability operate in both the plot of this chapter and selected scholarly interpretations of this chapter.

In Genesis 39, the Ishmaelites sell the Hebrew Joseph to Potiphar, who is "a eunuch of Pharaoh, captain of guard, an Egyptian" (39:1, au. trans.).[4] Joseph, described as "beautiful in form and in appearance," (39:6, au. trans.) is successful and is elevated to a position in charge of Potiphar's household. In Genesis 39:7, Potiphar's wife says to Joseph, "Have sex with me" (au. trans.). Joseph refuses, but Potiphar's wife propositions him repeatedly (39:10), although he refuses continually. One day, when Potiphar's wife is alone with Joseph, she grabs his garment and says again, "Have sex with me" (39:12, au. trans.). Joseph leaves his garment in her hand and runs outside. Potiphar's wife cries out to the other servants. She claims that Joseph attempted to rape her. She says, "See, my husband has brought among us a Hebrew to insult us! He came in to me to lie with me, and I cried out with a loud voice; and when he heard me raise my voice and cry out, he left his garment beside me, and fled outside." (39:14–15). When Potiphar comes home, she tells him a somewhat similar story, and he has Joseph imprisoned. Two issues that scholars often focus on in their discussions of this chapter are: (1) whether or not Potiphar was a eunuch (meaning a castrated male)[5] and (2) the behavior of Potiphar's wife.

Two biblical passages refer to Potiphar as a *saris* (Gen. 37:36; 39:1), a Hebrew word that we translated as "eunuch" in the previous paragraph. The NRSV often translates this word as "eunuch" elsewhere in the Hebrew Bible (e.g., 2 Kgs. 9:32; 20:18; 23:11; Esth. 1:10; 2:3; Isa. 39:7; 56:3; Jer. 34:19; 38:7; 41:16). Yet, in the case of Genesis 37:36 and 39:1, the NRSV refers to Potiphar as simply an "official," which suggests a non-castrated officer (cf. RSV, NAB). Scholars have made extensive arguments for both translation options.[6] We will not attempt to resolve this debate in this chapter. Instead, we focus on the particular significance that some scholars who interpret Potiphar as a eunuch find in this designation.[7]

Although the text refers to Potiphar as a eunuch in verse 1, Genesis 39 does not comment further on his physical status or capabilities. Other biblical texts reflect a stigma against eunuchs. Deuteronomy 23:1 (v. 2 in Hebrew) prohibits men with genital damage from entering "the assembly of the LORD," which may refer to the temple (cf. Isa. 56:3–5), an assembly of Israelite landowners (cf. Mic. 2:4–5), or the people of Israel in general (Num. 16:3; 20:4; 1 Chr. 28:8). In any case, Deuteronomy 23 bans various non-Israelite groups from this assembly (vv. 3–9; vv. 4–10 in Hebrew), including Egyptians until the third generation (vv. 7–8; vv. 8–9 in Hebrew). Thus, in Potiphar's case, the fact that he was an Egyptian would have prevented him from entering the assembly regardless of his physical condition. Although the Hebrew Bible mentions a handful of foreign eunuchs, biblical traditions tend not to denigrate them or to exhibit much concern regarding their physical status. Thus it is understandable that Genesis 39 mentions Potiphar's physical status only once. His physical status seems to have little, if any, explicit impact on the plot of the chapter. The fact that he is a eunuch does not provide the central conflict in the text. Instead, Potiphar's wife's actions toward Joseph introduce the major conflict in need of resolution. It is not her husband's body but her actions that create the crisis that pushes the story line forward.

According to Potiphar's wife, the introduction of a Hebrew into an Egyptian household provides the central crisis in Genesis 39. Unlike Potiphar's physical status, the chapter makes repeated references to the ethnic differences of the characters. For example, the narrator notes twice that Potiphar is an Egyptian (vv. 1, 2), and Potiphar's wife draws distinctions between the Egyptians and Joseph as a "Hebrew" (vv. 17, 19). While the text provides little evidence to support the assumption that Potiphar's status as a eunuch creates any reason for concern within his household, the emphasis on ethnic differences makes a large contribution to the plot of Genesis 39. Ethnicity plays a more significant role than disability in the text.

Nevertheless, some scholars have interpreted Potiphar's wife's actions in light of her husband's physical status while downplaying the role of ethnicity in this chapter. They treat Potiphar's disability as a reproductive crisis that provides a catalyst for the action in the story. At first, one might assume that a reproductive crisis provides the problem that his wife's behavior tries to address in Genesis 39, especially since some other Yahwistic narratives seem particularly concerned with infertility (cf. Gen. 11:30; 25:21; 29:31).[8]

In these interpretations, the crisis created by the presence of a character with a disability helps to explain questionable behavior by his nondisabled wife.[9] For example, Heather McKay interprets Genesis 39 as part of a larger sequence in Genesis, which involves women using various strategies for having children. Thus, according to McKay, as with Sarai (Gen. 16), Leah (Gen. 30:9), Rachel (Gen. 30:15), and Tamar (Gen. 38), Potiphar's wife desires a child, but unlike these Hebrew women, her plans fail. McKay contends that Potiphar, as a eunuch, was unable to deliver what Potiphar's wife wanted, "fertile sperm." Joseph was the "only" person who could provide it.[10]

McKay treats Potiphar's condition as a eunuch as a rationalization for Potiphar's wife's behavior toward Joseph. Potiphar's wife resorts to extreme measures because of her husband's disability. McKay connects Potiphar's wife with other women in Genesis who desire children. Downplaying the ethnic differences between these women, Potiphar's wife shares "normal" cultural values reflected elsewhere in Genesis that reward heterosexual intercourse resulting in pregnancy. Yet the presence of a eunuch, capable of sexual intercourse but not reproduction, does not affirm or conform to these (supposedly) normal cultural values.[11] In this interpretation, Potiphar's wife's motives conform to normal cultural values, whereas Potiphar's disability threatens these values. The supposed cultural deviancy of the character with disabilities reinforces the cultural normalcy of the nondisabled character.

Yet Genesis 39 never indicates that Potiphar's wife desires pregnancy. She does not mention children or issues of fertility. By contrast, the other women in Genesis that McKay discusses often make explicit their desire for children. For example, Rachel says to her husband Jacob, "Give me children or I shall die!" (Gen. 30:1). In the other cases, the issue of fertility or pregnancy is explicit, whereas Genesis 39 never mentions fertility or pregnancy.[12] Fertility and reproduction are not obvious concerns of Potiphar's wife. She may simply be interested in nonreproductive intercourse outside of marriage, which some would interpret as culturally deviant behavior that threatens the stability of her household. Yet McKay's interpretation downplays the behavior of the nondisabled that poses a more obvious threat to the household's stability by creating a reproductive crisis around a character with a disability.

Like McKay, Ron Pirson connects the story in Genesis 39 to a larger pattern involving female characters elsewhere in Genesis.[13] He links Genesis 39 with Genesis 38. In Genesis 38, Tamar goes to extreme measures to have a child after the death of her husband leaves her childless. Since Tamar focuses on having a child in the story that immediately precedes Genesis 39, Pirson questions whether the desire for a child might also be Potiphar's wife's motivation. To support his theory, Pirson reconsiders Potiphar's wife's testimony to the servants and to her husband in Genesis 39:17. Pirson interprets her testimony as an indication that since Potiphar was a eunuch, he purchased Joseph with the intention of having Joseph serve as a surrogate like the slaves Hagar, Bilhah, and Zilpah did for Sarah, Rachel, and Leah.[14]

Yet, in these other cases, Sarah, Rachel, and Leah each explicitly offer Hagar, Zilpah, and Bilhah respectively to their husbands to use as surrogates due to their infertility (Gen. 16:2; 30:3, 9). By contrast, there is no record of Potiphar offering Joseph to his wife as a surrogate. Nevertheless, Pirson implies that Potiphar follows the same cultural custom as these Hebrew women despite the fact that he is an Egyptian male and not a Hebrew woman. In this sense, Pirson's focus of the alleged crisis that Potiphar's disability provokes overshadows other aspects of his identity such as gender and ethnicity.

Pirson portrays Potiphar as knowledgeable and complicit in his wife's behavior despite the fact that Joseph tells Potiphar's wife that Potiphar has not "kept back anything from me except yourself, because you are his wife" (v. 9). For Pirson, both Potiphar and his wife seek to secure a child by using Joseph as a surrogate. As with McKay, the central crisis in the story becomes the threat that Potiphar's disability poses to "normal" cultural values. The crisis for Pirson is not the more obvious threat that Potiphar's wife's behavior may pose to the structure of their household, as Joseph implies when he objects to her advancements on the grounds that it will disturb the stability of their household (vv. 8–9). Moreover, Potiphar's alleged complicity presents him as affirming the deviance of his own body and mitigating for the nondisabled the supposed threat that he poses to cultural values that reward people capable of reproduction.[15]

The interpretations discussed in this section are certainly not representative examples of mainstream biblical scholarship on Genesis 39. Most scholars comment on textual issues such as the translation and interpretation of *saris*. Also, they tend to note the lack of a clear motivation behind Potiphar's wife's behavior in the text. Most leave aside more speculative claims. By contrast, the interpretations we reviewed reinforce the deviance of those who are unable (Potiphar) or unwilling (Joseph, according to Pirson) to provide children by any means necessary and thus affirm reproduction as a core value powerful enough to override all other values that also help to maintain social stability, such as honesty with members of one's household or avoiding false accusations against innocent parties.

We have used these somewhat extreme examples in order to illustrate how the issue of disability can serve to articulate particular ideals or values in ways unsupported by the text. The implicit associations that some scholars make between disability and threats to normative cultural values find little support in Genesis 39. Disability does not always create a crisis. In fact, in Genesis 39, the actions of the nondisabled pose the threat. Nonetheless, some scholars have normalized these actions by interpreting them as understandable responses to the imagined threat posed by the presence of a character with disabilities. The way that some scholars use the idea of disability in their interpretations of Genesis 39 reveals how the values or ideals that we attribute to disability imagery may not line up with the textual evidence from the Bible.

Our analysis of Genesis 39 and selected scholarship surrounding this text illustrates how disability studies contributes to biblical studies. In particular, our analysis uses a cultural model of disability, which does not assume that notions of disability and nondisability have the same meaning across all cultures. This model allows us to focus on the ways in which interpreters may assume or endorse particular cultural values in their use of disability and nondisability imagery. This approach focuses on the significance that we attach to this imagery and asks whether these interpretations are persuasive based on the evidence provided according to the method of biblical criticism employed.

CONCERNS REGARDING DISABILITY STUDIES OF THE BIBLE

This section addresses three frequently raised concerns regarding the critical study of disability in the Bible: (1) disability is a contemporary concept that is foreign to the biblical text; (2) disability studies has limited usefulness to biblical scholars since not all biblical texts contain explicit disability imagery; and (3) disability studies is a form of advocacy disguised as scholarship.

Biblical Hebrew does not have a word or phrase equivalent to the English word, "disability." This leads some to ask whether the concept of disability existed in the societies that produced biblical literature. The Hebrew word *mum*, usually translated as "blemish" in the NRSV, refers to many conditions that we may consider to be disabilities, such as blindness or lameness (Lev. 21:16–23). Yet *mum* does not cover every trait that we may consider a disability today. The Bible does not use the word *mum* for conditions such as deafness, muteness, or skin diseases, even though these conditions are sometimes paired with other conditions that qualify as a *mum* (e.g., the pairing of "blind" and "deaf" in Lev. 19:14; Isa. 29:18; 35:5; 43:8).[16] Thus a contemporary conception of disability seems foreign to biblical literature. It might not seem appropriate to use disability in relation to the Bible.

Nevertheless, just because the limited amount of Hebrew vocabulary contained in the Bible does not include a word for "disability" does not mean that the concept of disability would not have made sense to ancient peoples. The Hebrew Bible does not use a word equivalent to the English word "religion" either. Yet, the numerous studies of ancient Israelite religion show that the idea of religion was a meaningful concept in ancient Israel even if it was not used in a way that reflect any contemporary expressions of religion.[17]

Likewise, the idea of disability would have made sense to ancient Israelites even if the physical and cognitive traits and associations that they may have connected with disability would be different than the traits and associations that we might connect with disability. For example, unlike contemporary uses of the term "disability," not every culture would have one term that could apply to conditions as diverse as anorexia, blindness, and cerebral palsy. Furthermore, the Hebrew Bible frequently uses words for certain physical traits in clusters (such as "lame," "blind," or "deaf" in Exod. 4:11; 2 Sam. 5:8; Jer. 31:8; Mal. 1:8). These clusters suggest that ancient Israelites did not understand these particular conditions as isolated occurrences, but as belonging to a larger concept or idea. Instead of assuming that the idea of disability is a foreign concept that did not exist in ancient Israel, we might study how ancient Israelite societies understood the idea. The concept of disability seems well represented in the Bible, even if, as with religion, they applied this concept differently than we do today. These differences invite us to consider the cultural associations present in biblical representations of disability instead of dismissing disability as a concept foreign to ancient Israelite societies.

The fact that disability is a subject rather than a method presents another concern regarding the use of disability studies within biblical scholarship. We have multiple manuscripts of every biblical text. Also, these texts vary greatly in terms of their composition, redaction, and genre. Thus we could examine nearly any biblical text using textual criticism, redaction criticism, or form criticism. In contrast, not every biblical text contains representations of disability. In this sense, some would argue that disability studies may have limited use within biblical studies.

Yet, as suggested earlier in relation to the cultural model of disability, studying how biblical texts reflect cultural notions of disability also entails studying how biblical texts reflect cultural notions about nondisability. The idea of nondisability does not simply represent what is normal by default. Rather, nondisability expresses cultural expectations for normalcy, which may differ across cultures. Contemporary interpreters may not share the cultural expectations for normalcy reflected in biblical literature. For example, in the book of Genesis, God "opens" the wombs of Leah and Rachel so that they can produce children (29:31; 30:22) just as God "opens" a donkey's mouth so that she can speak (Num. 22:28) or "opens" a rock (Ps. 105:41) so that it produces water. Yet ancient Israelites would not consider speaking donkeys or water-producing rocks as normal. Likewise, even if human and animal fertility occurred frequently, some biblical texts suggest that fertility was a divine blessing that contravened a normal human condition experienced across ancient cultures (cf. Deut. 7:14).[18] This notion is very different from a contemporary understanding of fertility as normal and infertility as a deviation from this norm.

These types of differences caution us against reading contemporary standards for bodily normalcy into every biblical text that lacks obvious disability imagery or physical description. Along these lines, the book of Ruth does not contain any explicit disability imagery. Yet Ruth's ten year marriage produces no children (Ruth 1:4–5), the townspeople explicitly compare her to Rachel and Leah (4:11), and she only has a child after an explicit divine intervention following the townspeople's appeal to God (4:11–13; cf. Gen. 25:21). The lack of explicit disability imagery in the book of Ruth may not indicate that Ruth was fertile by default but that infertility was considered a normal human condition. Even in texts that do not deal with disability explicitly, the critical study of disability may help us to understand better the cultural expectations for human normalcy reflected in biblical literature.

Another common misconception is that critical scholarship on disability is a form of disability rights advocacy. Since disability studies grew out of the Disability Rights Movement, some might reasonably assume that biblical scholars who engage disability studies focus on using biblical literature to advocate for contemporary disability rights. This assumption may also arise from the fact that the biblical scholarship on disability focuses on a category of embodied identity like ethnicity, race, or gender. Over the last few decades, the general climate within biblical studies acknowledges that our scholarship is never completely objective or uninfluenced by our social locations. Some recent scholarship self-consciously analyzes or advocates for certain social, political, or confessional causes. Thus, considering the subject and scholarly climate in which work on disability in the Bible emerged, it is understandable that some people might assume that it self-consciously advocates for people with disabilities.

Yet, while some of the recent biblical scholarship on disability self-consciously promotes liberationist, confessional, and theological interpretations that advocate for persons with disabilities, most of the recent work focuses on how studying disability can help us to better understand biblical literature and the worldviews represented in them. In this sense, disability serves as a tool of scholarly analysis. In part, this recent work involves clarifying the many anachronistic scholarly interpretations of disability. Often, such interpretations come more from contemporary assumptions or biases about disability that scholars read back into the text than from evidence based on a careful reading of the text. As demonstrated by our examples from Genesis 39 and Ruth, we should not assume that ancient Israelite societies shared our contemporary ideas and stereotypes about disability or nondisability any more than they shared our contemporary ideas and stereotypes about other subjects such as kingship or sacrificial regulations. Such interpretations result in misconceptions about the text or the societies that produced the text. Critical examinations of disability improve our understanding of biblical literature and ancient Israelite societies substantially.

Biblical scholarship that engages disability studies is a relative newcomer to the field of biblical criticism, but it should not be dismissed as a trendy exercise. In some ways, the critical scholarship on disability has taken a fairly traditional exegetical approach to an untraditional topic. Although recent work on disability tends to avoid historical reconstructions of how ancient Israelites with disabilities lived, it still shares many of the goals and concerns of historical analysis of the Bible in that it accounts for ancient cultural assumptions reflected in this literature. This does not mean that biblical scholarship on disability cannot inform the work of disability rights advocates. Some disability advocates may find some of the scholarly correctives to popular misconceptions about disability in biblical literature helpful for their own projects. It does not seem problematic for disability advocates to engage biblical scholarship responsibly if they find such engagement useful.

CONCLUSION

Like all responsible biblical scholarship, if studying how cultural notions of disability operate in both biblical texts and in contemporary scholarship can help us to find new meanings in ancient texts, it is primarily because such study exposes and clarifies popular and scholarly (mis)conceptions about these ancient texts. If the burgeoning number of monographs and journal articles related to this subject are any indication, biblical scholarship on disability has a very exciting future.

KEY TERMS

cultural model of disability. This approach analyzes how a culture's representations and discussions of disability (and nondisability or able-bodiedness) help to articulate a range of values, ideals, or expectations that are important to that culture's organization and identity.

disability. Under the social model, disability refers to the social and structural discrimination that people with impairments experience. Under the cultural model, disability is the byproduct of a complex variety of cultural factors that shape and reinforce cultural understandings of mental and physical normality and abnormality.

impairment. A term used in the social model of disability for a biological anomaly that inhibits the body from functioning normatively. By this definition, a damaged limb or organ that makes activities such as walking or seeing difficult qualifies as an impairment.

medical model of disability. An approach that understands disability as an individual medical or healthcare issue that must be corrected or cured through treatment by healthcare professionals or lifestyle changes by the person with disabilities. This model locates the so-called "problem" of disability in the body of the individual.

social model of disability. Unlike the medical model, this approach interprets disability as a social issue rather than an individualized medical condition. The social model distinguishes the term impairment from the term disability. This model relocates the so-called "problem" of living with a disability from the individual body with impairments to the social and political structures that prevent people with impairments from full access to and participation in our social and political structures.

NOTES

1. Jeremy Schipper, *Disability Studies and the Hebrew Bible: Figuring Mephibosheth in the David Story* (Library of Hebrew Bible/Old Testament Studies 441; New York: T & T Clark, 2006), 15–16.
2. One finds a more detailed discussion of this point in Jeremy Schipper, "Embodying Deuteronomistic Theology in 1 Kings 15:22–24," in *Bodies, Embodiment, and Theology of the Hebrew Bible,* ed. Tamar Kamionkowski and Wonil Kim (Library of Hebrew Bible/Old Testament Studies 465; New York: T. & T. Clark, 2010), 77–89.
3. Rebecca Raphael, *Biblical Corpora: Representations of Disability in Hebrew Biblical Literature* (New York: T. & T. Clark, 2008), 119.

4. Joseph is sold by the Midianites according to Gen. 37:36. Many scholars account for this discrepancy with 39:1 as due to differences in sources. The Elohist refers to the Midianites, and the Yahwist refers to the Ishmaelites in 39:1.
5. One finds a discussion of male castration as a disability in Saul M. Olyan, *Disability and the Hebrew Bible: Interpreting Mental and Physical Differences* (New York: Cambridge University Press, 2008), 10–12, 28–29, 84–85.
6. One finds a concise review of scholarship on this issue in T. M. Lemos, "'Like the eunuch who does not beget': Gender, Mutilation, and Negotiated Status in the Ancient Near East," in *Disability Studies and Biblical Literature*, ed. Candida R. Moss and Jeremy Schipper (New York: Palgrave Macmillan, 2011), 47–66.
7. It is possible that the identification of the Egyptian who purchased Joseph as a eunuch named Potiphar in Gen. 39:1 may not have come from the Yahwist but from a later insertion that reconciled the purchaser's identity in Gen. 39:1 with the Elohistic account in Gen. 37:36. See Joel S. Baden, *The Composition of the Pentateuch: Renewing the Documentary Hypothesis* (New Haven, CT: Yale University Press, 2012), 220–24. This would explain why Potiphar's disability has little, if any, impact on the plot of Genesis 39 as noted below. Nevertheless, scholars who interpret Potiphar as a eunuch in Genesis 39 do not follow this source analysis. As we engage these scholars' interpretations in this section, we will read the text according to what they assume is included in this chapter.
8. On infertility in these other Yahwistic texts, consult Joel S. Baden, "The Nature of Barrenness in the Hebrew Bible," in *Disability Studies and Biblical Literature*, ed. Moss and Schipper, 13–27.
9. In fairness to the scholars discussed in this section, their explanations of Potiphar's wife's behavior serve as a corrective to interpretative traditions dating back to antiquity that have portrayed Potiphar's wife as an evil woman. For example, in *On Joseph* (5.22), Ambrose (*ca.* 339 CE–397 CE) regards Joseph as innocent but denounces Potiphar's wife as sinful and wicked because she gazed upon Joseph with evil intent (cf. Gen. 39:7).
10. Heather A. McKay, "Confronting Redundancy as Middle Manager and Wife: The Feisty Woman of Genesis 39," *Semeia* 87 (1999): 215–31 (227). McKay acknowledges the translation difficulties with the word *saris* but she identifies him as a eunuch (217). Similar explanations of Potiphar's wife's motivations for her behavior toward Joseph may have existed since antiquity. As James L. Kugel suggests, ancient interpreters may have concluded that, "Potiphar was a *saris* capable of sex, but simply sterile . . . . [Thus] to Mrs. Potiphar, unable to have children with her 'eunuch' husband, Joseph's allure might indeed be irresistible." James L. Kugel, *In Potiphar's House: The Interpretative Life of Biblical Texts,* 2nd ed. (Cambridge, MA: Harvard University Press, 1994), 76.
11. This implication reinforces a more explicit connection that has existed in some interpretations since antiquity. According to a talmudic passage, Potiphar acquired the good looking Joseph for his own sexual purposes, which were neither heterosexual nor reproductive. Thus the angel Gabriel castrated Potiphar as punishment for his sexual intentions toward Joseph (*b. Sotah* 13b; cf. *Gen. Rab.* 86:1, 3a). Similarly, the Islamic legends of al-Tabari and Tha'labi cite a source that describes Potiphar as "a man who did not have intercourse with women, though his wife Rail was beautiful and tender, and had property and possessions." Tabari, *The History of Al-Tabari: Prophets and Patriarchs,* ed. Said Amir Arjomand, trans. William M. Brinner, SUNY Series in Near Eastern Studies 2 (Albany: State University of New York Press, 1987), 154.
12. This textual silence leads Athalya Brenner to a different understanding of Potiphar's wife. Unlike McKay, Brenner concludes that Genesis 39 depicts Poti-

phar's wife negatively because, in contrast to other women in Genesis, she desires sexual intercourse for pleasure rather than reproduction. Athalya Brenner, *The Israelite Woman: Social Role and Literary Type in Biblical Narrative* (Sheffield: JSOT Press, 1985), 106–14.
13. Ron Pirson, "The Twofold Message of Potiphar's Wife," *Scandinavian Journal of the Old Testament* 18.2 (2004): 248–59.
14. Ibid., 256
15. Unfortunately, this interpretation of Potiphar reflects a common experience for many people with disabilities. People with disabilities may downplay the ways that their existence calls into question the cultural values and norms that reward the nondisabled by playing up or affirming the deviance of their own minds or bodies. One finds a discussion related to this issue in Robert McRuer, *Crip Theory: Cultural Signs of Queerness and Disability* (New York: New York University Press, 2006), 1–32.
16. Olyan provides a detailed discussion of those physical disabilities that do or do not qualify as a *mum* in the Hebrew Bible in *Disability in the Hebrew Bible*, 26–61.
17. Raphael, *Biblical Corpora*, 14–15.
18. Baden develops this point in "The Nature of Barrenness," 14–17.

FOR FURTHER READING

Avalos, Hector. *Illness and Health Care in the Ancient Near East: The Role of the Temple in Greece, Mesopotamia, and Israel.* Atlanta: Scholars, 1995.
Avalos, Hector, Sarah Melcher, and Jeremy Schipper, eds. *This Abled Body: Rethinking Disability and Biblical Studies.* Atlanta: Society of Biblical Literature, 2007.
Dorman, Johanna. *The Blemished Body: Deformity and Disability in the Qumran Scrolls.* Groningen: Rijksuniversiteit, 2007.
Melcher, Sarah, Mikeal Parsons, and Amos Yong, eds. *Disability and the Bible: A Commentary.* Waco, TX: Baylor University Press, forthcoming.
Moss, Candida, and Jeremy Schipper, eds. *Disability Studies and Biblical Literature.* New York: Palgrave MacMillan, 2011.
Olyan, Saul M. *Disability in the Hebrew Bible: Interpreting Mental and Physical Differences.* New York: Cambridge University Press, 2008.
Raphael, Rebecca. *Biblical Corpora: Representations of Disability in Hebrew Biblical Literature.* New York: T. & T. Clark, 2008.
Schipper, Jeremy. *Disability and Isaiah's Suffering Servant.* New York: Oxford University Press, 2011.
———. *Disability Studies and the Hebrew Bible: Figuring Mephibosheth in the David Story.* New York: T. & T. Clark, 2006.

Chapter 3

Ecological Criticism

Norman C. Habel

Ecological criticism, or ecological hermeneutics as it is more widely known, is a relatively recent second-level reading of a biblical text arising primarily in response to the current ecological crisis facing our planet. In general terms, ecological criticism in this presentation is an ecocritical reading of the text from the perspective of Earth or the Earth community.

Ecological hermeneutics, of course, may be understood more broadly than a specific ecocritical analysis of biblical texts. Ernst Conradie, for example, calls for a new "horizon," a hermeneutic that will enable us to interrelate the biblical roots of Christianity, the history of Christian tradition, the content of Christian faith, ethical categories, and the challenges of environmental degradation (2010, 311). In this chapter, however, I will confine ecological criticism to a critical, second-level interpretation of biblical texts employing appropriate tools of analysis, namely suspicion, identification, and retrieval.[1]

ORIGINS: PERSONAL

Where did this approach to reading the text begin for me? Some may argue that as an exegete born and raised among the emus and eucalypts of the Australian countryside, I was unknowingly nurtured as much by the Australian bush as by the discipline of a Lutheran exegetical tradition or a contemporary historical-critical tradition. It could also perhaps be argued that wandering with my brother for miles every weekend deep in the native bush, where I felt a kinship with snakes, eels, and goannas, I unconsciously developed a spiritual connection with the nonhuman Earth community.

Returning to Australia in 1974—after almost twenty years of city life in North America—I realized I would need to de-Americanize myself to be true to my Australian hermeneutical postcolonial context. In the late 1970s, I also did a little research into the life of my great grandfather Wilhelm Habel, in connection with a commemoration of his lifework. To my surprise and delight, I discovered that he was more than a German pacifist turned farmer.

My grandfather, it seems, objected to the endless clearing of land around two lakes between which he built his farmhouse. He chose, therefore, to plant local trees around the lakes to encourage new growth and the return of wild life—demonstrating that he was an "environmentalist" more than one hundred years before the term became popular! After planting native trees around Lake Linlithgow, he met strong opposition from the nearby farmers who banded together and pulled up all the young trees. They declared, "God intended this land for sheep not for trees. We don't want a sinful pleasure park here like those in the city of Melbourne"[2]

It is one thing to honor an ancestor who affirmed the intrinsic worth of trees, birds, land, and lakes; it is quite another to experience in person a genuine kinship with these members of the Earth community in any meaningful or spiritual sense. My second reorientation to Earth began during a close encounter with the world of Indigenous Australians. A group of Aboriginal elders from Queensland in northeast Australia invited me to function as a facilitator to prepare a written expression of their oral theology.

My preparation for this role included twenty years of academic study of the Aboriginal religions of Australia, my research into the land ideologies of the Hebrew Scriptures (Habel 1995), and my active participation in a national movement to effect reconciliation between indigenous and nonindigenous Australians, a movement now known in South Australia as "The Journey of Healing." In spite of this preparation, I experienced during my role as facilitator a new level of understanding of the nonhuman world that also demanded a reorientation to reading texts in my biblical heritage where the natural world was in focus.

The group of indigenous leaders involved designated themselves "Rainbow Spirit Elders" because their belief in a creator spirit, often associated with a primal rainbow snake, was a common element in the mythology of northeast Australia. My task was to listen to a local theology that was expressed in a set of predominantly oral beliefs that lay suppressed behind the official face of a shared Christian doctrine, despite denominational differences. The result was the text of *Rainbow Spirit Theology* (Rainbow Spirit Elders 1997).

In hindsight, I realize that a significant aspect of my reorientation was a transformation of an academic comprehension of how traditional indigenous peoples relate to Earth—and to land in particular—to a first-hand appreciation of this relationship as expressed in the personal faith and wisdom of elders who had survived Western attempts to destroy their indigenous culture. In this process of Westernization, many Christian missions were complicit agents of destruction.

For these elders the land was alive, spirit-filled, and life-nurturing. For each individual elder, specific parts of the land were kin, kin-filled, and kin-determining. These kin connections may be with indwelling ancestors or with animate or inanimate parts of the landscape.

I came to realize that the worldview many anthropologists and missionaries had derided as animism was, in fact, a sophisticated and complex articulation of the interconnectedness of all the natural forces and spiritual entities of Earth. My Western education had led me to view that natural world—however beautiful and bountiful—as a collection of objects. Human beings, I firmly believed, were beings of a radically different—and superior—order to the rest of creation.

This experience led me to ask the following questions: Are Earth and the components of Earth my kin in some sense? Is Earth my parent or partner? Is Earth merely a lump of stardust? Are rabbits my relatives, regardless of how much farmers may condemn them as vermin?

It needs to be emphasized that this orientation is not to be identified with a belief in Earth as a goddess like the classical Greek figure of Gaia. My experience of the indigenous world led me to recognize a dimension of life and thought that has been lost to most of us in the Western world, at least since the Enlightenment, if not before. The Earth community is not only a part of creation reflecting massive diversity; it is also an extensive family, a network of interconnected beings. Everything from the platypus to plasma is my kin in some way. I am an Earth being, kin with all other beings in the Earth community. When I read a biblical text, I can no longer ignore this dimension of my identity.

ORIGINS: PRO-EARTH PERSPECTIVES

A further contributing factor in the development of an ecological hermeneutic has been the emergence of what I am calling a new "Earth consciousness," a consciousness that assumes a variety of social, psychological, and spiritual forms of expression. These diverse expressions of awareness are responses to the ecological crisis facing Earth and appear in a wide range of disciplines and domains of contemporary society.

Planet Earth, after the initial trip of humans to the moon, was no longer viewed as an indestructible mass of matter that could be exploited for oil, soil, and endless resources selected for human consumption. Quite suddenly, Earth was a fragile green-blue planet that many sensitive and Earth-conscious humans regarded in a new way. Earth was no longer a cluster of conflicting countries; Earth was a habitat we call home. And a new question was posed: how should we relate to this precious planet, and why is it in such jeopardy now?

An early response was articulated by Lynn White (1967) in his now famous critique of Christianity as a major contributing factor in the exploitation and devastation of much of our planet home. White, as an Earth protagonist, argued that traditional Christian readings of the Bible had led to a destructive domination of Earth. For White and others, the salvation of Earth from this religious ideology lay in science and not with the churches—whose mission was frequently viewed as focused on saving souls for heaven, rather than on saving Earth for living. The latter focus became the mantra of conservationists and ecologists.

Another dimension of the wider pro-Earth movement is exemplified by the more philosophical and spiritual thrust of Thomas Berry (1988), Matthew Fox, (1983), and proponents of the Gaia hypothesis (e.g., Lovelock 1988). These scholars introduced what might be broadly called a new "Earth spirituality." In the work of these scholars, Earth was viewed as a spiritual entity, a source of sacred power, and a special living presence in the cosmos. Spiritual insights and intuitions from all ages, cultures, and wisdoms were cited and used to support this new pro-Earth perspective.

A number of writers have raised questions about particular aspects of the approach being outlined in this chapter. Tim Meadowcroft, for example, argues that seeking to retrieve the voice of Earth is itself an anthropocentric device and at the end of the exercise "the voice of the earth continues to look suspiciously like a human creation" (2000, 5–6). The Earth Bible Team responded by reiterating their suspicion that interpreters suppress the voice of Earth and by citing the experience of writers who read with an awareness of Earth as a subject and do indeed discern the voice of Earth (2001, 23–24).

Ernst Conradie argues that the principles enunciated in The Earth Bible project are inadequate because they represent a "radical this-worldly theology with no reference to divine presence in the world" (Conradie 2010, 308). He then proceeds to develop what he calls a more adequate doctrinal construct, a hermeneutical horizon that is shaped by an ecumenical Christian theology and its reading of the biblical text. That construct is being developed in a current research project titled Christian Faith and the Earth (Conradie 2010, 311). David Horrell tends to agree with Conradie, because the ecojustice principles represent the authority for the project rather than the Bible or Christian theology (2010, 120). He maintains that by adopting a doctrinal construct it becomes clear that "We are not simply claiming to read or present what the text "says," but are acknowledging that our reading of the Bible is a *construction*, shaped by certain priorities and convictions. (2010, 123)

Another type of construct is that enunciated by Douglas Hall, who selects the concept of stewardship as the lens with which to interpret the text and harmonize problematic passages in the light of a governing anthropocentric center, as the title of his article illustrates: "Stewardship as a Key to a Theology of Nature" (2006, 129–44).

In response to these approaches, it needs to be emphasized here that ecological criticism is not governed by a Christian doctrinal or theological orientation. Just as the approaches of historical criticism or rhetorical criticism are determined by the principles of historical or rhetorical analysis rather than a doctrinal construct, so ecological criticism is grounded in the principles of ecological analysis. The interpreter reads from the perspective of Earth and the Earth community with ecology as the determining lens rather than a doctrine of creation or a Christian construct.

Another approach that may well deserve consideration is that of Monica Melanchthon (2010). She maintains that empathy with Earth and members of the Earth community should also include empathy for the poor who are victims of environmental destruction. There is a necessary kinship between the oppressed Earth and the oppressed of Earth.

ORIGINS: AN ECOLOGY-INFORMED WORLDVIEW

We are also faced with the challenge of a new view of the natural world, a new understanding of the universe, a new cosmology that has little in common with the biblical, the geocentric, or the heliocentric cosmologies of the past. We are becoming aware of an ecocosmology, a worldview where ecology conditions our thinking.

What is ecology? According to Oxford's *A Dictionary of Ecology*, "Ecology is the scientific study of the interrelationships among organisms and between them and all aspects, living and non-living, of their environment" (Allaby 2003, 136). This definition reflects a very limited perspective that locates ecology as but one scientific discipline among many. In reality, ecology has now become an integral part of our social, political, and personal worlds. And if we are to face the challenge of ecology in biblical studies, we need to articulate what ecology really means as part of our emerging worldview and how we read texts from the perspective of that worldview.

Strange to say, most of the scholars who explore ecotheology, ecoethics, and similar fields rarely seem to begin by defining just what they mean by "ecology." They often take the meaning of ecology for granted. How might we describe the essence of ecology that informs this new worldview? One option is the formulation by Thomas Berry:

> In reality there is a single integral community of the Earth that includes all its component members whether human or other than human. In this community every being has its own role to fulfil, its own dignity, its inner spontaneity. Every being has its own voice. Every being declares itself to the entire universe. Every being enters into communion with other beings. This capacity for relatedness, for presence to other beings, for spontaneity

in action, is a capacity possessed by every mode of being throughout the entire universe. So too every being has rights to be recognised and revered. (1999, 4)

Taking this new ecological worldview seriously leads to what has been described as an ecological conversion. In his General Audience Address in January 2001, Pope John Paul II introduced the need for just such a reorientation. Catholic theologians such as Denis Edwards have promoted this concept as integral to the development of ecotheology (2006, 2–4). And, I would argue, this reorientation is crucial for a serious critical ecological reading of the biblical text.

The context of this concept is the growing ecological crisis and our emerging awareness of its implications. The dilemma before us is the way we understand this laudable reorientation. What are the parameters of this conversion experience? From what am I being converted? To what am I being converted? According to Edwards,

> Commitment to ecology has not yet taken its central place in Christian self-understanding. It is far from central in terms of its structure, personnel and money. As the church itself is called to conversion to the side of the poor in the struggle of justice and to the side of women in their struggle for full equality, so the church itself is called to conversion to the side of suffering creation. (2006, 3)

If this reorientation means taking a stand at the side of suffering creation, joining the struggle for ecojustice, and seeking to heal the wounds of our planet, then the process is indeed worthy and vital. In this context, the question at hand is how such conversion plays a role in reading the Bible. The "suffering creation" presumably relates to the current ecological crisis. How does this rich new ecological awareness influence our critical interpretation of that biblical tradition from the past that has contributed to the suffering of creation in the present?

In our new cosmology, our ecologically informed view of the natural world, and more particularly of Earth, I suggest that as we read we are conscious of Earth as a living planet that originated in cosmos space and evolved into a living habitat, as a fragile web of interconnected and interdependent forces and domains of existence, as a living community in which humans and all other organisms are kin who live and move and have their common destiny.

In short, the current ecological cosmology challenges us to read from within Earth as our habitat, with Earth as our partner, and with concern for a suffering Earth as we face the future.

ORIGINS: DUALISM AND FEMINISM

Ecological criticism acknowledges a significant debt to the approaches of feminism. I had long been aware that many of our Western theological thought patterns are governed by an underlying set of dualisms. These have been articulated very clearly by Val Plumwood (1993) and are summarized by the Earth Bible Team in volume 1 of The Earth Bible series (2000, 40–42).

Especially significant among these dualisms are the powerful polarities between culture and nature, human and (nonhuman) nature, reason and matter, spiritual and material, heaven and Earth, subject and object, male and female. In these pairings, the realities associated with the human and male pole of the pairing have long been considered superior to the opposing nature and female pole. Feminists have exposed these polarities as socially constructed and flawed, especially in relation to their presentation as either-or pairings, and the posited linkages between terms grouped at the female pole. Ecofeminists, like Sally McFague (2008) and Heather Eaton (2000), have extended aspects of the feminist approach that focus on the female/feminine in relation to nature and the physical realm.

In developing an ecological hermeneutic, The Earth Bible Team asked: are any of these dualisms inherent in the ancient biblical text, or have they been read into the text by subsequent generations of exegetes? An associated challenge faced the team: how are we to formulate appropriate questions to uncover the way various biblical texts compare humanity and nature, spirit and matter, heaven and Earth?

Much of our Western understanding of nature, it would seem, goes back to the influence of thinkers like Descartes (Ponting 1991, 147). Philosophers and scientists of the seventeenth and eighteenth centuries pressed the dualism of medieval Christianity to its logical conclusion. They viewed Earth as a machine, God as the great designer of the machine, and humans as fashioned to determine the workings of the machine and run it for the benefit of human beings. As modern interpreters, we in the West are often unconsciously influenced by this heritage.

The task of transcending dualistic forms of Western thinking is not easy. Our task is to find a sympathetic way of relating to Earth, nature, and components of the material world whenever they appear in the text. We are obliged to undertake a conscious paradigm shift in order to appreciate Earth as subject rather than object; kin rather than mere matter; partner rather than pawn to be dominated; an active and vocal participant rather than a silent, passive victim.

Feminist reading strategies, especially the work of Elisabeth Schüssler Fiorenza (1985), provided the model of a hermeneutic of suspicion and retrieval. This approach was adapted so that Earth/nature became the focus rather than the feminine/female. The suspicion aspect of this approach means that we may legitimately suspect that biblical texts and past interpretations of these texts—because they have been written by human beings—will probably reflect the interests of human beings, and focus on human well-being, human relationships with God, and the personal salvation of human believers. In short, we suspect that biblical texts are likely to be anthropocentric, as well as patriarchal or androcentric, because most writers and interpreters of the Bible in past periods were males socialized within dominant patriarchal traditions.

The second aspect of this approach involves discerning features in the text that facilitate a retrieval of traditions about Earth or the Earth community that have been unnoticed, suppressed, or hidden. The task before us is to reread the text and identify where Earth and members of the Earth community have suffered, resisted, or been excluded by attitudes apparent within the text or factors influencing its interpretation in particular historical contexts. We also need to consider the possibility that there are suppressed Earth traditions that resist the dominant patriarchal anthropocentric orientation of the text and that this resistance can be discerned and voiced.

PROCESS: THE EARTH BIBLE PRINCIPLES

The preceding discussion outlines some of the key factors that influenced the development of the ecojustice hermeneutic used in The Earth Bible series. After considerable debate the members of The Earth Bible Team adopted the following aims for The Earth Bible Project:

- to acknowledge, before reading the biblical text, that as Western interpreters we are heirs of a long anthropocentric, patriarchal, and androcentric approach to reading the text that has devalued the Earth and that continues to influence the way we read the text;
- to declare, before reading the text, that we are members of a human community that has exploited, oppressed, and endangered the existence of the Earth community;
- to become progressively more conscious that we are also members of the endangered Earth community in dialogue with ancient texts;
- to recognize Earth as a subject in the text with which we seek to relate empathetically rather than as a topic to be analyzed rationally;
- to take up the cause of justice for Earth to ascertain whether Earth and the Earth community are oppressed, silenced, or liberated in the text;
- to develop techniques of reading the text to discern and retrieve alternative traditions where the voice of Earth and Earth community has been suppressed.

To guide us in achieving these aims, we articulated a set of ecojustice principles. These principles were developed in dialogue with ecologists, such as Charles Birch (1990), and their writings over a number of years. The principles articulated below were refined in consultations and workshops concerned with ecology in general and ecological concerns linked to theology and the Bible more specifically.

The principle of intrinsic worth: the universe, Earth, and all its components have intrinsic worth/value.

The principle of interconnectedness: Earth is a community of interconnected living things that are mutually dependent on each other for life and survival.

The principle of voice: Earth is a subject capable of raising its voice in celebration and against injustice.

The principle of purpose: the universe, Earth, and all its components are part of a dynamic cosmic design within which each piece has a place in the overall goal of that design.

The principle of mutual custodianship: Earth is a balanced and diverse domain where responsible custodians can function as partners with, rather than rulers over, Earth to sustain its balance and a diverse Earth community.

The principle of resistance: Earth and its components not only suffer from human injustices but actively resist them in the struggle for justice.

When reading the text, the writers for the Earth Bible series asked critical questions provoked by these principles to ascertain whether there is justice for Earth in the orientation, ideology, or focus of the text or its interpreters: Is Earth viewed merely as a human resource or as a subject with intrinsic worth? Is Earth treated as a subject with a "voice" or as an object to be exploited? A detailed discussion of these principles and their usage is provided by The Earth Bible team in the opening volume of The Earth Bible series (2000).

The principles were not intended to be exhaustive or definitive. Ongoing dialogue with ecologists and those employing this approach have led to further refinements and modifications. These principles, moreover, are not articulated in terms of any specific religious tradition so that they may be used broadly across traditions.

PROCESS: ECOLOGICAL HERMENEUTICS

After consideration of the various critiques of The Earth Bible principles, dialogue within The Earth Bible team, and an analysis of so-called second-level hermeneutical approaches, such as feminism and postcolonial hermeneutics, a more precise set of steps were developed for testing and exploration as part of a Consultation on Ecological Hermeneutics at the annual meetings of the Society of Biblical Literature.

A revised ecological hermeneutic requires a radical reorientation to the biblical text. The task before us is not an exploration of what a given text may say *about* creation, *about* nature, or *about* Earth. In this context, Earth is not a topos or theme for analysis. We are not focusing on ecology *and* creation or ecology *and* theology (Habel 2000a). An ecological hermeneutic demands a radical change of posture in relation to Earth as a subject in the text.

A radical ecological approach to the text involves a critical hermeneutic of suspicion, identification, and retrieval. This progression bears obvious similarities with several approaches of well-known feminist hermeneutics. The difference, of course, is that we are not reading from within the worldview of women, but first and foremost from within the orientation of an ecosystem called Earth. We are reading as creatures of Earth, members of the Earth community, in solidarity with Earth. We are Earth beings, and Earth is our habitat.

Suspicion—Anthropocentric Bias

First, we begin reading with the suspicion that the text is likely to be inherently anthropocentric and/or has traditionally been read from an anthropocentric perspective. At the outset, "anthropocentric" needs to be distinguished from "anthropogenic"—a text originating from humans, and from "anthropotopic"— a text in which humans are a central topos or theme.

The anthropocentric bias that we are likely to find both in ourselves as readers and in the text we are reading has at least two faces. The first is the assumption or condition we have inherited as human beings, especially in the Western world, that we are beings of a totally different order than all other creatures in nature, or, in other words, in the hierarchy of things there is God, human beings, and the rest of creation.

Even where scholars have insisted that texts are theocentric rather than anthropocentric in character, the writer may ultimately be more concerned about God's relation to humanity or a group within humanity than about God's relation to the Earth or the Earth community as a whole. The Bible has long been understood as God's book for humans. And for those of us who have been reading biblical texts that way for years, this understanding has come to be self-evident. Should we not then, with a new ecological consciousness, legitimately suspect that the text and its interpreters have been understandably anthropocentric?

A second face of this anthropocentric bias relates to nature as "object." We have for so long viewed nature and all its parts, both animate and inanimate, as the objects of many forms of human investigation, of which scientific analysis is but one. This process has not only reinforced a sense of human superiority over nature, but has also contributed to a sense of distance, separation, and otherness. The rest of nature, especially the inanimate world, has been viewed as separate, other, and a force to be harnessed.

This phase of the hermeneutical process is related especially to the principle of intrinsic worth articulated in The Earth Bible. When viewed with a traditional anthropocentric bias, other parts of nature are considered of less value. Often they are seen merely as the stage, scenery, or background for God's relationship with humanity rather than as valued subjects in their own right.

When viewing the readings of past interpreters, our suspicion may be directed to many previous forms of criticism. A scholar may begin with a literary or narrative analysis, seeking to uncover the basic design of the narrator. In such analyses it is typical that the design revolves around human or divine characters and themes. Earth or members of the Earth community are not likely to be determinative characters or forces in any perceived plot, rhetoric, or design of the text.

When scholars explore the historical, cultural, or social background and dimensions of the text, they have a natural propensity to focus on human events, contexts, and relationships rather than the natural habitat, environment, or entities imbedded in the text. We read, therefore, with a suspicion that past scholars reflect an anthropocentric bias in most traditional forms of biblical criticism.

Identification—Empathy with Earth

The second element of a contemporary ecological criticism is the task of empathy or identification.

In the light of my experience as an editor and writer in The Earth Bible project, it has become clear that the activity of identification now deserves to be highlighted as a distinct step in the hermeneutical process. As human beings we identify, often unconsciously, with the various human characters in the biblical story, whether that identification be empathetic or antipathetic. We can identify with the experiences of these characters, even if they are not necessarily ones we admire or emulate.

Even before reading the narrative or poetry of the text, a reader using this approach must—at least to some extent—come to terms with his or her deep ecological connections. Before we begin reading and seek to identify with Earth in the text, we need to face the prior ecological reality of our kinship with Earth as outlined above. We are Earth beings, born of Earth, and living expressions of the ecosystem that has emerged on this planet. Our identities are influenced by the various environmental forces we experience in a given habitat. This step relates to the fundamental principle of interconnectedness that was explored in The Earth Bible.

Identification with Earth and members of the Earth community raises our consciousness to the injustices against Earth reflected in the text as they are portrayed at the hands of both humans and God. The exegete who pursues a radical ecological approach ultimately takes up the cause of the natural world seeking to expose the wrongs that Earth has suffered, largely in silence, and to discern, where possible, the way Earth has resisted these wrongs. Our aim is to read in solidarity with Earth. We are Earth beings reading in empathy with Earth.

Our approach is to move beyond a focus on ecological themes to a process of listening to, and identifying with, the Earth as a presence, character, or voice in the text. Our task is to take up the cause of the Earth and the nonhuman members of the Earth community by sensing their presence in the text—whether their presence is suppressed, oppressed, or celebrated. We seek indicators of ecological wisdom to identify with the Earth in its ecojustice struggle and move beyond merely identifying ecological themes in creation theology or.

A crucial dimension of this step is to identify with nonhuman figures in the narrative, empathizing with their roles, character, and treatment. By such a process we seek to discern the voices of the figures involved. Another dimension of this process is to locate ourselves in the habitat of the participants in the narrative. By so doing we may be able to discern multiple forces, whether positive or negative, interacting with the characters in the text and determining their identities. These interactions may reveal other indications of mastery where a given entity has been isolated, suppressed, or devalued by the dominant figures and forces in the habitat of the characters involved.

In this step, when we read the text as Earth beings, we identify with one or more of the nonhuman characters in the text and locate ourselves in their respective habitats to ascertain what forces or factors we might legitimately claim these characters have experienced.

Retrieval—The Voice of Earth

The third facet of this ecological criticism is that of retrieval. The process of retrieval is closely related to the prior steps of suspicion and identification.

As the interpreter exposes the various anthropocentric dimensions of the text—the ways in which the human agenda and bias are sustained either by the reader or the implied author—the text may reveal a number of surprises about the nonhuman characters in the story. Earth or members of the Earth community may play a key role or be highly valued in the text, but because of the Western interpretive tradition we have inherited, that dimension of the text has been ignored or suppressed.

Where we meet nonhuman figures communicating in some way—mourning, praising, or singing—we have tended in the past to dismiss these expressions as poetic license or symbolic language. Our anthropocentric bias leads to classifying these elements as mere anthropomorphisms.

Discerning Earth and members of the Earth community as subjects with a voice is a key part of the retrieval process. In some contexts their voice is evident but has been traditionally ignored by exegetes. In other contexts the voice of Earth is not explicit, but nevertheless present and powerful in a silent way. These subjects play roles in the text that are more than mere scenery or secondary images. Their voice needs to be heard, a voice that need not correspond to the language of words we commonly associate with the human voice.

Discerning this voice may even take the form of reconstructing the narrative—as a dimension of the interpretation process—in such a way as to hear

Earth as a narrator of the story. In the process, Earth becomes an interpreter. Such a reconstruction is, of course, not the original text, but a reading as valid as the numerous efforts of biblical scholars over the centuries to reconstruct the history, literary sources, social world, or theology behind a text.

The task before us is to reread the text to discern where the Earth or members of the Earth community may have suffered, resisted, or been excluded by attitudes within the text or the history of its interpretation. The task demands a strategy for reclaiming the sufferings and struggles of the Earth, a task that involves regarding the wider Earth community as our kin. The aim is to read as Earth beings in tune with Earth, the very source of our being.

There is a strong possibility that biblical texts may be more sympathetic to the plight and potential of the Earth than our previous interpretations have allowed, even if the ecological questions we are posing arise out of a contemporary Earth consciousness. We also need to consider the possibility that there are suppressed Earth traditions that resist the dominant patriarchal anthropocentric orientation of the text. By counter-reading the text it may be possible to identify alternative voices that challenge or subvert the normative voice of the dominant tradition. Whether these sub-texts point to the continuing voice of ancient traditions still in touch with the Earth, or whether these alternative perspectives arose as a mode of resisting the patriarchal orientation of monotheistic Yahwism is a task for future interpreters to explore.

Especially significant in this context is the contribution of feminists and ecofeminists. Not only have they focused on identifying the patriarchal orientation and bias of both text and interpreter, they have also developed techniques of "reading against the grain" and discerning traces of antipatriarchal resistance in the text. Clues are sought within the text that point to traditions where the suppressed voices of women resisting a patriarchal society can be detected and the tradition itself retrieved.

This technique of retrieval has been developed in a more "revolutionary" way by feminists such as Ilana Pardes, who discerns countertraditions—sub-texts that read against the grain of the dominant rhetoric of the main text. The patriarchy of the Bible is "continuously challenged by antithetical trends" that need to be uncovered (Pardes 1992, 51). Pardes's goal is to reconstruct, in the light of surviving remains, "antithetical undercurrents which call into question the monotheistic repression of femininity."

Similarly, interpreters employing an ecological hermeneutic may pursue counter-readings that seek to retrieve elements of resistance, hidden undercurrents, and suppressed voices that reflect the perspective of Earth or the Earth community and challenge the dominant anthropocentric voices of the biblical text. These suppressed elements provide the basis for reconstructing the voices of Earth and the domains of Earth that have been silenced by traditional reading. This step relates to the fundamental principle of voice that was explored in The Earth Bible.

THE NILE PLAGUE—AN ECOCRITICAL READING

Suspicion

If we consider the plague narrative in which the Nile is turned to blood (Exod. 7:14–24) we begin by suspecting that the text and efforts to discern the literary design of the text may be anthropocentric and pay little attention to the Nile as a character in the structure of the plot.

The plague cycle has been analyzed by source critics to determine whether there are several plague traditions imbedded in the cycle. Literary critics have identified these narratives as legends from Israel's past that introduce us to two main protagonists: Moses, who represents the God of the enslaved Israelites, and Pharaoh, who represents the gods of Egypt. The two protagonists represent two masculine human domains of power. Moses is even said to be "like God to Pharaoh" (Exod. 7:1).

In a typical plague cycle plot, Moses, at his God's behest, asks Pharaoh to let God's people go to worship in the desert. Pharaoh refuses and Moses' God sends a plague, via the agency of Aaron, that is intended to force Pharaoh to change his mind. Initially, he relents but then hardens his heart and forces the Israelites to stay.

In the plague under consideration, the Nile is turned to blood and all life in the Nile is destroyed. In spite of the fact that the Nile is pivotal to the plot, the Nile is not viewed as a character, partner, or victim by most literary analysts. The Nile apparently has no voice in the plot, but remains as a passive acquiescing tool of a divine power. Nor is there any indication of positive divine relationships with the Nile as a valued domain of creation.

Other scholars have sought to interpret this plague as a legendary version of a natural ecological disaster. They seek to read the text in terms of a plausible historical context that gave rise to the legend (Fretheim 1991). Their approach is based on the infrequent occurrence of an unusually heavy rainfall in the highlands of Ethiopia. The annual rise of the river that starts in July and reaches its peak in mid-September is said, on rare occasions, to result in catastrophe rather than fertility. The soil in the basin of the Blue Nile and its tributary, the Atbara, is tropical, red earth. This red sediment emerges along the Nile when floods from the highlands pour downstream and discolor the waters so that they look much like blood.

Similar natural explanations, based on this same flooding phenomenon, are given for the subsequent plagues. Whatever the natural phenomena, however, the text as it reads portrays the event as a blatant destructive act of God. What may have happened in natural terms is not the agenda of this text but a reconstruction of scholars. Such reconstructions are not ecological criticism, but efforts to discover a possible historical disaster behind the text that seeks to explain the text and, to some extent, excuse the overt devaluing of nature by the God of Israel.

Identification

If we now take a second step and identify with the Nile as a living subject in the narrative, we gain a sense of injustice and assault at what happens. We realize that we are an innocent victim, the object of a divine power play. When we look more closely at the text, we realize that the whole ecosystem of the land of Egypt is abused. The land becomes like a bleeding corpse.

A key text in question reads,

> The LORD said to Moses, "Say to Aaron, 'Take your staff and stretch out your hand over the waters of Egypt—over its rivers, its canals, and its ponds, and all its pools of water—so that they may become blood; and there shall be blood throughout the whole land of Egypt, even in vessels of wood and in vessels of stone.'" (Exod. 7:19)

Fretheim suggests that the image of water as shed blood anticipates the sea becoming red with Egyptian blood. He argues that this image is a sign, "more than just a bloody mess, a lot of dead fish and a headache for waterworks personnel." Blood, which will be a sign of deliverance for Israel (Exod. 12:13), here becomes a sign of disaster for Egypt (Fretheim 1991, 388).

If, however, I identify with the Nile or the land of Egypt, the blood is a sign of physical abuse and virtual murder. God striking the waters is a cruel blow that results in blood and death. It affects me personally. God strikes the waters, not because they are explicitly in league with Pharaoh or the oppressors. They are apparently collateral damage in the war of YHWH against Pharaoh and the gods of Egypt. There is no obvious ecological interconnection between the oppressors and the waters.

The waters of the Nile are a life-giving force, a massive ecosystem that sustains both humans and nonhumans along the length of the Nile. The waters of the Nile are the life-blood of several countries. The waters of the Nile flow for some 3,500 miles with a watershed that is estimated to be about a million acres. The Nile, and the ancient Nile god Hapi, represent the waters of life for millions of people, plants, and other living creatures.

Why should the Nile be polluted by God and all its life-giving waters turned to blood when all God had to do was change the mind of one man—Pharaoh? Why destroy millions of creatures in the Nile ecosystem? All God had to do was *not* to harden Pharaoh's heart. Why should the waters of the Nile be demonized when one human being called Pharaoh is the real demon?

Where scholars focus on the water events, they try to retrieve natural phenomena that could possibly explain the events. The waters of the Nile, however, are victims of divine pollution; they have been unfairly demonized as forces for a warrior God to conquer. These water ecosystems have been violated and their true character denied. Some may describe these water events as evidence of the sovereignty of God over nature (Sarna 1986, 115), but clearly God's sovereignty is here devoid of empathy. There is no rainbow at the end of these water events to suggest that God will never again violate the ecosystems of nature.

When I identify with the Nile and the creatures of the Nile I become angry and challenge the very portrayal of God in this legend as a power-hungry protagonist who is ready to destroy vast domains of life and living water. I also become aware that the violation of the Nile ecosystems by a less-than-compassionate deity also means untold suffering for the poor of Egypt who depend on the waters of the Nile for their very existence.

Retrieval

Is it possible to retrieve the voice of the Nile in this text? As we identify with the Nile we become aware of just how the Nile and the Nile community have been silenced. We also become aware of just how forcefully the legend focuses on the mighty protagonists of the plot and the resulting abuse of nature by a deity bent on demonstrating superiority.

Is there any indication that the narrative reflects an empathy with nature and does not simply reflect the dominant culture of the leading protagonists in the legend? Are there any clues in the language of the text that suggest we might be able to read another perspective by reading against the grain?

Significantly, the narrator does not merely indicate that the waters of the Nile will be miraculously turned into blood as Moses announced to Pharaoh when he planned his morning ritual bath. Rather, the account describes the instruction given to Aaron as stretching out his hand to curse rivers, canals, pools, and even water vessels so that blood is found throughout the land.

In addition, the outcome of the plague is described emotively as the waters of the Nile changing into blood, all the fish dying, and the river emitting such a putrid smell that the Egyptians are unable to drink the water. Given these clues, it seems we may well hear the suppressed voice rising from these verses as follows:

> I am the Nile, a rich source of life for numerous plants, peoples, and fish. I suffered a vicious unwarranted assault at the instigation of the God of Israel. I did not deserve it, nor did any of the creatures I sustain. And what made this assault even more disgusting is the plot announced by this God that, even before it happened, the plague would not be effective. This God had already planned to harden Pharaoh's heart and force further plagues that demonstrated a total disdain for the value of creation. I call on the God of Israel to demonstrate compassion and hear the groaning of creation across Egypt. It is one thing to find ways to rescue the people of Israel from slavery. It is quite another to debase domains of creation in the process.

CONCLUSION

I have applied the basic steps of an ecological criticism to a biblical narrative, relating how the waters of the Nile are changed into blood, and in so doing, I have exposed an anthropocentric heritage that focuses on dominating protagonists who represent the gods of Israel and Egypt. By identifying with the Nile, I have discerned a blatant injustice; the waters and life of the Nile suffer unjustly at the hands of the God of Israel. By listening to the suppressed voice of the groaning, bleeding Nile I believe I can hear cries of anguish—the Nile calling on the God of Israel to have compassion not only for God's people but also for God's creation.

I have elsewhere identified this as a "gray" passage because of the way in which nature is devalued (Habel 2009, xviii–xxi). There are numerous other texts in the Bible where identifying with Earth or domains of Earth reveals "green" texts where nature is valued but where that valuing has been traditionally ignored. One such text is Genesis 1:1–13, which describes the birth of Earth (Habel 2011).

The basic hermeneutic of suspicion, identification, and retrieval outlined above offers a model developed by a number of scholars in recent years. This approach need not by employed in a pedantic way, but in a manner that facilitates a genuine, critical, ecological interpretation of the text or book involved.

Our goal, however, is to discern more than ecological wisdom imbedded in the text. Our aim is to identify with Earth and other domains of Earth so that through critical analysis their presence, passion, and perspective are clearly identified.

KEY TERMS

Ecojustice means justice for Earth and members of the Earth community by enabling the voice of Earth to be heard and the rights of Earth to be represented in the context of the injustices perpetrated on Earth, past and present. Six ecojustice principles are enunciated in The Earth Bible series and serve as a guide for interpreters of biblical texts.

Identification is the second and pivotal step in ecological criticism. The reader, aware that he or she is an Earth being, informed by an ecological consciousness, empathizes and identifies with Earth and other members of the Earth community rather than with human characters only. The interpreter then reads from the perspective of Earth or a domain of Earth.

Gray texts are those passages in the Bible that not only reflect an anthropocentric bias but are also at odds with the principles of ecojustice and in the process reflect humans or God devaluing nature and creation.

Green texts are those consistent with the principles of ecojustice and in so doing affirm Earth, members of the Earth community, and all of creation as having intrinsic value and not merely as existing to be resources for human consumption.

Retrieval is a third step in the process of ecological criticism. The reader, while empathizing and identifying with Earth and the Earth community, may come to recognize these realities as more than objects in the text; they are subjects whose role and voice deserve to be heard. Retrieval is the process of recovering the latent or suppressed voices of Earth and members of the Earth community.

Suspicion refers to an initial step in the hermeneutical process of ecological criticism. Approaching the text, the reader suspects that most past interpreters and probably most biblical writers have written from an anthropocentric perspective; that is, generally human readers have focused first of all on human interests and relegated the interests of Earth and domains of Earth to the background.

NOTES

1. The analysis that follows represents, in part, a revision of my previous writings on this subject (Habel 2000a, 2000b, 2000c, 2003, 2008, 2009, 2011). In *Ecological Hermeneutics,* edited by David Horrell et al. (2010), few of the authors seek to articulate the tools of analysis appropriate to an ecological hermeneutic.
2. From a letter to the editor of the *Hamilton Spectator,* 16 October 1879. The letter bore the signature "Ratepayer" with no other name.

SOURCES

Allaby, Michael. 2003. *A Dictionary of Ecology.* 2nd ed. Oxford: Oxford University Press.

Berry, Thomas. 1988. *The Dream of the Earth.* San Francisco: The Sierra Club.

———. 1999. *The Great Work: Our Way into the Future.* Sheffield: Sheffield Phoenix Press.

Birch, Charles. 1990. *On Purpose.* Sydney: University of New South Wales Press.

Conradie, Ernst. 2010. "What on Earth Is an Ecological Hermeneutics? Some Broad Parameters." In *Ecological Hermeneutics: Biblical, Historical and Theological Perspectives,* ed. David Horrell, Cherryl Hunt, Christopher Southgate, and Francesca Stavrakopoulou, 295–313. London: T. & T. Clark.

Earth Bible Team. 2000. "Guiding Ecojustice Principles." Pages 38–53 in *Readings from the Perspective of Earth.* The Earth Bible. Edited by Norman C. Habel. Sheffield: Sheffield Academic Press.

———. 2001. "The Voice of God: More Than Metaphor." Pages 23–28 in *The Earth Story in the Psalms and the Prophets.* The Earth Bible. Edited by Norman C. Habel. Sheffield: Sheffield Academic Press.

Eaton, Heather. 2000. "Ecofeminist Contributions to an Ecojustice Hermeneutics." Pages 54–71 in *Readings from the Perspective of Earth.* The Earth Bible. Edited by Norman C. Habel. Sheffield: Sheffield Academic Press.

Edwards, Denis. 2006. *Ecology at the Heart of Faith: The Change of Heart That Leads to a New Way of Living on Earth.* Maryknoll, NY: Orbis Books.

Fretheim, Terrence. 1991. "The Reclamation of Creation: Redemption and Law in Exodus." *Interpretation* 45:354–65.

Fox, Matthew. 1983. *Original Blessing: A Primer in Creation Spirituality.* Santa Fe, NM: Bear and Co.

Habel, Norman C. 1995. *The Land Is Mine: Six Biblical Land Ideologies.* Minneapolis: Fortress.

———. 2000a. "The Challenge of Ecojustice Readings for Christian Theology." *Pacifica* 13:125–41.

———. 2000b. "Geophany: The Earth Story in Genesis 1." Pages 34–48 in *The Earth Story in Genesis*. The Earth Bible. Edited by Norman C. Habel and Shirley Wurst. Sheffield: Sheffield Academic Press.

———. 2000c. "Guiding Ecojustice Principles." Pages 38–53 in *Readings from the Perspective of Earth*. The Earth Bible. Edited by Norman C. Habel. Sheffield: Sheffield Academic Press.

———. 2003. "The Origins and Challenges of an Ecojustice Hermeneutic." In *Relating to the Text: Interdisciplinary and Form-Critical Insights on the Bible*, ed. Timothy Sandoval and Carleen Mandolfo, 141–59. London: T. & T. Clark.

———. 2008. "Introducing Ecological Hermeneutics." Pages 1–8 in *Exploring Ecological Hermeneutics*. Society of Biblical Literature Symposium. Edited by Norman C. Habel and Peter Trudinger. Atlanta: Society of Biblical Literature.

———. 2009. *An Inconvenient Text. Is a Green Reading of the Bible Possible?* Adelaide: ATF Press.

———. 2011. *The Birth, the Curse and the Greening of Earth: An Ecological Reading of Genesis 1–11*. Earth Bible Commentary. Sheffield: Sheffield Phoenix.

Hall, Douglas J. 1990. *The Steward: A Biblical Symbol Come of Age*. Grand Rapids/New York: Eerdmans/Friendship Press.

———. "2006. Stewardship as a Key to the Theology of Nature." In *Environmental Stewardship: Critical Perspectives—Past and Present*, ed. R. J. Berry, 129–44. New York: T. & T. Clark.

Horrell, David. 2010. *The Bible and the Environment: Towards a Critical Ecological Theology*. London: Equinox.

Lovelock, James. 1988. *The Ages of Gaia: A Biography of our Living Earth*. New York: Bantam.

McFague, Sally. 2008. *A New Climate for Theology: God, the World, and Global Warming*. Minneapolis: Fortress.

Meadowcroft, Tim. 2000. "Some Questions for the Earth Bible." Paper presented at the Australian and New Zealand Association of Theological Schools Conference, Christchurch, New Zealand.

Melanchthon, Monica. 2010. "The View from the Margins: Identifying with the Colonized Peoples/Earth." Paper delivered at an Ecological Hermeneutics Session of the Society of Biblical Literature, September.

Pardes, Ilana. 1992. *Countertraditions in the Bible: A Feminist Approach*. Cambridge, MA: Harvard University Press.

Plumwood, Val. 1993. *Feminism and the Mastery of Nature*. New York: Routledge.

Ponting, Clive. 1991. *A Green History of the World: The Environment and the Collapse of Great Civilizations*. London: Penguin.

Rainbow Spirit Elders. 1997. *Rainbow Spirit Theology*. Melbourne: Harper Collins.

Sarna, Nahum. 1986. *Exploring Exodus: The Heritage of Biblical Israel*. New York: Schocken Books.

Schüssler Fiorenza, Elisabeth. 1985. "The Will to Choose or to Reject: Continuing our Critical Work." In *Feminist Interpretation of the Bible*, ed. Letty Russell, 125–36. Philadelphia: Westminster.

White, Lynn. 1967. "The Historical Roots of Our Ecological Crisis." *Science* 155:1203–7.

FOR FURTHER READING

Fretheim, Terrence. 1999. "The Plagues as Ecological Signs of Historical Disasters." *Journal of Biblical Literature* (1999): 110:385–96.

Habel, Norman C., ed. *Readings from the Perspective of Earth*. The Earth Bible. Sheffield: Sheffield Academic Press, 2000.

Habel, Norman C. "Introducing the Earth Bible." In *Readings from the Perspective of Earth*. The Earth Bible, edited by Norman C. Habel, 25–37. Sheffield: Sheffield Academic Press, 2000.
———, ed. *Readings from the Perspective of Earth*. The Earth Bible. Sheffield: Sheffield Academic Press, 2000.
———. "Playing God or Playing Earth? An Ecological Reading of Genesis 1:26–28." In *"And God Saw That It Was Good." Essays on Creation and God in Honor of Terence Fretheim*. Word and World Supplement Series 5, edited by Frederick Gaiser and Mark Throntveit, 33–41. St. Paul: Word and World, Luther Seminary, 2006.
Habel, Norman C. and Peter Trudinger, eds. *Exploring Ecological Hermeneutics*. Society of Biblical Literature Symposium. Atlanta: Society of Biblical Literature, 2008.
Horrell, David, Cherryl Hunt, Christopher Southgate, and Francesca Stavrakopoulou, eds. *Ecological Hermeneutics: Biblical, Historical and Theological Perspectives*. London: T. & T. Clark, 2010.

Chapter 4

New Historicism

GINA HENS-PIAZZA

Some have observed that there is something inherently odd if not outright contradictory about the label "New Historicism." The word "history" conjures up images of what is old, what has come before now, what is past. The concept of "new," on the other hand, signals the novel, what is to come, what we can expect in the future. To complicate matters further, New Historicism arose among a group of literary critics who claimed to be committed to making a difference in the present. So what is the New Historicism?[1]

During the first half of the twentieth century, traditional historical criticism held sway in biblical studies as the dominant mode for the interpretation of texts. Here, factors external to the text were considered integral in the production of meaning. Authorial intention, context, sources, editorial process, and literary form constituted the loci of study. A host of historical approaches was developed for systematic analysis of these factors in the service of interpretation. Many of these methods are still practiced today. Specialization in historical studies continued to grow, reaping important gains. Biblical scholars regularly began to rub shoulders and collaborate with colleagues in other areas of the humanities. These influences and exchanges became especially evident in the second half of the twentieth century.

Mirroring shifts in the larger academy, historical methods of interpretation eventually gave way to literary approaches in the biblical field. The rise of various methods from schools of literary criticism created what some termed a "paradigm shift" and what others labeled a "revolution" in biblical interpretation. Meaning, once tied to the text in relation to its context, was now consigned to the text alone. Analysis of the biblical stories for literary coherence, rhetorical elements, narrative design, deep structures, poetics, and all other kinds of literary pursuits challenged the sovereignty of historical critical inquiry. In 1992, Mark Allen Powell's anthology of modern literary studies on the Bible attested to the burgeoning status of the literary field.[2] Cataloging research from the 1970s to 1990s, Powell identified well over a thousand studies on biblical texts that employed a vast array of literary methods. And these studies were matched in number by other explorations that discussed the theoretics of literary approaches to the Bible by biblical scholars and literary critics alike. Given the dramatic shift from historical explorations to a literary focus, the rise of a literary school called New Historicism on the campus of the University of California at Berkeley in the late 1980s was something of an anomaly at first glance. Even odder was the lack of agreement about what to call it.

While the term "New Historicism" can be traced to an essay by Michael McCanles in 1980,[3] Stephen Greenblatt, the *chef d'école* of the movement in the United States, claims to have coined the label somewhat arbitrarily.[4] Earlier, in his *Renaissance Self-Fashioning*, which is generally taken as the programmatic work in this area, Greenblatt described his way of working as a "poetics of culture."[5] Others had other labels. "The new history," "historical-materialist criticism," "cultural materialism," and "critical historicism" were among the candidates. Lee Patterson even went so far as to observe that "no single label can be usefully applied to the historicist enterprise as a school, least of all the already assigned, hotly contested, and irredeemably vague 'New Historicism.'"[6]

This reticence about what to call it was not the only oddity about the new literary activity. There was an intrinsic resistance among its practitioners to setting forth an operational definition that might domesticate this literary nova for straightforward public consumption. Greenblatt referred to New Historicism as a "trajectory" rather than a "set of beliefs."[7] Louis Montrose called it an "orientation" rather than a prescription of practices in interpretation.[8] Joel Fineman defined it as an "intellectual posture."[9] And Catherine Gallagher described it as a "phenomenon of apparent political indeterminacy."[10] Yet a common thread runs through all this reticence. At the start, New Historicism is best comprehended as less a theory and certainly not a method of interpretation. Adopting Daniel Boyarin's suggestion, New Historicism might be aptly understood as a sensibility or perspective on literature.[11] It views texts as caught up in the social processes and contexts out of which they emerge. Though identified with a single author, texts are generated by communities. One community produces a text, while another community interprets it, thereby producing another text. Hence the text is constantly under production.

As a sensibility rather than a method, New Historicism views literature (including the biblical texts) as integrally tied to and identified with other material realities—cultural practices, relics, data from a context, and so on—that make up social contexts. Of interest here is how historical, social, economic, biographical, sexual, aesthetic, and psychological forces are disclosed by this material evidence. New Historicism investigates these forces by crossing disciplinary boundaries, venturing into such territories as economics, medicine, and psychology to offer its interpretations.

As sensibility, New Historicism views literature and history as essentially the same. Traditionally, a constructed history formed the stable backdrop against which unstable literary texts were read and interpreted. New Historicism abandons these distinctions between literature and history. It views both as story and involved in the fashioning of each other. Hence distinctions between foreground and background, superstructure and substructure, cultural reality and mirror image no longer function to delineate the boundary between a story and its context. Instead, literature and social context are thought to reside in a dynamic relationship of mutual shaping and defining of one another. How literature impacts the construction of social context on the pages of history and how social context impacts the production of literature defines New Historicism's interests.

Finally, as sensibility, New Historicism presumes that all constructions of the past are intimately tied to the present. Thus it resists hard and fast distinctions that separate now/then, author/reader, what the text meant/what the text means, and even composition/interpretation. All these long-standing categories that separate and reinforce distinctions between the past and present begin to erode in the New Historicist's view.

ANTECEDENTS OF A NEW HISTORICISM

Tracing the development of New Historicism crafts one of many stories that could be told about it. If an identifiable theoretical base could be established for the tenacious resistance to theory itself among New Historicists, it would most certainly be the work of Michel Foucault.[12] In the years immediately preceding its rise in the Department of English Literature of the University of California at Berkeley, Michel Foucault, a reluctant theorist himself, was a visiting professor there. Foucault laid the basis for a New Historicism with his emphasis on literature as discourse, his insistence on history as made up of numerous discourses, and his explorations of the relationship between discourse and power.[13] New Historicists also manifest a theoretical kinship with Marx. The frequent preoccupation with struggle, contestation, and power relations in texts and the social processes that produced them suggests the Marxist influence.[14] Moreover, this turn toward the social processes involved in a history's production suggests a great deal of anthropological torque. The influence of anthropologist Clifford

Geertz and his approach to culture with "thick description" echoes resoundingly across essays by New Historicists.[15] As Geertz studies culture as text, New Historicists study texts as culture. Finally, this movement acknowledges the influence that feminists and voices of the tri-continental world[16] have had in their persistent attention to articulated hierarchies of value and power resident in texts. Hence, New Historicism attends to voices excluded from the texts, the fragmentary elements of a story, a passing comment of a character, unanswered questions, and the places where texts lacked cohesion. Consequently, as New Historicism gained momentum across the academic terrain of the 1980s, its range of practitioners extended beyond the confines of departments of literature. It included those interested in feminism, Marxism, ethnic and cultural studies, and history, as well as literature. Though separated by different disciplines, what joined together this loose if not aberrant confederacy of critics was their return to history after a long exile and their lively production of a *new* historicism.

RECURRING FEATURES OF A NEW HISTORICISM

Unlike a method of interpretation, no blueprint or set of steps exists for how to proceed in conducting a New Historicist study of a biblical text. Still, the situation is not hopeless. In the New Historicist's studies on Renaissance literature, several features recur often enough to suggest characteristic proclivities of the enterprise. Three of them are discussed here.

First, New Historicist studies frequently involve ways of reading and interpreting that look less at the center and more at the borders of a story or literary work. Instead of pursuing rhetorical integrity or literary unity, New Historicism attends to the cracks, the undersides, and the signs of disarray latent in a work. Convinced that whole readings are but a self-satisfying illusion, New Historicism opts for more fragmentary kinds of considerations. Resisting the tendency to integrate dominant images, dialogues, and characters into a single, master discourse, it attends to fleeting references, incongruities, or unanswered questions resident at the edges or margins of the text. For example, instead of focusing on whether King Josiah's religious reform (2 Kgs. 24) was religiously grounded or politically motivated, New Historicism might wonder about the peasants who lost their jobs when the this king ordered the dismantling of the local shrines. Instead of being captivated by the details of this king's centralization of cult, it would inquire about how hierarchical forms of power become the enabling conditions of such detailed representations. Attention to such borders often discloses a complicated past that resists the coherence of reigning historical reconstructions, while unaddressed questions lurking in the margins disrupt the artificial integrity of unified reading. Rather than producing an outcome that conforms to the monological tendencies of traditional historical or even literary interpretations, New Historicism uncovers "a past of competing voices, values and centers of power. . . ."[17] This focus on the edges or more fragmentary elements of a text leads easily to a second recurring feature—a focus on the tensions and struggles in a text. New Historicism theorizes the relation between the material/political world, on the one hand, and the textual/representational world, on the other, and the way they closely and mutually fashion one another. Influenced by Foucault, New Historicism assumes a concept of discourse that commingles the linguistic, cultural, sociopolitical, and material realms. And it is within this commingling that echoes of struggle, contestations, and tension can be heard. All texts are caught up in the complex and contestatory processes by which a society defines and maintains its organization and its institutions as well as its self-understanding. All societies are caught up in the struggles whereby one segment of culture defines itself as dominant. In the process, segments of culture construct discourses that distinguish themselves from a subservient segment defined as "the other."

For example, a story that celebrates a monarch's wisdom, such as the tale of Solomon and the Two Mothers (1 Kgs. 3:16–28), probably represents reality in a way that serves the interests of the dominant culture. Girded with the gift of wisdom bestowed by none other than God, the king adjudicates between two women subjects arguing before him. In contrast to the one woman's frantic, wordy oration and the forensic deadlock evoked when both women speak, the king practices an economy of words. In Hebrew, his two-worded command, "Bring me the sword" (v. 24), not only elicits immediate obedience but also ruptures the impasse of the women's wordy exchange. While the women speak more words than the king, his words count more in the story. While the women are portrayed as incapable of resolving their differences, the king dislodges the deadlock. Thus, this contrast in characterization between the women and the king suggests the tension. The depiction of these subjects as women and then as harlots contrasts sharply with and distances them from the depiction of the sovereign as male and as "wise king." Here, the biblical texts participate in constructing and reinforcing a version of reality that represents a dominant culture within which members of a subservient culture understand themselves. Furthermore, a New Historicist reading might inquire why the women here and elsewhere in the biblical tradition are depicted at odds with one another in stories that address and illustrate the sovereignty of kings, especially those whose rule is questionable (e.g., Jehoram and the two cannibal mothers, 2 Kgs. 6:24–33). Or, to put it another way, do women working together pose a threat to maintaining the hierarchical elevation of sovereigns?[18] But the struggle in the texts is not confined to the works themselves. Those who read, interpret, and preach the biblical texts down through the ages participate in these contestations.

Third, New Historicist studies are marked by their attention to the interests, voices, and forces that crisscross and rebound across cultures and across generations. New Historicism recognizes that the questions we ask of the past are invariably tied to the questions we ask about the present as we make our way toward the future. In fact, the crux of our orientation toward texts resides within this explicit entanglement of past, present, and future. Hence, New Historicism investigates the multitude of forces, the myriad of voices, and the variety of interests and concerns that traverse and synapse along the continuum of history and within the web of culture. Attention to these exchanges as we read and write about the past in the present enables us to envision change in the future. As Daniel Boyarin notes, while we cannot change the past, we can change our understanding of the past. This in turn enables us to live differently in the present and "puts us on a trajectory of empowerment for transformation"[19] for the future.

With this orientation, biblical texts are not identified with one particular group or author in the past. Instead, they are viewed as acts of engagement with a vast and ever-changing reality made up of different and even opposing beliefs, values, biases, and investments. As representations of such a reality, a text both bears witness to and is imprinted with the complexity of its fashioning. When a text arrives in our lap, it bears the accumulation of effects from its own production as well as all of its former receptions. Needless to say, these two processes are difficult to separate. As the text moves across generations, cultures, and even religious traditions, it absorbs the amalgam of these influences. For example, as the tradition of the Exodus/Settlement in the Land has made its way across generations, it has narrated the liberation of the Israelites from bondage at one time, the early Christians' escape from the enemy of death at another, and most recently the release of Latin Americans from political oppressors. At the same time, it has attested to the terrible fate of the Canaanites and even the fate of Native Americans in the face of Manifest Destiny.

Gradually, the complexity of these interchanges spans spatiotemporal webs of time, place, peoples, and culture in the ongoing production and reception of a text. Subjectivity in the production thus spills over into subjectivity in reception. This slippage obscures the distinction not only between production and reception but also between text and reader and between past and present.

GENESIS 18:1–16a—AN ILLUSTRATION

The Background

Beginning in Genesis 12, the Abraham-Sarah traditions introduce Israel's salvation history with rich and variegated story units.[20] Dominant among the central ideas crafting this first ancestral saga (Gen. 12–25) is the theme of Sarah's barrenness. Even before God calls Abraham and tells him to take his family and leave Mesopotamia for the land he will be shown, we learn that the matriarch is barren. At the very first mention of her name, unprecedented as it is in the patriarchal genealogy, Sarah is introduced to us as childless (11:30). Just a few verses later, the record of Abraham's age at 75 and Sarah's age at 65 suggests that this childlessness has had a long history (12:4). Moreover, this barrenness is not just a passing sidebar that, in tandem with the very few other details we are afforded, rounds out the character of Sarah. Rather, her barrenness introduces a crisis warranting the plot that unfolds in the subsequent chapters. Now alongside this introduction to these first ancestors, and in conjunction with the alert to their infertility problem, comes a divine pledge. God promises Abraham that he will have descendants. The first pronouncement of the promise comes soon after the problem of infertility is established (12:7). Next, the promise is reiterated in 15:4. Finally, it receives its fullest and most graphic exposition in 15:5 when Abraham is not only promised descendants, but "descendants as numerous as the stars." This creates a problem and a plot with a good deal of narrative tension. When all these factors are taken together—the couple's ages at 65 and 75, the matter of Sarah's barrenness, and a divine promise to Abraham of descendants as numerous as the stars—the plot thickens. It pulsates with a heightened sense of urgency and promises a narrative with a bit of comic relief.

In response to the crisis of urgency that old age imposes on conceiving offspring, Sarah takes matters into her own hands. In accordance with accepted practices of surrogacy in the ancient world, she offers Hagar, her maidservant, to Abraham (16:1–4). And though this action proves immediately successful, the outcome is apparently not acceptable to the divine one making the promise. Hence we are hurled deeper into the growing complexity of the story line, skippered by the intensifying crisis of offspring of old Abraham and Sarah.

A glimmer of hope dawns in Genesis 17:15–21, and then again in Genesis 18:1–16a. We encounter not one but two birth announcements from God addressed to these desperate, wannabe parents. With the formality of this twice employed genre of the "birth announcement," God promises to overturn Sarah's barrenness and fulfill the promise of offspring to this couple.

That there are two birth announcements is especially encouraging. While the setting and circumstances of these proclamations differ, parallel features yoke them together, urging the reader to hear them as real assurance. Abraham is featured in the first and Sarah eventually assumes center stage in the second. Both accounts carry the explicit announcement that Abraham and Sarah will have a son. In both accounts the parent-to-be laughs in the Lord's presence on hearing the news. As each laughs, they both express the reason for their incredulity. Abraham says to himself, "Can a child be born to a man who is a hundred years old? Can Sarah, who is ninety years old, bear a son?" (17:17). And Sarah says to herself, "After I have grown old, and my husband is old, shall I have pleasure?" (18:12). They both keep their skepticism to themselves. Moreover, both responses serve as anticipation and affirmation regarding the child's name: Isaac, which in Hebrew (*yitzhaq*) means "he laughs." Later, when the child is named, Sarah underlines the personal significance of the name by exclaiming, "God has brought laughter for me; everyone who hears will laugh with me" (21:6).

A New Historicist reading of Genesis 18:1–16a takes a turn away from finding parallels to the preceding birth announcement in Genesis 17:15–21 or attending to the literary congruity of the tale. Rather, as this study will show, it fixes attention on incongruities (God's response to Abraham in ch. 17 vs. God's response to Sarah in ch. 18). It resists pursuit of rhetorical integrity and instead notices how the prolonged introduction threatens to overshadow the actual birth announcement to Sarah. It attends to cracks, to fleeting comments, to the underside of a story where Abraham's dominance as character threatens to obscure the major role Sarah plays. Convinced that "whole readings" are but a self-satisfying illusion, New Historicism opts for the more fragmentary. It attends to fleeting references (e.g., a laugh), and to unanswered questions or issues at the borders of the text, (i.e., *Why* did Sarah laugh?). Finally, it muses about the liberating role that laughter and comedy play in granting place and importance to characters/persons who are often relegated to the margins in both the biblical or contemporary "historicity of texts and in the textuality of history."[21] Genesis 18:1–16a is considered to be originally a self-contained unit consisting of two easily identifiable parts: first, the visit of the three men to Abraham (vv. 1–8) and second, the promise of a son (vv. 9–16a). In part one, Abraham is sitting outside his tent pitched near the great trees of Mamre in the heat of the midday sun when three visitors approach. Though the narrator informs the reader that this is a divine visit, Abraham only knows them to be "three men standing near him" (v. 2). This quiet opening abruptly shifts to a story narrated in haste (v. 2b). With no formal introduction or exchanges of identity, Abraham runs to greet the three, bows down before them, and urges them to stay. He offers them water, food, and a place for resting, to which they are receptive (vv. 3–5). Despite the heat of the day, Abraham moves about quickly and hurries others about in order to prepare a sumptuous refreshment for these three strangers. He runs to the tent and hurries Sarah to make cakes (v. 6). He races to the cattle and secures a nice tender calf (v. 7a). He gives it to his servant, who prepares the meat "in haste" (something our visitors might have been leery of had they known) (v. 7). Then he takes milk and curds, which he prepares along with the calf. He sets all the food before the visitors, who then feast on homemade bread, "veal, milk, and curd" (v. 8). In the meantime, Abraham positions himself nearby, ready to wait on them and respond to their every need. To us this hospitality appears extreme. We might even be suspicious that some strings are attached to such unsolicited kindness. Some even interpret this as a gift offering for the promise of the child that is to follow. However, nothing in the story indicates Abraham knows who these visitors are or the reason why they came. A more likely interpretation is founded on social-scientific studies, which disclose that such gestures of hospitality were characteristic of sedentary peoples in these early settings.

The second half of the story opens when the visitors ask Abraham a question: "Where is Sarah, your wife?" (v. 9). With no segue, and at this juncture in the story, the question is peculiar. How do they know about Sarah, and how do they know that she is his wife? Since Abraham has been hurrying about and hosting this whole event himself, why are they even asking about her? Given the patriarchal context, perhaps it is precisely because he has been doing so much of the preparing and serving that they want to know where his wife is. Whatever the reason, Abraham seems unfazed. He answers straightaway, "There in the tent"

(v. 9). At this point one of the visitors makes the birth announcement: "I will surely return to you in due season and Sarah will have a son" (v. 10).

Next, the scene shifts to inside the tent for the first time. Only the reader is allowed to enter and see what is going on in this domestic enclosure. Sarah is listening at the entrance to the tent behind the one who is speaking (v. 10). She laughs! Then she muses about her physical status being all used up, about the possibility for her sexual pleasure, and about her husband's age and her own.

Then something unexpected happens. The messenger, identified only to the reader as the Lord (v. 13), turns to Abraham and asks, "Why did Sarah laugh. . . . Is anything too wonderful for the LORD?" (vv. 13–14a). This is quite strange, because Sarah was in the tent when she laughed and the Hebrew description, *beqirbah*, qualifies her laughter as laughing "inside herself." In the tent, out of sight, out of earshot of Abraham, and by herself, Sarah laughs inside herself. How is Abraham supposed to know that she laughed, much less why she laughed? The Lord speaks again to Abraham and reiterates the promise made just previously. "At the set time, I will return to you in due season and Sarah shall have a son" (v. 14).

Now Sarah, who evidently suspects the identity of the stranger, is afraid and quickly tries to make a correction: "I did not laugh" (v. 15). That she was afraid discloses further her hunch about God's identity. As the story draws to a close it creates a further complexity. Someone responds to Sarah: "And he said, 'Oh yes, you did laugh'" (v. 15). However, the text leaves unspecified whether "he" refers to God or to Abraham. Most translations and the story line itself assume it to be God, since Abraham had no knowledge of her laughter. Finally, the account concludes as starkly and abruptly as it began: "Then the men set out from there" (v. 16a).

Our close look at this story discloses some glaring peculiarities, the kinds of matters that interest New Historicists. In the first half of the tale, Abraham appears as the protagonist. He is in charge of the action. He issues commands and initiates the dialogue. However, the second half unfolds quite differently and is almost unrelated to the first half. While Abraham continues to be addressed, he has no idea what is going on. He does not know who the messengers are. He does not know about Sarah's laughter. Thus he surely does not know why she laughed. And he must be incredibly perplexed when, in response to Sarah's denial, the visitor retorts, "Oh yes, you did laugh" (v. 15), suggesting that the visitor has knowledge about his wife, Sarah, that Abraham himself does not even possess. Moreover, despite all the parallels noted by scholars between the birth announcements in chapters 17 and 18, the contrast between the attention Sarah's laughter commands in contrast to the passing reference to Abraham's laughter invites attention.

Read through a New Historicist's lens, this story line and its literary arrangement are more than peculiar; the story, with all its cracks and gaps, approaches being downright funny. Hence, as Sarah's laughter rings across the history and tradition of interpretation, we are invited to hear it as an expression of amusement at something other than merely the incomprehensible announcement that she and old Abraham are about to conceive a child. The multidimensional nature of this laughter and interrogation embrace much more.

Sarah's Laughter as Discursive Force

From a literary standpoint the organization and balance of the story are odd enough to be noteworthy. The whole first half of the story is introduction (vv. 1–8). It is so detailed (greeting, time of day, food preparation, menu, and so forth) as to be determinative of the story's identity. Numerous commentaries refer to this tale in 18:1–16a with such titles as "Abraham Entertaining the Three Messengers from Heaven" or "Abraham and the Three Messengers" or "Abraham and the Visitors at Mamre."[22] Such headings are already interpretations and have shaped the text's reception. As a result, readers experience this introductory half of the tale as integral to the heart of the story, even though without it the account of the annunciation of Isaac's birth in verses 9–16a could stand on its own.

While these opening verses relate the encounter between Abraham and the three visitors, they do not govern and constrain the story line. Rather, they function only as introduction. And as introduction, we might note how nonessential this first part is. What could have been introduced in one sentence, "And three men came to visit Abraham and Sarah," would then have been a more appropriately parallel component to the conclusion, "The men set out from there" (v. 16a), giving the story a clear envelope shape. Instead, the lengthy introduction with its elaborate detail (vv. 1–8) creates a very uneven envelope structure. The detailing of food preparations bears no relationship to the story at hand. In fact, in another story where a divine messenger delivers a birth announcement to Manoah, Samson's father, the divine emissary declines food offered by Manoah (Judg. 13:15–16). At best, the exceedingly long introduction of our tale appears to create its own story but with no real plotline—visitors, gathering food, preparing food, serving, eating, resting. Not much of a story! At worst, this long, unrelated description delays the commencement of the real plot—the birth announcement that Sarah will have a son—but it hardly builds suspense. Moreover, these opening eight verses threaten to overshadow the story that unfolds in the second part, but without poetic purpose. The introduction focuses on the character of Abraham even though the plotline will ultimately feature Sarah. Hence the introduction actually competes with the plot, overshadowing it and rendering it secondary. This is a most awkward literary arrangement. Such an imbalance suggests a struggle to rewrite this story of a birth announcement to Sarah as another birth announcement to Abraham.

At the same time, we can identify discursive forces that oppose and resist both the dominance of this long introduction and the centrality of Abraham's character. The first of these is the mention of the "tent." There are five references to the tent in this story, with most of them occurring in the first half of the tale. The first time Sarah is mentioned, we hear that she is in the tent (v. 6). In fact, this first reference to Sarah constitutes the focus and establishes the center around which the other references to the tent revolve, making her the centerpiece of these iterations. After Sarah is identified with the tent, she is named again every time the tent is mentioned,

> 18:1 He was sitting at the opening of his **tent**.
> 18:2 He ran from his **tent**.
> 18:6 Abraham hurries to *Sarah* in the **tent**.
> 18:9 *Sarah* is in the **tent**.
> 18:10b *Sarah* is listening in the **tent**.

In the midst of Abraham rushing around greeting visitors, fixing food, serving, and being something of a distraction to the real story at hand, the narrative references to "tent" persist in soliciting the reader's curiosity and fixing it on this site in the story. One is reminded of a good suspense movie where the camera keeps cycling back to an ashtray with a tiny stub of a cigarette resting on its edge while everyone in the scene is involved in an animated discussion about how that dreaded cigarette-smoking intruder could never break into this apartment. Moreover, the pattern fashioned by the iteration of the "tent" transgresses the outer limits of the introduction and navigates our attention to the story following in part two (vv. 9, 10b). And when that story finally begins, the spotlight moves to Sarah herself in place of the tent where she has been concealed. The question, "Where is Sarah, your wife?" opens this section. Following, we hear, "Sarah was listening," "Sarah laughed," "Why did Sarah laugh?" "Sarah is to have a son," "Sarah feared," and "Sarah denied." The narrative is riveted on Sarah. This is her story, and the birth announcement is intended for her.

Another element that works to raise questions and shift our attention away from Abraham and this introduction is the matter of genre. The genre here, "birth announcement," is a familiar occurrence in the biblical stories. For his part, Abraham has already received a visitation from God in the preceding chapter, with a birth announcement attached. Given the recurrence of this literary form across the biblical traditions, we could expect Sarah to be visited and told the same news. This format of an announcement to one parent and then to the other has its counterpart in the book of Judges. Like Sarah, Samson's mother is barren, and she receives a messenger from God promising her a child (Judg. 13:3). Soon after, the messenger returns to confirm this same news to her husband, Manoah (Judg. 13:11–14). More characteristically, however, women are the recipients of these visitation and announcements. The barren Hannah receives assurances from the priest Eli and is granted a son (1 Sam. 1:12–18). The childless Shunammite woman receives the same promise at the word of Elisha the prophet (2 Kgs. 4:13–17). The genre continues on into the New Testament, where Mary (though a virgin, not barren) receives a proclamation of a child (Luke 1:26). Well documented across biblical narratives as well as other ancient Near Eastern traditions, this genre of the "birth announcement" characteristically features an announcement or revelation to the mother-to-be.

In our story, when the announcement finally occurs, the shift in language indicates this was to be a birth announcement for Sarah. When God spoke to Abraham in chapter 17, the patriarch was promised "I will give you a son by her [Sarah]" (17:16). A few verses later the rhetoric emphasizes Abraham again: "No, but your wife Sarah shall bear you a son and you shall name him Isaac" (17:19). Here the direct address in "give you" and "bear you" designates Abraham as the recipient of the announcement. Later in the story, however, the language of the messenger changes. After trying to establish the whereabouts of Sarah, the messenger delivers to Abraham what is formulated to be her announcement: ". . . Sarah shall have a son" (18:10). Parallel to the birth announcement to Abraham, it is reiterated again in v 14: "Sarah shall have a son." The rhetoric, "your wife Sarah shall bear you a son" in the preceding chapter, in contrast to "and Sarah shall have a son" here, encourages us to hear the earlier announcement as to Abraham and this one as to Sarah.

Yet another, more integral element works against the dominance of the introduction as the heart of the story. It is the matter of plot development. Typically plot entails the exposition of a conflict/problem, climax, and resolution. However, in our text the exposition does not occur until the second half of the story. The conflict/problem is introduced with the question, "Where is Sarah?" focusing on the tent where she is located and will soon be laughing in response to the promise of a son for her. The climax occurs when the Lord asks, "Why did Sarah laugh?" and the resolution takes place when the visitor manifests an extraordinary knowledge about what went on in the privacy of the tent and counters Sarah's denial with "Oh yes, you did laugh." The visitors' departure parallels their arrival to form the bookends—introduction and conclusion—to the story within.

We now turn our attention to this climax and consider in detail *why* did Sarah laugh. First we might note, at least from the contemporary reader's vantage point, an all-too-familiar scene in our own legislative bodies of government. It is a bit comical and unsettling to watch and listen in on a group of men sitting around a meal discussing matters of conception, especially in regard to women. Something equally surprising and humorous takes place in our ancient text as well. When Sarah laughs, she says, "After I have grown old and my husband is old, shall I have pleasure?"(v. 12). This English translation does not convey the full force of her words. The Hebrew is more graphic and blunt. The verb *belah*, "to be worn out" ("used up" as of old clothes in Josh. 9:13 and of bones dried up in Ps. 32:3), in the context of *ednah*, referring to "sexual pleasure," communicates Sarah's private amusement.[23] Her thoughts are first fixed on the process leading to the conception, which at this stage is a bit of a hurdle. "Now that I am used up, shall I have pleasure? And my husband is old." When the messenger repeats what Sarah said to herself, he strips Sarah's musing of its bluntness. By recasting it as "Shall I indeed bear a child now that I am old?" he makes private thoughts more palatable for public consumption. This need not be heard as a censure of Sarah. Actually, in a somewhat humorous vein, it might best be heard as an illustration of just how differently men and women think about these matters.

The theological linchpin of this announcement is the messenger's follow-up query, "Is anything too wonderful for the LORD?" This is the first time God has been referenced in the conversation among the characters. Sarah's laughter here plays a pivotal role in unmasking the divine presence in this tale. Up to this point only the reader knows of God's presence in the story. However, the detection of Sarah's laughter inside herself discloses that all-knowing quality characteristic of the divine on the part of the messenger who is speaking. Hence Sarah's laughter reveals God's presence in these awkward circumstances. Veiled in the character of the messenger, God's presence at this meeting is disclosed. Sarah seems to get it. When the messenger accuses her of laughing, "fear" prompts her denial. Fear is one of the most frequently acknowledged responses on the part of those who encounter God. For example, when the midwives disobeyed Pharaoh in Exodus 1:17 they did so because of their fear of the Lord. Hence Sarah's laughter and fear verify the divine backing of the promise in this story.

Finally, we return to the question whose trajectories we have been chasing: "Why did Sarah laugh?" Out of sight, and out of earshot, this woman's silent little snicker catapults her to the center of the tale. When she laughs, she becomes present to the narrative. When she laughs, her confinement in the tent ends. When she laughs, her husband recedes to the sidelines. When she laughs, the divine presence in the episode is unveiled. With her laughter, she finally assumes her rightful place in this tale. When a laughing Sarah enters as an essential player in this story she is no longer easily relegated to the margins of the story or absent altogether. As testimony to the role laughter plays here, Sarah's laughing places her front and center in a story that otherwise tries to obscure her. Caught laughing, Sarah commands our attention and the attention of others in the scene.

In classical literature, comedy perennially takes up arms against the forces that stifle life, silence voices, or shut out the deserving. It ridicules the arrogant and boastful. It deflates the pretentious and pompous. And it does so with humor, all in the interest of celebrating life and its players. This little story of the birth announcement to Sarah hardly qualifies as comedy in the classical sense, but it does depend on some of comedy's dynamics. Stifling the forces that keep her out of sight and out of earshot in the tale, Sarah's laughter makes a case for her role as central rather than peripheral in this story. And that should teach us something about the enduring and transforming power of a good laugh not only in the ancient world but especially in our own.

New Historicism discloses other histories in conjunction with a story or within the story itself. While we cannot know the world that beheld this ancient Genesis text, New Historicism directs our attention to another story resident there. While attending to rhetorical devices, narrative features, intertextual connections, and so on, New Historicism marks a turn away from the pursuit of literary integrity or literary unity. Rather, it attends to the cracks, to subtle comments, to the underside of a story, and to signs of disarray latent in a work. Resisting the tendency to integrate dominant images, dialogues, and characters in a single, master narrative, it hosts the playfulness in texts. It attends to fleeting references (e.g., a laugh), incongruities (God's response to Abraham in ch. 17 versus God's response to Sarah in ch. 18), or unanswered questions (why did Sarah laugh?) resident at the borders of the text. Turning attention away from the dominance of the visitors and Abraham's hospitality, New Historicism fixes our gaze on the periphery: for example, on the tent. As a result, Sarah, who seems sidelined, actually emerges as a significant player in the story. Moreover, her silent little snicker discloses more than even Abraham himself understands about the unfolding events. As New Historicism takes up the seemingly innocuous but unanswered question, "Why did Sarah laugh?" it unveils another story. A woman lightly sketched in the background of this tale laughs. And that laughter moves her to the front and center of a story world that would otherwise obscure or erase her. Her extra-linguistic response functions as interruption of the traditional frameworks of thought, speech, and activity. Her laughter testifies to the existence of Sarah's autonomous self and her story. It may even level a blow to the patriarchal status quo dominating this tale. Hence, even for an old barren Sarah hidden in the tent, laughter is "freedom made visible."[24]

PERILS AND PROSPECTS OF A NEW HISTORICISM

For some, the machinations of a New Historicism and other such orientations (postmodernism, cultural studies, and so forth) signal perils. Collapsing the distinction between the world of the text and the world of the reader risks abandoning the long, hallowed distinction between "what the text meant" and "what the text means." It would allow for the commingling of what some still assume to be the objective investigation of historical studies with the subjective bias of the reader's contemporality. It risks tainting the exegesis of the text with what might become an exegesis of the reader and the reader's context.

For others, the perils of a New Historicism lie in the unlimited disciplinary horizons of inquiry that such an orientation allows. Instead of confining history's lens to matters of the past and its constructions, a New Historicism risks broadening the scope of investigation to include such questions as, Whose history does criticism relate? What transactions take place in the ancient and contemporary context in history's production? How does that history get told? Who is empowered to do the telling? What changes in the social fabric does biblical studies effect or fail to effect? For those who sense peril on the horizon of a New Historicism, anything beyond a one-dimensional totalizing explanation of history, context, or even the biblical text itself becomes suspect.

Unlike the justifications for the rise of many new methods or approaches, the prospects and interests in New Historicism do not stem from the assessment of how past and current methods have failed. The harvest from traditional historical methods and the harvest from the variety of literary approaches in biblical studies have been richly successful. But as the parameters of individual historical methods are defined and the theoretical boundaries of newer literary and cultural approaches are sketched, the gap between these two arenas widens. The possibility of arriving at an integrated grasp of our subject fades. Synchronic approaches seem at odds with diachronic methods. A focus on context contrasts with a focus on text. Literary analysis frequently involves setting aside the research and conclusions of historical critics. Different approaches to interpretation engender polarization as to the determinacy or indeterminacy of meaning. While such disagreements can be productive, they can also encourage fragmentation. Methodological specialization in biblical studies often seems to have bred methodological ghettos. Even during these first decades of the twenty-first century, biblical studies still appears to be a profession of specialists, refining and defending their methods, parsing these sophisticated approaches further into subspecialties.

Along with other newer orientations, New Historicism resists such specialization. It crosses boundaries separating the different disciplinary specializations and ignores the dividing line between the world of the text and the world of the reader. It invites critics to address the political consequences, economic ramifications, social functions, and the ethical import of the texts in both their historical and their contemporary contexts. It assumes that any social-historical construction that one might compose is not only founded on a production of the past but also results in a production about and by a reader. Consequently, such a construction must be seen in relation to the ancient writing and the contemporary reading as well as the ideological and institutional agendas that lie behind the writing and the reading practices.

One final explanation looms large, explaining the appeal and the need for a New Historicism. Whether in the biblical guild or at the level of the institutions where biblical studies is taught—colleges, universities, communities, seminaries—a sea change has taken place in how business is conducted. The homogenous character of these institutions has all but vanished. Under the banner of cultural diversity, the curricula, pedagogy, administrative models, and even financial packages have had to undergo major renovation. Globalization has given way to world systems, world economy, global frames of knowledge, and a demand for new ways of knowing and understanding. The emphasis on specialization has been supplanted by the urgent need to prepare persons to participate in this global setting. Educational institutions themselves have become "markets of exchange." Whether engaged in the study of complex moral issues, questions of doctrine, or a challenging biblical passage, students are constantly exchanging information across national, ethnic, cultural, sexual, and class borders and attending to the cultural transactions at the heart of these exercises. Instead of mastering a specialized pool of knowledge, students learn how religious knowledge transmutes into forms of political power and back again. In concert with appreciating the biblical text as a confessional or an aesthetic work, students must learn how these texts can also function as oppressive or hegemonic forces.

The appeal of a New Historicism in biblical studies is thus more than the product of a theoretical argument in literary studies. Rather, its rise is seeded by changes in the very institutions where it is being practiced. Exchange and negotiation across the cultural histories and identities of seminary and university populations concerning the very cultural histories and identities in the biblical writings are at the heart of our efforts. We cannot do otherwise in a world where boundary crossing has become requisite not only for economics, politics, and communication, but also for ministry, for biblical and theological understandings, and for knowledge itself.

KEY TERMS

Discourse. A way of speaking or writing that includes the complex interaction between the formal/theoretical and the practical component of the topic under discussion.

Representation. Refers to a new understanding of mimesis whereby a text becomes a lens on human experience that shapes rather than reflects our experience and our understanding of it.

Textuality. In poststructuralist terms, refers to a text as not aloof or disengaged from the surrounding context but contiguous with it, both forming and being formed by it.

Thick Description. A term cultural anthropologist Clifford Geertz borrowed from Gilbert Ryle to narrate Geertz's approach to the study of culture. This approach strives to discover, sort out, and detail all the features, incoherences, ellipses, interactions, faded elements, contrasts, contradictions, behaviors, and so on that together help capture the potential meaning of social reality itself. Like close readings, Geertz reads culture like a text. Similarly, like thick description, New Historicists read texts like culture.

NOTES

1. Portions of this article have appeared in a previous work by the author, *The New Historicism* (Minneapolis: Augsburg Fortress, 2002) and are used with permission of the publisher.
2. Mark Allan Powell, *The Bible and Modern Literary Criticism: A Critical Assessment and Annotated Bibliography* (New York: Greenwood, 1992).
3. Michael McCanles, "The Authentic Discourse of the Renaissance," *Diacritics* 10 (1980): 85.
4. Stephen Greenblatt, "Introduction" in *Forms of Power and the Power of Forms*, ed. Stephen Greenblatt (Norman, OK: Pilgrim Press, 1982), 3–6.

5. Stephen Greenblatt, *Renaissance Self-Fashioning* (Chicago: University of Chicago Press, 1980), 5.
6. Lee Patterson, "Introduction: Critical Historicism and Medieval Studies," in *Literary Practice and Social Change in Britain, 1380–1530*, ed. Lee Patterson (Berkeley, CA: University of California Press, 1990), 1.
7. Stephen Greenblatt, *Learning to Curse: Essays in Early Modern Culture* (New York: Routledge, 1990), 3.
8. Louis Montrose, "Renaissance Literary Studies and the Subject of History," *English Literary Renaissance* 16 (Winter 1986): 6.
9. Joel Fineman, "The History of the Anecdote: Fiction and Fiction," in *The New Historicism*, ed. H. Aram Veeser (New York: Routledge, 1989), 52.
10. Catherine Gallagher, "Marxism and the New Historicism" in *The New Historicism*, ed. Veeser, 37.
11. Daniel Boyarin, "Rabbinic Resistance to Male Domination: A Case Study in Talmudic Cultural Poetics," in *Interpreting Judaism in a Postmodern Age*, ed. Steven Kepnes (New York: New York University Press, 1996), 118–41.
12. For an extended and clear exposition of Foucault's work, see Alan Sheridan, *Michel Foucault: The Will to Truth* (London: Travistock, 1980).
13. For an overview of Foucault's contribution to historical study, see Mark Poster, "The Future According to Foucault: The Archaeology of Knowledge and Intellectual History, in *Modern European Intellectual History: Reappraisals and New Perspectives*, ed. Dominick LaCapra and Steven L. Kaplan (Ithaca, NY: Cornell University Press, 1982), 93.
14. For a discussion of Marxist tradition as it influences New Historicism, see Pierre Machery, *A Theory of Literary Production*, trans. Geoffrey Wall (London: Routledge and Kegan Paul, 1978); Louis Althusser, "Ideological State Apparatuses," in *Lenin and Philosophy and Other Essays*, trans. Ben Brewster (New York: Monthly Review Press, 1971), 123–73; and Terry Eagleton, *Criticism and Ideology: A Study in Marxist Literary Theory* (London: New Left Books, 1976).
15. Clifford Geertz, "Thick Description: Toward an Interpretive Theory of Culture," in *The Interpretation of Cultures* (New York: Basic Books, 1973), 3–30.
16. Frequently in writing, the terms "Third World" or "Two-Thirds World" are enlisted to distinguish between the developed and the undeveloped/underdeveloped continents. Since these distinctions echo colonialism and, thus, are resisted by theorists especially from these parts of the world, the term "tri-continental" is preferred by people doing this work and is used here to refer to Africa, Latin America, and Asia.
17. Brian Rosenberg, "Historicizing the New Historicism: Understanding the Past in Criticism and Fiction," *Modern Language Quarterly* 50 (1989): 376.
18. See Gina Hens-Piazza, "Forms of Violence and the Violence of Forms: Two Cannibal Mothers before a King (2 Kgs 6.24–33)," *Journal of Feminist Studies in Religion* 14.1 (1998): 91–104.
19. Boyarin, "Rabbinic Resistance to Male Domination," 119.
20. An earlier edition of this interpretative study by the author exists in a collection of essays under the title "Why Did Sarah Laugh?" and is used here by permission of the publisher. See Holly Hearon, ed., *Distant Voices Drawing Near* (Collegeville, MN: Liturgical Press, 2004) 57–67.
21. Louis Montrose, "Renaissance Literary Studies and the Subject of History," 8.
22. E.g., see Ephraim A. Speiser, *Genesis*, Anchor Bible 1 (Garden City, NY: Doubleday, 1983), 124–31; Gerhard von Rad, *Genesis*, Old Testament Library (Philadelphia: Westminster, 1972), 203; and Claus Westermann, *Genesis 12–36: A Commentary*, trans. John Scullion, S.J. (Minneapolis,: Augsburg, 1985), 272.

23. Andrew A. McIntosh, following Pseudo-Jonathan, proposes the meaning "sexual pleasure or conception" in "A Third Root in Biblical Hebrew?" *Vetus Testamentum* 24 (1974): 454–73.
24. Jacqueline Bussie, *The Laughter of the Oppressed: Ethical and Theological Resistance in Wiesel, Morrison, and Endo* (New York: T. & T. Clark, 2007), 41.

FOR FURTHER READING

Boyarin, Daniel. *Carnal Israel: Reading Sex in Talmudic Culture*. The New Historicism: Studies in Cultural Poetics 25. Berkeley: University of California Press, 1993.

Gallagher, Catherine, and Stephen Greenblatt. *Practicing New Historicism*. Chicago: University of Chicago Press, 2000.

Hens-Piazza, Gina. *The New Historicism*. Guides to Biblical Scholarship. Minneapolis: Augsburg Fortress, 2002.

Moore, Stephen D., ed. New Historicism issue, *Biblical Interpretation* 5. Leiden: Brill, 1997.

Schipper, Jeremy. *Disability Studies and the Hebrew Bible: Figuring Mephibosheth in the David Story*. New York and London: T. & T. Clark, 2006.

Sherwood, Yvonne. *A Biblical Text and Its Afterlives: The Survival of Jonah in Western Culture*. Cambridge, UK, and New York: Cambridge University Press, 2000.

Chapter 5

The Bible and Popular Culture

LINDA S. SCHEARING AND VALARIE H. ZIEGLER

What do the video game *Bioshock,* a print ad for Absolut Vodka, and a joke about God's gender have in common? They all take ancient biblical characters and story lines and turn them into contemporary cultural commodities. Such usage of the Bible raises an interesting issue for biblical scholars: how important is popular culture's appropriation of the Bible, and how should it be analyzed? In this chapter we will explore the concept of popular culture and its relationship to biblical studies. We will then take two genres of popular culture—advertising and humor—and present several case studies in which we analyze examples of each. But before we do this, we need to address two deceptively simple questions: *Just what is popular culture, and why in the world should scholars (and students) study it?*

POPULAR CULTURE

Definition of Popular Culture

Noted historian Asa Briggs once remarked that "it is easier to participate in, to enjoy, to deplore, or to explore popular culture than it is to define it."[1] After all, to define "popular culture" one has to deal with the multiple meanings inherent in the terms "popular" and "culture." The complexity of this issue, however, does not deter scholars from *attempting* to define it. For example, in his work on cultural theory and popular culture, John Storey identifies at least six different definitions:

1. "Popular culture is simply culture which is widely favored or well liked by many people."[2]
2. Popular culture is "the culture which is left over after we have decided what is high culture."[3]
3. Popular culture is "mass culture."[4]
4. Popular culture is "the culture which originates from 'the people.'"[5]
5. Popular culture, seen from the perspective of hegemony theory, is "a terrain of ideological struggle between dominant and subordinate classes, dominant and subordinate cultures."[6]
6. "A sixth definition of popular culture is one informed by recent thinking around the debate on postmodernism. . . . The main point to insist on here is the claim that postmodern culture is a culture which no longer recognizes the distinction between high and popular culture."[7]

Another scholar, Holt Parker, admits that Storey's work is "still the most systematic discussion of attempts to pin down popular culture," but argues that his sixth definition ends with "something of a whimper."[8] Instead of focusing on Marxist models of production—the underlying assumption of many prior understandings of popular culture—Parker argues that we need to take a more Weberian approach and look at consumption. Such a turnabout means that we should think less of "class" when dealing with popular culture and more of "status." Parker thus offers some tentative definitions:

1. "Popular culture consists of the productions of those without cultural capital, of those without access to the approved means of symbolic and cultural production."[9]
2. "Popular culture consists of products that require little cultural capital either to produce or else to consume."[10]
3. "Popular culture is unauthorized culture."[11]

But, in spite of his diligence in unpacking the term "popular culture," Parker concludes that "a precise definition of popular culture is elusive, perhaps delusive."[12]

The very fact that scholars like Storey and Parker think popular culture is worth defining and studying, however, is revelatory. In the past, scholars have questioned whether popular culture deserved "serious consideration at all."[13] In the introduction to their book, *Rethinking Popular Culture*, Chandra Mukerji and Michael Schudson make this startling observation:

> Popular culture studies have undergone a dramatic change during the last generation—from an academic backwater to a swift intellectual river where

expansive currents from different disciplines meet. Anthropologists, historians, sociologists, and literary scholars have mounted impressive intellectual challenges to basic assumptions in their own fields, which had previously barred close attention to popular forms.[14]

Today, popular cultural artifacts—video games, comics, advertisements, jokes, Internet chat rooms (to name only a few)—are the focus of academic research, the subject of course curricula, and the objects of discussion in classrooms.

Why Study Popular Culture?

Popular culture not only reflects its social context, but shapes it as well. This is especially true in the twenty-first century with its expanding communication technology and resulting information explosion. In this atmosphere, popular culture becomes a means of storytelling that shapes our own identities. As Mary Hess notes, ". . . human storytelling, at least in this time and place, is thoroughly embedded in and permeated by mass-mediated popular culture. Pop culture shapes our narratives in multiple ways, including our explicitly religious narratives."[15]

Popular culture, it is argued, is now one of the most important influences on the "values, beliefs and behaviors"[16] of people today. Indeed, the question confronting students and scholars shouldn't be "Why should we study popular culture?" but "How can we justify ignoring it?"

THE BIBLE AND POPULAR CULTURE

The Bible has always been an elitist object—produced, consumed, transmitted, and studied by elites variously defined: "I wonder whether we Bible scholars shall be brave enough to focus on the Bible's heritage in our culture. . . . The gain of doing cultural/biblical studies so-called, outside organized religion especially, may be enormous. Who knows, this way the Bible may continue to exist as a book for life, an identity cultural marker."[17]

In 2006, the "The Bible and American Popular Culture" section debuted in the Society of Biblical Literature's (SBL) annual meeting program. Prior to this, popular culture topics had appeared in a variety of other sections (e.g., Bible and Cultural Studies, Bible and Ancient and Modern Media, and so forth), but now, for the first time in SBL's history, a regularly convened section was created to routinely address popular culture and the Bible. In 2008, one of the section's sessions examined Mark Roncace and Patrick Gray's new book, *Teaching the Bible through Popular Culture and the Arts* (2007). Its publication highlighted the fact that not only were biblical scholars studying popular culture, they were using it (or being encouraged to use it) in their pedagogy and classrooms.

Since more and more biblical scholars are studying popular culture artifacts, one would expect that they would have developed by now a clear methodology.

But they have not. In the introduction to her coedited book, *The Bible in/and Popular Culture: A Creative Encounter*, Elaine M. Wainwright finds it surprising that "given the penchant in biblical studies for hermeneutical and methodological issues, there is as yet no systematic study of the interrelationship between the Bible and popular culture."[18] She concludes that "one comprehensive theoretical framework for the nexus of the Bible and popular culture may not be possible. The media are too diverse and the possible approaches too numerous...."[19]

How does one designate a single methodology for analyzing a video game, advertisement, joke, fashion trend, and so on? And what kind of academic training is best suited for this work? The discipline in which the researcher is located also shapes the theoretical approach. Popular culture artifacts are analyzed by scholars from diverse academic fields, each of whom brings to their analyses their own discipline-shaped expertise and theories. Yet, as Mukerji and Schudson note, "no single discipline has or will ever have a monopoly on the study of popular culture."[20]

What tools do biblical scholars bring to the analysis of popular culture? First and foremost they bring a focus—the Bible. Another asset biblical scholars have is their utilization of interdisciplinary methods in their scholarship. Some of these methods are routinely used in critical studies of popular culture. Here are but a few of the useful concepts and approaches that both cultural and biblical critics employ:

1. *Rhetorical Criticism.* Rhetorical criticism is not limited to biblical studies. The focus of a rhetorical critical analysis of a cultural artifact is to address what the text is doing "inside of the text" (e.g., direct tactics, implied strategies, structure)[21] as well as looking at the "real world within which texts do their work" (e.g., metonymies, empowerment/disempowerment, etc.).[22] Communication experts like Barry Brummett find rhetorical criticism helpful in analyzing popular culture texts. For Brummett, popular culture texts "wield their rhetorical influence by affecting the meanings that people attribute to the world."[23] Moreover, since meaning is complex, Brummett finds that "texts are often sites of struggle over what the world means."[24]

2. *Feminist Analysis.* Feminism addresses the issue of gender in the reading and production of texts—whether biblical texts or those of popular culture. Popular culture, after all, both reflects social experience and artifacts and helps to shape their meaning. As Lana Rakow notes,

> Though contemporary feminists have taken a diversity of approaches to popular culture, they have shared two major assumptions. The first is that women have a particular relationship to popular culture that is different from men's.... The second assumption is that understanding how popular culture functions both for women and for a patriarchal culture is important if women are to gain control over their own identities and change both social mythologies and social relations.... Feminists are saying that popular culture plays a role in patriarchal society and that theoretical analysis of this role warrants a major position in ongoing discussions.[25]

As a movement, feminism doesn't just "address" gender and its meaning; it also seeks to identify and challenge gender bias.

3. *Semiology*. Semiotics is the study of signs, symbols, and the ideology and power inherent in their meanings. One of the pioneers of applying semiotics to the study of popular culture is the French semiologist Roland Barthes. Drawing on the earlier works of Ferdinand de Saussure, who studied the role of signs as part of social life, Barthes developed a model for using semiology to read popular culture. In his book *Mythologies* (1973) he adds a second level of signification to Saussure's idea of signifier/signified—that of consumption. For Barthes, how a person "reads" a text is dependent on "the location of the text, the historical moment and the cultural formation of the reader."[26] He cautions his readers, however, against thinking that they have found the meaning of a sign. In the end, one must remember that signs are polysemic and have the potential for a multiplicity of significations.

4. *Intertextuality*. Intertextuality is the interpretation of one text by another text. In traditional biblical studies this usually means an earlier biblical passage being used/interpreted by a later biblical one. Cultural critics, however, also use this term to describe how a cultural artifact (a "text") is using/interpreting another. When interpreters talk about intertextuality between the Bible and popular culture, one "text" is the Bible, while the other "text" is the cultural artifact (e.g., advertisements, jokes, and so forth). The result is that meanings associated with the biblical text often add to the cultural artifact's impact.

5. *Reception History/History of Interpretation*. Biblical scholars are quite used to looking at the history of a biblical passage's interpretation. Within the last few decades, scholars have increasingly turned from their study of the world behind the biblical text to the one in front of it. In her paper, "What's the Use of Reception History?" Mary C. Callaway explores the history behind the terms "reception history" and "history of interpretation" and suggests that while these terms are different, in both their historical origins and in their orientation, there is a possibility of collapsing these differences:

> . . . the term History of Interpretation is used in general for studies that take an exegetical approach and have a theological interest. The object of study may be a work of art or a piece of music, so long as the approach is exegetical and explores the hermeneutic by which the biblical text was interpreted. The term Reception History, as its origins in *Wirkungsgeschichte* imply, should describe studies that employ a mixture of historical, sociological and anthropological approaches to illuminate the mutual interplay of *effects* that a biblical text has had on a given culture and that a culture manages to encode in a biblical text. It may well be that the two approaches will be collapsed into a single new approach that is productive for the synagogue and the church in the postmodern world, and for a culture grappling with an identity shaped by the Bible but not versed in it.[27]

Some areas and approaches to analyzing popular culture and the Bible have drawn more attention from Bible scholars than others. Art and film, for example, have been the focus of a number of treatments.[28] But popular culture is more than simply art and film. While a chapter of this length cannot hope even to touch superficially on all the important genres of popular culture, it will address two that are significant in their appropriation of biblical materials but have drawn little attention from biblical scholars: advertising and humor.

CASE STUDY: ADVERTISING AND THE BIBLE

In his article "What Is Advertising?" William M. O'Barr discusses the difficulties encountered when trying to define the term "advertising":

> We know it when we see it. We are exposed to it thousands of times every day. Most of us are reasonably good, although seldom perfect, at distinguishing it from other kinds of messages. It is something that we tend to take for granted, seldom thinking about what it is or how it came into existence. But what is this thing called advertising?[29]

After surveying attempts at definition—from "a device to arrest attention" to "selling Corn Flakes to people who are eating Cheerios"—he concludes with a quotation from Sal Randazzo's book, *Mythmaking on Madison Avenue*:

> Myths are more than entertaining little stories about gods, goddesses, and heroic characters. The universality of myths, the fact that the same myths recur across time and many cultures, suggests that they originate somewhere inside of us. . . . Advertisers sell products by mythologizing them, by wrapping them in our dreams and fantasies. . . . Advertising is not simply in the business of "selling soap." . . . Advertising turns products into brands by mythologizing them—by humanizing them and giving them distinct identities, personalities, and sensibilities that reflect our own . . . . Advertising has discovered a powerful truth: Dreams sell.[30]

If Randazzo is correct, it is no wonder that Madison Avenue uses the Bible!

In the analysis below we will look at an ad for ASICS running shoes and one for Smirnoff's Green Apple Twist vodka. While the first will employ a semiotic analysis, the second will use a history of interpretation/text reception approach.

Semiotic Analysis of Ad: ASICS

ASICS is a leading manufacturer of running shoes. Its title is the acronym for the Latin phrase "*Anima Sana In Corpore Sano*—a sound mind in a sound body"[31]—which is understood to reflect the company's philosophy that "the best way to create a healthy and happy lifestyle is to promote total health and fitness."[32] In 2009, ASICS launched a new campaign. The ad campaign was titled "Left and Right" and promoted: ". . . the SportStyle leisure footwear range

... using unique pairings and relationships that together create something more than the sum of their two parts. Four pairings, Adam & Eve, Up & Down, Art & Science and East & West, are brought to life in modern artistic expressions and feature the end line: 'What's a left without a right?'"[33]

Since our guiding focus in this chapter is how advertisements use biblical characters and themes, the only ad in ASICS's campaign that we will analyze is the Adam and Eve ad. The analysis below employs a semiotic approach. A semiotic analysis pays close attention to elements such as visual signs, linguistic signs, aural signs, the implied communication situation, textual structure, information structure, visual emphasis, genre, binary opposition and contrast pairs, and communication codes.[34]

The Ad

Title: Adam & Eve

Campaign Name: Left & Right

Company: ASICS B.V.

Product: ASICS Footware

Advertising agency: Amsterdam Worldwide

Artist: Johan Kleinjan

Release Date: March 2009 [35]

Description: A naked young man and woman are standing on either side of a fruit tree with a host of objects surrounding them. The woman is on the viewer's right, with a purple background and pink tree with red leaves (with a white and red snake interwoven in its branches); the young man is on the viewer' s left, with a blue background and a brown tree with green leaves. On the bottom is a pair of shoes with the ad copy "What's a left without a right?" ASICS. (To see the illustration, go to http://theinspirationroom.com/daily/print/2009/3/ASICS_Adam_Eve.jpg.)

The Analysis

Visual Signs. What signs are used in the ad? What do they signify? The signs in the ad consist of a naked male (with a tattoo, "Eve") and a naked female (with a tattoo, "Adam"), each standing on a different side of a tree. They are surrounded by a host of objects. Around the male are a car, baseball bat, video game control, camera, headphones, and grass. Around the female are a snake, a butterfly, cupcakes, jewelry, rabbits, and flowers. All of these objects signify lifestyle activities associated with men and women. Clearly men play video games, drive cars, and so on, while women cook, wear jewelry, and like rabbits and butterflies (and snakes?). Thus the objects reinforce cultural stereotypes of what it means to be a man and a woman and function as extensions of the "self."

The Implied Communication Situation. Who is the ad's intended target? Given the age of the figures and the types of objects surrounding them, one can conclude that it is a younger rather than an older audience being targeted.

Visual Emphasis. Neither male nor female in the ad seem to be aware of the viewing audience. The male is standing straight (to the viewer's left of the tree) and looking off to the right in a rather uninterested or bored manner (in spite of all the things surrounding him). The woman is imaged a bit differently, leaning against the tree with her right arm raised above her head. But she too is gazing off to the right, a bit uninterested or bored. Visually the emphasis seems to be on their binary opposition.

Binary Oppositions and Contrast Pairs. This ad, like all the ads in the ASICS Left and Right campaign, is structured around the concept of binary opposition/contrast. This structure can be seen in a number of the ad's visual and verbal elements. Visually, the fact that the image is split into two results in an optical and semiotic contrast. This contrast is emphasized by color—the main colors of the male's side being blue, green, white, and brown while the female's colors are pink, red, purple, and white. The objects arrayed around the male and female further develop this contrast by exploiting the stereotypical associations with gender: male with technology versus female with nature. Verbally, contrast is achieved by the ad's question: "What's a left without a right?" (left and right being binary opposites).

Communication Codes. The uninterested looks on the male and female's faces and the verbal ad copy ("What's a left without a right?") send a strong message of incompleteness to the viewing audience: Men and women are incomplete without each other; a left shoe is incomplete without a right shoe; the viewing audience is incomplete without a pair of ASICS shoes!

Intertextuality. How does the ad use Genesis 2? Tattoos aside, most readers would recognize the basic symbol system of the Adam and Eve story: a naked man, a naked woman, a tree with "fruit," and a snake dangling from its branches. And if they were slow to do so, the tattoos on the characters' arms—"Adam" and "Eve"—would clinch the association. A bit more subtle is the allusion to Gen 2:18: "Then the LORD God said, 'It is not good that the man should be alone; I will make him a helper as his partner.'" Is a left shoe any good by itself? No—you need a "helper"—a "right" shoe for its partner! Can you have a happy, healthy life without ASICS running shoes? The ad's creators are trying hard to persuade you that you can't.

What Do a Pair of Running Shoes Have in Common with Adam and Eve?

On the surface—not much. But then again, they don't have to have much in common for this ad to "work." Moshe Cohen-Eliya and Yoav Hammer point out that "Under semiotic theory, visual imagery is a picture that represents and suggests a particular meaning, idea or conception.... Such imagery encourages leaps of imagination in the viewer's mind from one meaning to another, without much attention to whether there is any logical connection among them."[36]

This ad "works" because it employs well-known figures—Adam and Eve (the first *pair* of humans)—from a powerful story of origin, Genesis 2–3. For many readers it is a story that defines gender roles as well as advocating heterosexuality. The ad builds on the idea that the viewing audience assumes the correspondence of male with female, not male with male or female with female. Indeed, it is hard to see the ad's creators even considering having footwear made up of two right or left shoes.

History of Interpretation Analysis of Ad: Green Apple Twist

As part of its flavored vodka line, Diageo launched in 2002, Smirnoff's "Green Apple Twist." Hital Pandya, one of the campaign's art directors in India, explains, "For Smirnoff's Green Apple Twist, we came up with a series of print advertisements that focus on popular themes revolving around apples. One print ad, for instance, shows Isaac Newton sitting under a tree holding a green apple, while another focuses on Adam and Eve and the forbidden fruit angle. The theme running through all these ads is 'old story, new twist.'"[37] What is interesting is that this ad, being created for an Asian market, used a biblical theme—the garden story—as its marketing tool.

The Ad

Title: Old Story, New Twist: Adam and Eve

Campaign Name: Smirnoff Green Apple Twist

Company: Diageo

Product: Flavored Vodka—Green Apple

Advertising agency: JWT, Mumbai, India

Art Directors: Debojyoti Purkayashta and Hital Pandya

Copywriter: Senthil Kumar and Arkadyuti Basu

Creative Director: Senthil Kumar and Debojyoti Purkayashta

Release date: November 2002[38]

Description: The middle of the ad focuses on a fruit tree with green apples set against a blue background. A woman attired only in leaves is reaching for an apple while looking at the man squatting to the viewer's left on the ground. The man's attention is fixed on a female snake with a lump in its torso and curved around the tree. At the ad's bottom right is the copy: "Old Story, New Twist" and the name of the product: "Green Apple Twist." (To see the illustration, go to http://adsoftheworld.com/media/print/smirnoff_green_apple_twist_adam_eve.)

The Analysis

The Snake. Genesis 3:1 introduces a new character into the garden story: "Now the serpent was more crafty than any other wild animal that the LORD God had made. He said to the woman, . . ." Some artists who have depicted this scene often portrayed the snake as male or gender neutral. But others have stressed the femaleness of the snake.[39] This resulted in making females (both reptilian and human) doubly guilty for the disobedience that followed. The Smirnoff ad appears in the trajectory of this interpretation. The snake's visage, with its soft gentle eyes, appears female to the viewer. Moreover, its lips (all the better to speak with?) appear in close proximity to the male, as if we are viewing the moments before a kiss.

What is different about the snake is the suspicious lump (the size of one of the apples) in its body. Did the snake eat the forbidden fruit before Eve? Did the snake "fall" before Eve? Of course, for the ad's creators there is another message here as well. Even snakes can't stay away from green apples—just like viewers can't resist Smirnoff's Green Apple Twist.

The Male. In the ad, Adam appears squatting with a bemused look on his face as he gazes into the eyes of the snake. His mouth is open and appears to be on the verge of a kiss. The idea of the snake having a sexual relationship with one of the first humans is not new. However, the snake's sexual relationship is usually understood as being with Eve, not Adam (*Yebam.* 103b). One rabbinic source even attributes the friction between Cain and Abel to the fact that they have different fathers—one, the snake and the other, Adam (*Pirqe R. El.* 21–22). But in the Smirnoff ad, there seems a reversal of sexual partners with the snake now pairing with Adam not Eve. Is this reversal an allusion to the ad's copy: "Old Story, New Twist"?

The Female. Eve is imaged in the ad as about to pick an apple behind Adam's back. In Genesis 3:6, however, the text stresses that Adam was "with her" when she spoke to the snake and subsequently ate the fruit. Writers like John Milton (*Paradise Lost*, book 9) stress the distance between Adam and Eve when she speaks to the snake, but this runs counter to the actual text. In the ad, however, a sense of distance is achieved by having Adam's back turned away from Eve. Another interesting aspect of the ad deals with the leaves covering Eve. Are we looking at the garden scene *after* the disobedience? Or is the ad's intent simply to meet marketing decency standards?

The Fruit and Tree. In the ad, the tree is an apple tree that produces green apples. But in Genesis the identity of the fruit is never specified. In 2:9 it simply says that "Out of the ground the LORD God made to grow every tree that is pleasant to the sight and good for food, the tree of life also in the midst of the garden, and the tree of the knowledge of good and evil." While in the following chapter they both eat the forbidden fruit, the reader is not told what *kind* of fruit it was. In antiquity, readers filled in that gap with a host of suggestions: the Carob/Tamarind (*1 Enoch* 32.4), fig, or wheat (*Gen. Rab.* 15.7).

Adam, Eve, and Vodka: A New Twist on an Old Story?

The ad's copy "A new twist on an old story" is a wordplay on Green Apple Twist Vodka. Ironically, however, the association of alcohol as the "forbidden fruit" isn't so new after all. When, in antiquity, the fruit of the garden was identified as grapes (*Gen. Rab.* 19.5), the "sin" of the garden was caused by wine (*Sanh.* 70a). Of course, Eve made the wine (*Gen. Rab.* 19.5). In the contemporary world of marketing, the forbidden fruit—with its taboo status—has been a "fruitful" way to advertise beer, wine, and hard liquors.

CASE STUDY: HUMOR AND THE BIBLE

There are numerous genres of humor (e.g., cartoons, comic strips, anecdotes, humor columns, parody, puns, satire, and so forth) and a variety of mediums for its delivery. Humor can be found in oral, print, and a host of visual formats. In this case study we will look at narrative jokes about Adam and Eve found on the Internet. Narrative jokes can be defined as "a short narrative, meant to amuse, with a punch line."[40] They have a formal pattern that progresses in a linear fashion to its conclusion. In "What's In a Joke: A Micro-analysis," Arthur Asa Berger describes this structure: "The punch lines generates [sic] some kind of meaning . . . which elicits laughter (when the joke is a good one). We move from a linear narrative or syntagmatic structure . . . to a paradigmatic structure in which there is meaning that is unexpected and a set of simple binary oppositions that can be elicited from the text."[41] The jokes in this case study are analyzed using a rhetorical-critical approach. Rhetorical criticism analyzes language aimed at persuasion. A key concern is to answer the questions, How does this text "work?" What is its intent? Often a rhetorical-critical analysis will identify the speaker, audience, and subject of a text. But the nature of the Internet makes it difficult indeed to discover the joke's original speaker and context or the form of the "anchor" joke from which subsequent variants are descended. The one area of the rhetorical triangle (speaker, context, and subject) that can be identified about the jokes in this case study is their *subject*. Both jokes being studied here are narrative in structure and similar in content. Both focus on stereotypes of gender characteristics/roles and link these to Genesis 2. By linking the jokes to a story of humankind's creation, these gender characteristics/roles take on the aspect of essential—not simply cultural—features. Both work intertextually with Genesis and either support or challenge cultural assumptions about men and women.

The first joke in this analysis focuses on Adam, while the second switches the focus to Eve. This shift significantly alters the content that follows, though the structure of the joke remains basically the same. Both jokes use gender stereotypes and are pejorative, at points, to both men and women.

Joke 1

Adam was walking around the Garden of Eden feeling very lonely, so God asked Adam, "What is wrong with you?"

Adam said, "Lord, I don't have anyone to talk to."

God said, "Then I will give you a companion, and she will be called a 'woman.' This person will cook for you and wash your clothes, she will always agree with every decision you make. She will bear your children and never ask you to get up in the middle of the night to take care of them. She will not nag you and will always be the first to admit she was wrong when you've had a disagreement. She will never have a headache and will freely give 'love' and compassion whenever needed. She will never question your behavior or the company you keep. She will support you and understand that you have important decisions to make throughout your life and don't have time for nonsense."

Adam asked God, "What will this woman cost?"

God said, "An arm and a leg."

Adam said, "What can I get for just a rib?"[42]

The Analysis

Setting. The narrator's "voice" occurs only briefly in the first line to set the stage for the dialogue between Adam and God that follows. It establishes that we are in the garden of Eden and that Adam is lonely.

Dialogue. Three characters "speak" in the joke: the narrator, Adam, and God. After the brief introduction by the narrator, the rest of the joke is a dialogue between Adam and God in which they both speak three times. God initiates the dialogue by asking Adam "What is wrong with you?" The bulk of the rest of the dialogue occurs in God's second speech to Adam. After Adam reiterates what the narrator said at the beginning—that he is lonely/has no one to talk to—God responds with a solution. God will make Adam a "companion." The new creation is called "woman," and the description that follows reflects the stereotypical way women are often defined—as housewives and sex objects:

Housewife

cook for you

wash your clothes

always agree with every decision you make

bear your children

never ask you to get up in the middle of the night to take care of them

will not nag you

will always be the first to admit she was wrong when you've had a disagreement

will never question your behavior or the company you keep.

will support you and understand that you have important decisions to make throughout your life and don't have time for nonsense

Sex Object
will never have a headache

will freely give "love" and compassion whenever needed

Following God's offer, Adam judiciously asks what such a companion will cost him. God responds, "An arm and a leg." The joke ends with Adam's last reply, the punch line of the joke: "What can I get for just a rib?"

Intertextuality. Although the joke is based on Genesis 2, it makes changes in the story to fit the joke's purpose. In Genesis 2 Adam never complains that he is lonely. Indeed, it is God who says that it is not good for humans to be alone (2:18a). Nor, in Genesis 2, does God immediately make woman to assuage the loneliness of man. Directly after God's pronouncement about being alone, God creates animals. What is the function of woman? According to 2:18b God says: "I will make him a helper as his partner." Genesis has no detailed description of woman as the ideal passive housewife/sex object, nor are there negotiations between God and Adam concerning her "cost." Although the joke is ostensibly about Adam and Eve, these changes in the garden story's content are crucial to the joke's message and intent.

Subject of the Joke. This joke is about gender roles and characteristics. In their analysis of gender in popular Internet humor, Limor Shifman and Dafna Lemish note that "comedic texts draw on prevalent ideologies, stereotypes, and cultural codes."[43] As Charles G. Kelly notes in his analysis of Adam and Eve jokes, use of the iconic Genesis 2 story of the first man and women serves as a "perfect springboard for sexist jokes"[44] because it presents readers with the prototype of male-female relations. Indeed the garden account is often cited in contemporary discussions as a proof text for what it means to be a man and a woman.

Readers recognize the description of woman as an ideal passive housewife and available (24/7) sex object because they are familiar with this cultural stereotype of a "perfect" companion vis-à-vis a male point of view. Shifman and Lemish identify four types of sexist humor and note that humor targeting women can be "implicit (i.e., uses stereotypical feminine prototypes . . . without signifying explicitly that the joke deals with gender)."[45] Indeed, since this joke is talking about the first woman, then the description given by God to Adam ostensibly gives readers the intended prototype for all women. Of course, women are no more like this prototype now than they were in antiquity. Genesis 3, with its account of the first human disobedience, reflects the fracturing of male-female relationships. While this is not mentioned in the joke, one could argue that it is implied in the joke's punch line.

The punch line significantly changes the cause of contemporary problems *between* men and women. When Adam asks how much it will cost him to get this companion, God responds "an arm and a leg"—an idiom meaning a very high price indeed. This answer is crucial, for it indicates that she is not only costly but also perhaps overpriced. Thus Adam asks what he can get for a rib. The implication, of course, is that the companion he gets is "less than" the one God would have given Adam. The irony here is that the joke actually belittles both Adam and Eve. Adam, because contemporary relational problems can be attributed to his own stinginess and Eve, because she is not what God had originally intended as Adam's companion. The humor (and irony) in the punch line is that Adam, not Eve, is at fault.

Joke 2

One day in the Garden of Eden, Eve called out to God, "Lord, I have a problem!"

"What's the problem, Eve?"

"Lord, I know you've created me and have provided this beautiful garden and all of these wonderful animals, and that hilarious comedic snake, but I'm just not happy."

"Why is that, Eve?" came the reply from above.

"Lord, I am lonely. And I'm sick to death of apples."

"Well, Eve, in that case, I have a solution. I shall create a man for you."

"What's a 'man,' Lord?"

"This man will be a flawed creature, with aggressive tendencies, an enormous ego and an inability to empathize or listen to you properly. All in all, he'll give you a hard time. But he'll be bigger, faster, and more muscular than you. He'll also need your advice to think properly. He'll be really good at fighting and kicking a ball about, hunting fleet-footed ruminants, and not altogether bad in the sack."

"Sounds great," says Eve, with an ironically raised eyebrow. "What's the catch, Lord?"

"Yeah, well, . . . you can have him on one condition."

"What's that, Lord?"

"You'll have to let him believe that I made him first."[46]

The Analysis

Setting. The narrator establishes for the reader that we are in the garden of Eden.

Dialogue. After a brief introduction by the narrator, the rest of the joke is a dialogue between Eve and God in which each speaks six times. Eve initiates the dialogue by telling God that she has a problem. When God asks what the problem is, Eve says she is not happy (in spite of the beautiful garden, wonderful animals, and comedic snake). God asks why she's not happy and Eve replies that she's lonely and she's bored with apples. The bulk of the rest of the dialogue occurs in God's fourth speech to Eve where God's solution is to make a "man" for her. When Eve asks what a "man" is, God's description of "man" employs the stereotypical ways men's faults and strengths are often discussed by women. The description starts with man's flaws and then moves to the more positive aspects of having a man:

The "Cons" of Having a Man

will be a flawed creature

will have aggressive tendencies, an enormous ego, and an inability to empathize or listen to you properly

will give you a hard time

The "Pros" of Having a Man

will be bigger, faster, and more muscular than you

will need your advice to think properly

will be really good at fighting and kicking a ball about, hunting fleet-footed ruminants, and not altogether bad in the sack

Eve says the offer sounds great but immediately suspects "a catch," and asks what it is. God responds by admitting that she's right. The joke then moves to the punch line: "You'll have to let him believe that I made him first."

Intertextuality. Like the previous joke, this joke switches the comment about loneliness from God's mouth to that of the human. Unlike the previous joke, however, that human is not Adam but Eve. Thus, from the outset, the reader knows that something is amiss. How can Eve be lonely when the Genesis account has Adam created before her? But the reader's attention is drawn away from this incongruity when God begins describing the solution to Eve's loneliness (evidently her boredom with apples isn't an issue). The changes between the garden story and the joke that follow, once again, are in sync with the joke's intent.

Subject of the Joke. Like the first joke we analyzed, this joke is about gender roles/characteristics. Unlike the first joke, however, it focuses on stereotypes about men, not women. Is this feminist humor? Shifman and Lemish identify certain types of humor as "feminist" and argue that such humor critiques "the patriarchal structure of society and aspires to reform it."[47] M. Crawford defines such humor as that which "challenges traditional views of gender by targeting men and resisting dominant constructions of femininity"[48] Whether this joke can been classified as "feminist" or not, the key is the joke's punch line. Throughout the history of the interpretation of Genesis 2, much has been made of the fact that Eve was created after Adam. Her derivative nature and the order of her creation have served to fuel arguments about her subordination to men and her "secondary" status. This joke's punch line, however, implies that it was Eve, not Adam, who was created first. Such a proclamation undercuts those arguments that mandate her subordination based on the order of her creation. Of course it does so by making man secondary and the dupe of some kind of conspiracy between woman and God. Is this some reverse sexism?

Kelly, in his article "Laughing In and Out of Eden: An Analysis of Adam and Eve Jokes," remarks that "Since Eve is the 'mother of all races' and Adam is the 'father of us all,' by association we are automatically connected with their plight. Consequently, Adam and Eve become prime subjects and targets of numerous sexual, religious, political and racial jokes that touch a universal thread in all of us and appeal to a wide range of joke tellers—and listeners."[49] He ends the article with the observation that "Jokes about Adam and Eve are jokes about us . . . ."[50] In spite of the frequently heard comment—"it's only a joke"—jokes are often not simply about laughter. As Berger explains, "humor is a double valenced agent: it can be used, in some circumstances, as a means of control and regulation, but it is also a force of resistance."[51] While it could be argued that both jokes in this case study use gender stereotypes, the second joke can be said to offer resistance to some of the more oppressive interpretations of Genesis 2.

CONCLUSION

Popular Culture Studies and Biblical Studies: A Match Made in . . .?

Of course, some scholars are apprehensive about popular culture's entrée into the field of biblical studies. Stephen Moore raises many of these concerns. Moore remarks that cultural studies are "the literary studies phenomenon that most tellingly sets the fox among the chickens; likewise in biblical studies, cultural studies constitutes the most serious (and salutary) threat to the inherited identity of the discipline."[52] Popular appropriations of the Bible, in short, disregard scholars' authority as biblical interpreters. But Moore sees this as an opportunity for biblical studies. He challenges biblical scholars to "acknowledge their own fetish for methodology, understand what impels it, and move beyond it."[53] Philip Culbertson strikes a similar note when he observes that "popular culture not only influences biblical interpretation but also opens up new perspectives and challenges and confronts the conventional, stylized hermeneutical frameworks of the 'industry' of the academic study of biblical texts."[54]

The study of the Bible and popular culture is a challenge, but one with great potential. As Laura Copier, Jaap Kooijman, and Caroline Vander Stichle remark in their article "Close Encounters: The Bible as Pre-Text in Popular Culture,"

Recognizing the Bible in . . . popular culture . . . opens up a space not only for exploring how the Bible as pre-text informs much of the culture we live in and consume every day, but also for critically engaging with the diffused and slippery boundaries that characterize contemporary audiovisual culture. Such an approach calls for creative encounters between the Bible and popular culture, thereby providing ever-new perspectives on this ancient book and revealing its continuous cultural relevance.[55]

Biblical scholars have already either "tentatively or with confidence"[56] started working with the Bible and popular culture. Such work just might, in Athalya Brenner's words, "save us Bible scholars from socio-political insignificance . . . while allowing for great fun, of the serious and light-headed types, in the process.[57]

In conclusion, biblical scholars should be attentive to popular culture and the Bible because, quite frankly, we cannot afford not to be. Consider these realities:

- Contemporary culture has been shaped by the Bible; studying popular culture appropriations helps us to examine and appreciate this continued relevance.
- The move from written texts to the world of visual appropriation (art, film, comics, and so forth) is an important change of medium that impacts the Bible's ongoing interpretation.
- Today's expanding communication technology and resulting information explosion makes popular culture's use of the Bible ubiquitous to anyone on the Internet. In other words, biblical scholars in the twenty-first century not only study the *worlds of the text* and *the worlds behind the texts*, but also the *worlds in front of the text*. Just as understanding the context of ancient texts is important to traditional biblical scholarship, so studying the contexts in which the Bible is currently understood should be just as important. As such, the question should not be, "Why should we, as biblical scholars, study popular culture and the Bible" but rather, "How can we justify ignoring it?"

KEY TERMS

binary oppositions. Pairs of mutually exclusive signifiers that represent logically opposed categories and together define a complete universe of discourse, e.g., alive/not-alive. "In such oppositions each term necessarily implies its opposite and there is no middle term."[58]

communication codes. "One of the fundamental concepts in semiotics. Semiotic codes are procedural systems of related conventions for correlating signifiers and signifieds in certain domains. Codes provide a framework within which signs make sense: they are interpretative devices which are used by interpretative communities. They can be broadly divided into social codes, textual codes and interpretative codes. Some codes are fairly explicit; others . . . are much looser."[59]

intertexuality. "Refers to the various links in form and content which bind a text to other texts. Each text exists in relation to others. Although the debts of a text to other texts are seldom acknowledged, texts owe more to other texts than to their own makers. Texts provide contexts such as genre within which other texts may be created and interpreted. The notion of intertextuality problematizes the idea of a text having boundaries: where does a text begin and end?"[60]

reception history. Focuses on readers as opposed to authors and examines "what happened to the texts after the authors had finished with them as opposed to what was in their mind or what was going on around them when they wrote them."[61]

semiology. "Involves both the theory and analysis of signs and signifying practices. Beyond the most basic definition, there is considerable variation amongst leading semioticians as to what semiotics involves, although a distinctive concern is with how things signify, and with representational practices and systems (in the form of codes). In the 1970s, semioticians began to shift away from purely structuralist (Saussurean) semiotics concerned with the structural analysis of formal semiotic systems towards a 'poststructuralist' 'social semiotics'—focusing on 'signifying practices' in specific social contexts."[62]

NOTES

1. Asa Briggs, "What Is the History of Popular Culture," *History Today* 35 (1985): 39.
2. John Storey, *Cultural Theory and Popular Culture: An Introduction*, 4th ed. (Athens: University of Georgia Press, 2006), 4.
3. Ibid., 5.
4. Ibid., 6.
5. Ibid., 7.
6. Ibid., 8.
7. Ibid., 9.
8. Holt N. Parker, "Toward a Definition of Popular Culture," *History and Theory* 50 (2011): 148.
9. Ibid., 161.
10. Ibid.
11. Ibid., 165.
12. Ibid., 169.
13. Chandra Mukerji and Michael Schudson, "Popular Culture," *Annual Review of Sociology* 12 (1986): 47.
14. Chandra Mukerji and Michael Schudson, *Rethinking Popular Culture: Contemporary Perspectives in Cultural Studies* (Berkeley: University of California Press, 1991), 1.
15. Mary E. Hess, "The Bible and Popular Culture: Engaging Sacred Text in a World of Others," in *The Bible in/and Popular Culture: A Creative Encounter*, ed. Philip Culbertson and Elaine M. Wainwright (Atlanta: Society of Biblical Literature, 2010), 209.

16. Pei-Ling Lee, "The Critical Characteristics of Rhetorical Criticism: Analyzing Texts in Popular Culture," *The Review of Communication* 8 (2008): 214.
17. Athalya Brenner, "Foreword," in *Culture, Entertainment and the Bible*, ed. George Aichele, *Journal for the Study of the Old Testament* Supplement 11 (2000): 11.
18. Elaine M. Wainwright, "Introduction," in *The Bible in/and Popular Culture*, 1–2.
19. Ibid., 8.
20. Mukerji and Schudson, *Rethinking Popular Culture*, 4.
21. Barry Brummett, *Rhetoric in Popular Culture*, 2nd ed. (Los Angeles: Sage Publications, 2006), 117.
22. Ibid., 131–32.
23. Ibid., 134.
24. Ibid.
25. Lana Rakow, "Feminist Approaches to Popular Culture: Giving Patriarchy Its Due," quoted in Storey, *Cultural Theory and Popular Culture*, 106.
26. Storey, *Cultural Theory and Popular Culture*, 95.
27. Mary C. Callaway, "What's the Use of Reception History?" (paper delivered at the Society of Biblical Literature annual meeting, San Antonio, 2004), http://bbibcomm.net/files/callaway2004.pdf (accessed October 2, 2011).
28. Stephen D. Moore, "A Modest Manifesto for New Testament Literary Criticism: How to Interface with a Literary Studies Field That Is Post-Literary, Post-Theoretical, and Post-Methodological," *Biblical Interpretation* 15 (2007):19, note 44.
29. William M. O'Barr, "What Is Advertising?" *Advertising and Society Review* Supplement Unit 1, http://muse.jhu.edu/journals/asr/v006/6.3unit01.html.
30. O'Barr, "What Is Advertising?" quoting Sal Randazzo, *Mythmaking on Madison Avenue* (Chicago: Probus Publishing, 1993).
31. ASICS, "About Us," http://www.asicsamerica.com/about-us/.
32. Ibid.
33. ASICS, "Left and Right" http://theinspirationroom.com/daily/2009/asics-left-and-right/.
34. Rachel Lawes, "Demystifying Semiotics: Some Key Questions Answered," *International Journal of Market Research* 44 (2002): 256.
35. "Left and Right" campaign for ASICS SportStyle, *Design nl*, http://www.design.nl/item/left_and_right_campaign_for_asics_sportstyle.
36. Moshe Cohen-Eliya and Yoav Hammer, "Advertisements, Stereotypes, and Freedom of Expression," *Journal of Social Philosophy* 35 (2004): 168.
37. "Jamming it up at JWT," Rediff News, India—http://specials.rediff.com/getahead/2007/may/08slid3.htm.
38. Ads of the World, "Smirnoff Green Apple Twist: Adam and Eve," http://adsoftheworld.com/media/print/smirnoff_green_apple_twist_adam_eve.
39. Peter M. Daly, "Adam and Eve in the Garden of Advertising," in *European Iconography East and West: Selected Papers of the Szeged International Conference, June 9–12, 1993*, ed. György E. Szőnyi (New York: Brill, 1996), 77.
40. Arthur Asa Berger, *Manufacturing Desire: Media, Popular Culture, and Everyday Life* (Piscataway, NJ: Transaction Publishers, 2008), 73.
41. Ibid., 74.
42. "Adam's Rib," Really Funny Jokes, http://reallyfunnyjokes.tumblr.com/post/5820256/adams-rib.
43. Limor Shifman and Dafna Lemish, "Between Feminism and Fun(ny)mism: Analyzing Gender in Popular Internet Culture," *Information, Communication & Society* 13, no. 6 (2010): 870. Business Source Complete, EBSCOhost, http://www.ebscohost.com/academic/business-source-complete.
44. Charles G. Kelly, "Laughing In and Out of Eden: An Analysis of Adam and Eve Jokes," *Midwestern Folklore* 14 (1988): 94.

45. Shifman and Lemish, "Between Feminism and Fun(ny)mism," 873.
46. "And God Made Man," CrocJokes.com, http://www.crocjokes.com/dirtyjokes.php?ID=1370&o=8&cat=%.
47. Shifman and Lemish, "Between Feminism and Fun(ny)mism," 873.
48. As cited in Shifman and Lemish, 873.
49. Kelly, "Laughing In and Out of Eden," 91.
50. Ibid., 96.
51. Berger, *Manufacturing Desire*, 80.
52. Stephen D. Moore, "A Modest Manifesto for New Testament Literary Criticism," 1.
53. Ibid.
54. Culbertson and Wainwright, *The Bible in/and Popular Culture*, 71.
55. Laura Copier, Jan Cooijman, and Caroline Vander Stichle, "Close Encounters: The Bible as Pre-Text in Popular Culture," in Culbertson and Wainwright, *The Bible in/and Popular Culture*, 195.
56. Brenner, "Foreword," 11.
57. Ibid., 11–12.
58. Daniel Chandler, Semiotics for Beginners, Glossary of Key Terms, http://www.aber.ac.uk/media/Documents/S4B/sem-gloss.html.
59. Ibid.
60. Chandler, "Glossary."
61. John F. A. Sawyer, "The Role of Reception Theory, Reader-Response Criticism and/or Impact History in the Study of the Bible: Definition and Evaluation," http://bbibcomm.net/reception-history.
62. Chandler, "Glossary."

FOR FURTHER READING

Books

Aichele, George, ed. *Culture, Entertainment and the Bible. Journal for the Study of the Old Testament* Supplement 11. New York: T. & T. Clark, 2000.

Brummett, Barry. *Rhetoric in Popular Culture*. 3rd ed. Los Angeles: Sage, 2011.

Culbertson, Philip, and Elaine M. Wainwright, eds. *The Bible in/and Popular Culture: A Creative Encounter*. Atlanta: Society of Biblical Literature, 2010.

Roncace, Mark, and Patrick Gray, eds. *Teaching the Bible through Popular Culture and the Arts*. Atlanta: Society of Biblical Literature, 2007.

Sawyer, John F. A., ed. *The Blackwell Companion to the Bible and Culture*. Oxford: Wiley-Blackwell, 2006.

Storey, John. *Cultural Theory and Popular Culture: An Introduction*, 4th ed. Athens, GA: University of Georgia Press, 2006.

Periodicals

Journal of Religion and Popular Culture. Journal published three times a year by the University of Toronto Press. Available online at http://utpjournals.metapress.com/content/u8w570v6u233/?p=977e9d719af2483c97616066d024a96d&pi=0.

Chapter 6

Postcolonial Biblical Criticism

WARREN CARTER

Postcolonial biblical criticism began to emerge in the 1990s. Like numerous forms of biblical criticism, it draws from other academic fields. For example, postcolonial studies embrace literature, film, history, human geography, political science, sociology, race, and gender theory, to name but some. It is a vibrant, complex, diverse, expansive, and unfolding area of study.[1]

It is widely recognized, though, that nearly everything about postcolonialism is disputed and unstable. Is postcolonialism a field of study, a step-by-step method, or a fragmented cluster of various theories that provides an "optic" or ways of looking that are portable to any number of disciplines? Should there be a hyphen between "post" and "colonial," and if so, what might the hyphenated and unhyphenated forms signify? Who can be a postcolonial reader: only those who know colonial oppression firsthand, or anyone (including someone from the so-called first world) who cares about what is just and fair and dignifying in the human experience? And how might postcolonial criticism be employed in biblical studies? Perhaps the term "postcolonial" is, as some have suggested, so debated and contested as to be meaningless. One scholar has helpfully proposed renaming it "imperial-colonial studies."[2]

This chapter will discuss some explanations of postcolonial criticism (section 1), briefly distinguish this "optic" from several other methods used for studying the Bible (section 2), and provide examples and some evaluation of postcolonial New Testament criticism (section 3).

SECTION 1: WHAT IS POSTCOLONIAL CRITICISM?

In this section I sample four explanations of postcolonial criticism randomly identified from the 515,000 hits I got (today) by googling "postcolonialism." Why google when there are numerous good books about postcolonial criticism? The act of googling has symbolic value. The cluster of theories that constitutes postcolonial criticism often emerges from academics. This is appropriate since the issues are complex, and thinking in careful ways about them matters. Much of the discourse, though, is difficult and esoteric with, in one scholar's opinion, "vagueness a cardinal virtue."[3] Ultimately, I would contend, postcolonial criticism not only comprises thinking and writing about the geopolitical issues of imperial-colonial formations and the complex and interconnected issues of power, gender, class, race/ethnicity, and sexual orientation but also involves "proactive moral involvement," addressing "the needs and aspirations of the exploited,"[4] *doing* justice across the world. It is about ways of living on our planet that are good for all people. Googling the World Wide Web turns us, at least symbolically, in a global, more "democratic," and praxis-oriented, direction.

First Posting

The World Literature Website of Dr. Fidel Fajardo-Acosta provides a glossary of literary terms that includes the following entry for "postcolonialism":

> A cultural, intellectual, political, and literary movement of the twentieth and twenty-first centuries characterized by the representation and analysis of the historical experiences and subjectivities of the victims, individuals and nations, of colonial power. Postcolonialism is marked by its resistance to colonialism and by the attempt to understand the historical and other conditions of its emergence as well as its lasting consequences.[5]

While the website's focus is on literature, this entry rightly emphasizes the cross-disciplinary nature of postcolonial studies. It recognizes that across these various disciplines, postcolonialism is concerned with unjust power relations as they are expressed in various geopolitical situations involving imperial-colonial power and/or represented in cultural products like novels, films, or histories. The glossary rightly locates the postcolonial optic as emerging out of anticolonial and anti-imperial struggles and concerned with ways in which the colonizing experience is represented. It locates the emergence of this focus in the twentieth century. While it is true that postcolonial criticism emerged in the second half of the twentieth century, it would be misleading to think that the imperial-colonial experience occurred only during that century.

By focusing attention on "victims, individuals and nations," the glossary entry indicates that these representations of the imperial-colonial experience will be varied. The foregrounding of the word "victims," a term denoting the damaging misuse of colonizing power, indicates that injustice involving the powerless or subalterns, and opposition to that injustice, are to the fore. The focus, then, is on the colonized but with vast implications for assessing the impact of Western power. Postcolonial work often disputes "official" and "benign" accounts that the powerful construct whereby literary, political, nationalistic, and religious representations of "civilizing" and "humanitarian" missions are shown to mask harmful exploitation of indigenous peoples. The claim that postcolonialism is "marked by resistance to colonialism" is central in recognizing both the sources and the goals of postcolonial criticism. Postcolonial criticism thus aligns with other liberationist (e.g., feminist) reading strategies. The last sentence of the glossary entry rightly recognizes that postcolonialism engages the whole of the colonizing experience, including its emergence and legacy, as formerly colonized peoples reclaim and redefine their past and construct identities for the future.

Second Posting

Among Answers.com's several explanations of "postcolonial" is one from the *Oxford Dictionary of Geography*. This posting also denotes postcolonialism's concern with the whole of the colonizing experience. And it locates the emergence of postcolonialism among colonized peoples in struggles against colonizing powers, specifically European ones:

> Stemming from the work of F. Fanon (1961) and E. Said (1978, 1993), the examination of the impact, and legacy, of the European conquest, colonization, and dominance of non-European cultures, lands, and peoples, together with the analysis of the ideas of European superiority inherent in European colonization. Other key features are: the exploration of the part played by representation in inaugurating and reproducing such ideas within both colonies and decolonized states; challenging the binary, homogeneous categories of the colonizing and colonized, and the recovery of the voices and agency of colonized peoples.[6]

Frantz Fanon (1925–1961) and Edward Said (1935–2003) are two key figures who laid a foundation for much of the postcolonial discourse of recent decades. Their work emerged from experiences and analysis of the impact of Western/European colonial power on local peoples, lands, material resources, and cultural structures in particular situations and circumstances, Fanon in Algeria and Said in the Middle East. They resist the imperializing xenophobia and racism that construct the subjugated "other" as inferior and the colonizer as superior.

Fanon wrestled with racism and French colonial power, first as he experienced it in Lyon, France, and subsequently in French-occupied Algeria during its fight for independence from France where he worked in the 1950s as head of a hospital psychiatry department. He observed the psychological damage and alienation caused by racist colonization whereby, for instance, oppressed locals yearned to exercise the power of their colonial overlords even while they simultaneously despised and opposed it. They felt overwhelmed and paralyzed by the oppressive control of colonial domination, yet they often directed toward each other the hatred and violence they felt for their oppressors. Drawing from these observations, Fanon's work challenges a simple binary of colonizer and colonized. His two most well-known books are *Black Skin, White Masks* (1952) and *The Wretched of the Earth* (1961).

Edward Said developed Fanon's insights in a number of works, especially *Orientalism* (1978) and *Culture and Imperialism* (1993). In *Orientalism*, he showed how the discourse of Western (British, French, American) authors constructed a West/East binary comprising the Occident and the Orient. Literature reflected and reinforced these constructions with the West presenting itself as superior and the East ("Arab" culture) presented as a negative "Other" that was inferior and subordinated. The West deceived itself in thinking that its construction of "the Orient" as monolithic, eccentric, menacing, untrustworthy, dishonest, sensual, irrational, passive, and anti-Western was objective and impartial, even while this construct participated in and functioned to embolden and sustain its imperialist agenda. Said saw the postcolonial struggle for the future as involving a people's right to define itself and develop its own culture and social institutions without interference.

This explanation from Answers.com, accordingly, construes the complex colonizer-colonized relationship in terms of recent European/non-European interactions. A focus on European power centers and non-European margins has certainly been the major emphasis in postcolonial discourse. Yet it by no means exhausts the subject. For example, the explanation does not recognize a recent concern with the global reach of the American economic, military, and cultural empire. Nor does the explanation recognize that assertions of imperial power over subordinated peoples took place long before the eighteenth century. Important for readers of the Bible are the Persian (sixth–fourth centuries BCE) and Roman empires (first century BCE–fifth century CE).

The explanation recognizes the key role that claims or depictions of superiority—whether European or any colonizing power—along with constructions of native inferiority play in the interactions between colonizer and colonized. And in challenging a simple binary depiction of colonizer-colonized, it recognizes that this interaction consists of much more than a one-way, "power over" dynamic. Increasingly, postcolonial criticism has recognized the complexities of interactions between colonizer and colonized. Various analyses have recognized that colonizer and colonized impact one another to create mixed or hybrid identities and cultural syntheses (so Homi Bhabha[7]) and that dynamics of imitation, accommodation, elite benefit, mutual dependency, and transformation exist alongside resentment, resistance, and opposition.

The last clause of the explanation names a vital contribution of postcolonial work: namely, its creation of space and discourse to recover "the voices and agency of colonized peoples." Subjugated colonized peoples—subalterns—always "write back" or "speak back" to dominating powers, naming for themselves the contours of their experience and contesting the colonizer's self-serving depictions and deceptive normalizing strategies. The postcolonial theorist Gayatri Chakravorty Spivak, an Indian scholar teaching at New York's Columbia University and active in training teachers to bring literacy to rural areas of India and Bangladesh, has especially highlighted the experience and voices of subaltern people. She has named the difficulty of recovering such marginalized voices (in an essay titled "Can the Subaltern Speak?")[8] and, with many others, has recognized the diversity or heterogeneity of subaltern groups. There is never one colonized experience or voice. Spivak has advocated the controversial approach known as "strategic essentialism," whereby subalterns temporarily downplay their diversity to create a somewhat stereotypical or essentialist group identity of marginalization so as to enable those from dominating powers to understand their experience of subjugation.

Third Posting

Answers.com also cites the entry on "postcolonialism" from the *Oxford Encyclopedia of the Modern World*. The first two paragraphs read,

> Postcolonialism is a critical concept within contemporary cultural studies characterized by attempts to explain the development, conditions, and consequences of the experience of modern colonialism. Postcolonial theorists generally focus on the empires of European nation-states that were consolidated in the nineteenth century and were largely dismantled in the mid-twentieth century. America's growing empire during the same period has also increasingly been subject to postcolonial cultural analysis.
>
> As a field of inquiry, postcolonialism asks both how unequal relationships of political power are represented in cultural institutions such as literature, art, popular media, and the academy and how these representations work to create, destabilize, or understand the differences between individuals and among social groups. Its critical theories endeavor to come to terms with the legacy of the modern era's racism, primitivism, territorial conquest, sexual exploitation, slavery, and mass violence, as well as the influence of that legacy on the contemporary world.[9]

In using the term "cultural studies," this entry begins by recognizing the multidisciplinary nature of postcolonial studies, and employs the more expansive view of postcolonialism's concerns with "the development, conditions, and consequences" of colonization. Yet it also focuses only on modern European and American assertions while neglecting empires of the so-called ancient world. It sees that at the heart of postcolonialism is a concern with representations of unequal power relationships and their varying and continuing impacts on all participants noted above. While the entry favors cultural representations, it downplays historical/material realities. It does, though, helpfully elaborate something of the extent and complexity of postcolonial interests in the colonial experience: "racism, primitivism, territorial conquest, sexual exploitation, slavery, and mass violence." That is, the imposition of colonizing power is not just about who has the more powerful navy or more extensive trade networks. Theories concerning racism and violence, for example, expose fundamental dynamics operative in colonization. We should add to this catalog, at least, concerns with gender and social status.

Fourth Posting

Whenever one googles, Wikipedia is sure to appear. Its ten-page entry on postcolonialism begins with a brief description that highlights "the cultural legacy of colonialism," and identifies the multidisciplinary nature of this "set of theories."[10] The entry emphasizes the goals of postcolonialism in praxis terms: namely, transforming the world so that racist, imperialist interactions no longer occur:

> The ultimate goal of post-colonialism is combating the residual effects of colonialism on cultures. It is not simply concerned with salvaging past worlds, but learning how the world can move beyond this period together, towards a place of mutual respect.... Post-colonialist thinkers recognize that many of the assumptions which underlie the "logic" of colonialism are still active forces today. Exposing and deconstructing the racist, imperialist nature of these assumptions will remove their power of persuasion and coercion. Recognizing that they are not simply airy substances but have widespread material consequences for the nature and scale of global inequality makes this project all the more urgent.[11]

This emphasis underscores that postcolonialism's "set of theories" is not disinterested theoretical knowledge for its own sake, but that the discourse is "committed" or "liberative," concerned to expose the dynamics, structures, and continuing expressions of colonization, so as to repair its material, cultural, and psychological damage and construct a different and just future based on "mutual respect" and the common humanity of all people.

The article also notes a concern expressed in previous explanations: namely, that "a key goal of post-colonial theorists is clearing space for multiple voices ... previously silenced by dominant ideologies—[those of] subalterns." It references Said's work along with Spivak's in discussing the difficulties of and strategies for doing so. Then it observes that "[s]ome postcolonial theorists make the argument that studying both dominant knowledge sets and marginalized ones as binary opposites perpetuates their existence as homogenous entities. Homi K. Bhabha feels the post-colonial world should valorize spaces of mixing; spaces where truth and authenticity move aside for ambiguity. This space of hybridity, he argues, offers the most profound challenge to colonialism."

Bhabha's notion of hybridity has proven very useful in foregrounding the complexities of colonizing interactions.[12] It troubles a simple binary construct of colonizer and colonized marked only by "power over" or one-way traffic from superior to inferior. Rather it recognizes that spaces of interaction—the "Third Space"[13]—are much more ambivalent and liminal with multiple interactions, identities, and cultures.

While appreciating Bhabha's work, the article notes that Frantz Fanon was not positive about such hybridity. He argued that "previously colonized peoples would remain hybrids with a miserable schizophrenic identity unless they revolt violently against their oppressors," thereby cleansing themselves of inferiority complexes and building collective pride.[14]

Against this, the Wikipedia article sets the different approach of Cameroon-born Achille Mbembe expressed in an interview titled "What Is Postcolonial Thinking?"[15] Mbembe argues that postcolonialism is not just a critique and exposure of European domination that exploited, violated, silenced, and extinguished the subjugated. Rather it seeks the end of the "inhuman" and the reinvention of a new humanity whereby "those who were on their knees not long before, bowed down under the weight of oppression . . . arise and walk." It looks to the future, to "humanity-in-the-making" after colonial structures have disappeared and justice has been done. It strives for "a politics of the fellow-creature" that recognizes the Other as fundamentally human, that speaks with and to the Other rather than speaking "in the place of the Other." In this hopeful framework, the prefix "post" of postcolonialism does not merely mean the time after a colonial power has been removed, but it expresses a vision of a new world in which colonizing realities have no place in shaping human interaction.

The Wikipedia article moves on to identify a wide range of postcolonial "subject matters," much of which we have noted already. It outlines, for example, postcolonialism's agenda of "destabilizing Western ways of thinking" (racist superiority, exploitative power, oriental stereotypes, and so forth) and "creating space for the subaltern, or marginalized groups to speak and produce alternatives to dominant discourse." As a literary theory, postcolonialism analyzes literature produced by authors of both colonizing and colonized nations to examine how colonizing experiences are constructed. Studies also expose the heterogeneity of colonized peoples and places by attending to the diverse and uneven impact of colonization and to the various interactions with it. The discourse examines cultural identities in colonized societies and the challenges of developing national identities in contexts where colonial legacies remain after colonial powers have been removed and historical roots have to be remembered and reasserted. Nations remain economically dependent and culturally indebted even though they have political independence. It briefly discusses notable theorists (Said, Spivak, Fanon), and the tasks of (re-)constructing national identities.

From our discussion of these four googled explanations, what can we say about postcolonial criticism? Clearly it is not a simple, step-by-step method. At the risk or reductionism, we might mention:

- Postcolonialism is a multidisciplinary cluster of theories and a resistant discourse. It analyzes assertions and representations of unequal power relations of domination and subordination that comprise complex, geopolitical, imperial-colonial experiences.
- This cluster of theories, this different way of seeing, this optic, places non-Western interests first and resists any attempt to view them as inferior to Western interests. It opposes oppressive power. It looks from below.
- Postcolonial criticism recognizes that while political independence from colonizing powers was a major accomplishment, it was only a first step. The legacies of colonization continue, for example, in cultural representations, learned cultural inferiority, economic inequalities, and political instabilities. Postcolonialism continues to resist this colonial past.
- Postcolonial criticism creates space for subalterns in which their voices and experiences are valued, not subjected or eradicated. It provides space for the subaltern or subjugated to speak, to rename, and to redefine.

We will add the results of a more analytical discussion of postcolonial criticism to this somewhat random and impressionistic survey generated by a google search.

Contested Areas of Focus

Fernando Segovia has surveyed postcolonial criticism to "map the postcolonial optic." He identifies five significant but contested areas of focus.[16] In each area he names the issue and discusses several different approaches, with the last option being his own preference. I will summarize his helpful discussion of these five areas.

Force of the Term.[17] Segovia surveys debate about the prefix "post" in the term "postcolonial" and identifies three ways of understanding it. (1) "Post" is understood in a basic chronological sense to signify "what comes after the end of colonialism." (2) "Post" refers to a wider span of political and historical experience that includes colonization as well as decolonization. (3) "Post" refers to "conscious awareness and problematization of the relationship of domination and subordination in colonization"; this third sense of "conscientization" holds together both critical awareness and a historical-political focus.

Nomenclature Deployed.[18] Segovia notes the prominence of the terms "colonialism" and "imperialism" in postcolonial discourse. Some discussions use the terms interchangeably, while, more commonly, others distinguish them. The classic distinction comes from Edward Said in which "imperialism" refers to the practice, theory, and attitudes of a dominating center over distant territory, while colonialism refers to the center establishing settlements in the distant territory.[19] This definition recognizes the center's physical presence in the colony. It does not, though, recognize that the exertion of power does not always require physical presence (neocolonialism). Another (Marxist) approach draws the distinction in terms of economic practices. Colonialism implies mercantilism and denotes extraction from the colony for the center's benefit; imperialism indicates capitalism and redrawing economic structures. But this privileging of economics ignores the various expressions of imperial power and inappropriately confines imperialism to capitalist practices. A third approach focuses on civilizational developments, with colonialism being more local and loose and imperialism having more structural and global coherence. But the assumption that imperialism entails "advanced organizational coherence" is not necessary. A fourth approach centers on power and space, defining imperialism in terms of the originating and dominating center and colonialism in terms of the receiving and subordinated margins. This focus on power leaves open the possibility of its various expressions and recognizes diverse interactions between center and margins.

Terrain Surveyed.[20] Controversial in postcolonial work is the matter of where attention is to be focused. As we have seen, one approach (associated with Said, Spivak, and Bhabha) concerns literary or textual representation and cultural production in imperial-colonial frameworks. A second approach emphasizes historical context, particularly social conditions analyzed by disciplines such as economics, politics, and sociology. A third approach combines both emphases in attending to the complexity of interactions between cultural production and social conditions.

Referential Quandry.[21] How is the relationship of colonizer and colonized, of center and periphery/margins to be construed? One approach emphasizes the history and experience of the periphery, but in terms of the history and experience of the center. This approach highlights the intrusion of the dominant West on the dominated non-West. But it frames the subjugated in terms of the dominant center, privileging the center's outlook and control. Another approach analyzes the impact of the center on the periphery where domination and subordination are undeniable, but it also recognizes analysis of the periphery "in its own terms, away from the center," including "its own reality and experience, cultural production and social context, structures and contradictions." That is, it recognizes that colonized locations and peoples have histories, community, and life apart from the center.

Nature of Encounter.[22] What is the nature of the encounter between center and periphery in an imperial-colonial framework? Segovia identifies three approaches. One approach, the homogenizing, employs one dynamic—oppressive power and constant resistance—for all imperial-colonial situations. A second approach highlights a particular local situation rather than theoretical discussions. A third approach borrows from both approaches. It attends to the specific and local, but recognizes some recurring elements across the numerous variations of particular situations. Likewise, this approach recognizes "considerable ambiguity in both center and periphery, ranging from oppression-resistance to attraction-seduction."

Beyond discussion in these five areas, Segovia identifies two significant limitations in much postcolonial discussion that have implications for postcolonial *biblical* criticism. First, Segovia notes that "discussion centers prominently on the imperial-colonial formations of the West from the eighteenth through to the twentieth centuries,"[23] and frequently on the British Empire. But study of imperial-colonial formations within Latin America, Asia, the Caribbean, Russia and the Union of Soviet Socialist Republics, and the United States is often missing. Especially important for biblical studies is the relative absence of attention to empires such as those of Assyria, Babylonia, Persia, Macedonia, and Rome. Such neglect significantly impacts study of the emerging Jesus movement in the imperial-colonial context of the Roman Empire, and study of the role of Christianity in various imperial formations over the last two millennia.

Second, Segovia notes that it is rare to find postcolonial discussions of religion, whether as cultural productions (texts) or social matrix (institutions, practices).[24] The constitutive role of religion, especially Christianity, in numerous imperial-colonial formations indicates that this is a significant neglect.

SECTION 2: POSTCOLONIAL BIBLICAL CRITICISM AND CRITICAL METHODS

How does postcolonial biblical criticism compare with other methods used in biblical studies?

Postcolonial work is concerned with imperial-colonial experiences and so will employ aspects of historical criticism. Yet the two approaches have important differences. Historical criticism, at least as it has been commonly utilized in biblical studies in its classic Eurocentric form, frames its work largely, though not exclusively, as neutral and impartial inquiry. It assumes a text provides access to the time and circumstances of its composition, the text's "background." For New Testament texts, these circumstances are often construed as ecclesial conflicts. It usually assumes that the text has one meaning—or a limited range of meanings—related to its originating circumstances. Meaning is often authorized in terms of the author's intention.

Postcolonial criticism, however, is explicit about the context and commitments of interpreters. Readers, conditioned by diverse sociocultural, postcolonial locations and by their particular interests and ideological investments in postcolonial agenda are not controlled by an author's intentions. Rather they construct meanings from the representations of the sociopolitical reality of imperial-colonial situations and of their various power dynamics involving the center and the margins.

The interpreters' experiences and social locations are not seen as intrusions into the interpretive process but as crucial elements of it. Awareness of the various power dynamics of the imperial-colonial experience informs such reading. Texts are generally regarded as constructions or representations that participate in and reflect the historical and ideological perspectives of their origins and are examined in terms of postcolonial agenda. These presentations can be "read" in numerous ways, do not present one definitive "meaning" to be discovered in or behind the text, and do not control the interpretive process. Multiple readings enter into critical analysis and dialogue as partial, perspectival, and situated.

This emphasis on the invested and located reader also expresses a crucial difference between postcolonial criticism and forms of narrative criticism that have been practiced in biblical, especially Gospel, studies. Narrative criticism focuses more on the text as a literary work.[25] It sees the text not as a means of access to the world behind it but as a medium or means of communication between author and reader. To the fore are the text's formal features, its plot, characters, settings, and artistic or literary techniques. In some forms of this approach, the reader is viewed as the implied reader, constructed by the text and able to execute all the interpretive moves required by the text to actualize its communication. This reader is not entirely passive because texts are understood to have gaps that readers fill.[26] Such gaps can be filled in different ways so more than one reading is possible. But with the text very much as the driver, interpretive options are limited and the role of the readers circumscribed; such readers are textually constituted much more than they are socially/historically/culturally located. The social locations of readers, let alone the power dynamics of imperial-colonial situations, play little acknowledged part in interpretation.

SECTION 3: EXAMPLES AND EVALUATION

So what does postcolonial biblical criticism look like?[27] What sort of readings does it produce?[28]

Not surprisingly, given the expansive interests of postcolonial criticism noted above, postcolonial biblical criticism is not monolithic. And, not surprisingly, there is some dispute about how it *ought* to be practiced. Fernando Segovia sets out a threefold scheme: postcolonial biblical criticism embraces "analysis of the geopolitical relationship of power on the worlds of antiquity, modernity, and postmodernity."[29] By this he means postcolonial biblical criticism has three areas of focus: (1) analysis of the imperial-colonial formations of the biblical texts, (2) analysis of interpretations of these texts in relation to the imperial-colonial formation of "western hegemony and expansion," and (3) analysis of interpretations in relation to imperial-colonial formations of contemporary globalization. R. S. Sugirtharajah offers a similar three-part grid: (1) the "scrutiny of biblical narratives for their colonial involvement," (2) the rereading of biblical texts "from the perspective of postcolonial concerns such as liberation struggles of the past and present," and (3) drawing "attention to the inescapable effects of colonization and colonial ideals on interpretive works."[30]

These agenda are huge. While the areas overlap, most postcolonial biblical criticism will offer only a partial engagement, some foregrounding biblical narratives and their imperial-colonial worlds, and others foregrounding contemporary struggles. I will briefly offer some examples, beginning with several that focus on the first aspect of both schema.

Some efforts have concentrated on exposing the rootedness of biblical writings in imperial-colonial structures and in rereading these texts. For example, studies have explored New Testament (NT) writings—Paul's letters, the Gospels, Revelation—primarily in relation to the structures of the Roman Empire.[31] Segovia and Moore express hesitancy about recognizing these studies as postcolonial, identify them as "empire" studies, and locate them with other historical critical works that include empire in their reconstructed "backgrounds." They comment that most of the scholars producing these works eschew the postcolonial label.[32]

However, these works cannot be pushed aside so easily, especially since doing so contradicts aspects of both Segovia's and Sugirtharajah's discussions. First, they do what Segovia names as "a first dimension of a postcolonial optic," namely they analyze NT texts in relation to the "overwhelming sociopolitical reality" of Rome's empire.[33] Such analysis that constructs the Roman Empire as the foreground (not the "background") of the early Christian movement has not been common in much NT scholarship. Scholars regularly avoid political-imperial readings, preferring to view NT texts as religious writings about individual faith and located in ecclesial contexts divorced from imperial-colonial structures. By examining NT writings as productions of the power structures of the Roman Empire, these approaches employ a postcolonial optic whether they explicitly identify as "postcolonial" or not. They focus on how the margins—small communities of Jesus-believers in various locations in the Roman Empire—negotiate assertions of the center's imperial power.

Moreover, we should also recall Segovia's preferred definition for postcolonialism. For Segovia it concerns, as we have seen in section 1 above, not primarily a time and space location, but "conscientization," or awareness, of the power dynamics of domination and subordination in imperial-colonial representations. There is no doubt that some NT scholarship has seen the Roman Empire as the "background" of the early Christian movement and discussed it without any awareness of power dynamics. But these writings focusing on NT texts and the Roman Empire, by contrast, exhibit awareness of, and commitment to, exposing the power inequities of imperial-colonial situations. They are informed by postcolonial insights as well as by classical and historical studies of the Roman Empire.

An interpreter attuned to imperial-colonial dynamics understands the Gospels, for example, to be both products of as well as sites that negotiate imperial-colonial dynamics. That is, such an interpreter will not construct the texts as "religious and ecclesial" writings concerned only with religious issues and isolated from imperial-colonial dynamics. This postcolonial optic understands that religion can legitimate imperial power ("Rome is chosen and blessed by God/ the gods") as well as imitate and oppose it ("God's empire or kingdom has come near").

The Gospels, then, are understood to be representations that oppose as well as assume and encode imperial dynamics as part of their various strategies of negotiation. The Gospels emerge as writings from relatively powerless groups that are both somewhat accommodated to imperial structures as a basic form of survival, yet are also committed to a different understanding of the world and its transformation according to God's purposes (or empire!). The texts participate in these imperial dynamics in various ways, at times embracing and mimicking them as products and producers of empire and at other times resisting them. Interestingly, the transformation of the world is often presented in ways that, ironically, imitate imperial power; God's empire will impose its rule over all. Some readers might find such a notion to be comforting—but all empires present themselves as benign toward the cooperative and subordinate. Interpreters attuned to imperial-colonial dynamics identify the complex interactions in which the texts are involved, recognizing that these texts are not "pure" or idealized. They construct readings that expose the various ways in which texts negotiate the power differential.

By exposing such dynamics, these readings remove the delusion that NT texts are neutral or apolitical (a-imperial) or solely "spiritual." They deflate the persuasive power of pervasive contemporary reading strategies that construct readers who are oblivious to intersections between the NT texts and damaging political, economic, social, and cultural representations and structures. They refuse to leave untroubled strategies of reading the Bible that divert attention from global injustices by turning readers toward such matters.[34]

What sorts of interpretations do these approaches produce? One type of postcolonial reading of Matthew 2, for example, the birth of Jesus as the agent of God's saving purposes (1:21–23), exposes the structures of Roman imperial-colonial power sustaining the story.[35] Those structures center on Herod, puppet king of Judea as Rome's ally and representative, along with his allies, the Jerusalem-based chief priests and scribes. Herod employs a repertoire of provincial imperial techniques—lies, spies, allies, and violence—by which he seeks to maintain his power in killing Jesus who is also (imitatively) identified as "king of the Jews" (2:2). Yet the narrative also presents the divine thwarting of Herod in mentioning three times *Herod's* death, not Jesus' (2:15, 19, 20). The chapter's presentation seems to construct a divine opposition to and thwarting of imperial-colonial power. Yet it also constructs God as callous and powerless in being able to protect Jesus but not the male infants around Bethlehem killed by Herod's troops (2:16).

This reading exposes a typical imperial-colonial dynamic in highlighting Rome exercising its rule over the colonial margins/periphery through alliances with local elites like Herod and the Jerusalem leaders. Other scenes in Matthew encode other imperial dynamics. For example, Matthew 4:18–22 is commonly construed as a religious "calling of disciples." At the sea of Galilee, Jesus calls Peter and Andrew, then James and John, from fishing to "follow me," and commissions them to evangelize people. Seen through a postcolonial optic, various imperial-colonial dynamics are at work in this scene.[36]

First, its location at the sea of Galilee is not "innocent" or "neutral." It is on the periphery, a site where imperial power is asserted and contested, and where many are disempowered. Galilee was Roman-controlled territory, where Galileans and Judeans fought Roman troops in the 66–70 war. After the war, the emperor Vespasian confiscated much land to reallocate to his allies. Three verses previously, the Gospel has presented Galilee as "Galilee possessed by the Gentiles" (4:15, a genitive of possession, au. trans.) and has described it by evoking scriptural traditions concerning the Assyrian Empire's possession of it and God's deliverance of the people from Assyrian rule (4:16, evoking Isa. 9:1–2).

Second, in 4:17, Jesus has asserted in this place claimed by Roman power that "the kingdom [empire] of heaven has come near." Jesus' words and actions manifest God's rule. The scene of calling the disciples that immediately follows provides one example of what it looks like when God's rule or empire comes near. It disrupts people's priorities and activities and redirects lives in relation to God's purposes. But of course the image of God's empire/rule is not a neutral one. While it contests Rome's empire, it reinscribes imperial-colonial structures by mimicking imperial practices in asserting control over these fishermen's lives.

Third, a postcolonial optic will notice the scene's gender construction. It includes, at least at this point in the Gospel story, only males as disciples of Jesus. It inscribes imperial patriarchy by rendering women invisible.

And a fourth dimension highlights a clash of empires. The presentation of these men as fishermen does not just mean that they were "ordinary" folks going about their everyday business. Rather, being attuned to imperial-colonial dynamics means recognizing that fishing was an industry that participated in and was subject to imperial control. Rome's empire was a "proprietary" empire in that Roman power meant control not only over people's loyalties and labor, but also over land and sea and their production.[37] Hence, fishing was licensed and taxed because "every rare and beautiful thing in the wide ocean, in whatever sea it swims, belongs to the Imperial treasury."[38] Jesus' call of these fishermen away from their fishing "interferes" with and counters these imperial claims to ownership of people, sea, and resources. Yet in asserting the empire of God over these men's lives, Jesus' call matches and reinscribes imperial ways.

Are such readings postcolonial? Who is a postcolonial biblical critic? Do readings have to include an explicit section of postcolonial theory or an "altar-call" to resist contemporary imperial-colonial experiences and global inequities in order to be designated "postcolonial?" Sometimes both elements are helpful or necessary. But it can also be argued that in drawing from postcolonial criticism while foregrounding and exposing NT texts as imperial-colonial experiences, these readings "do" postcolonial criticism by troubling a significant source of religious construction that is oblivious to imperial-colonial experiences. The Bible has long been read as a source of legitimation for patriarchal, racist, and colonizing power structures. Imperial-critical readings resist at their source religious construals that reinscribe or make invisible such structures and their harmful effects. They challenge contemporary readers to resist such use of power and develop alternative structures and practices in living into God's new creation, which is passionately concerned with the needs and well-being of all people.

Postcolonial scholars have frequently engaged the scene in Mark 7:24–30 (cf. Matt. 15:21–28) concerning the Syrophoenician (Canaanite in Matthew) woman and her daughter. Richard Horsley discusses the Mark scene under the heading "Women as Representative and Exemplary." In Horsley's reading, the Syrophoenician woman represents three entities: (1) non-Israelites—as a Greek in a "mixed frontier area" in "the region of Tyre" (Mark 7:24), she is a "double outsider, culturally and ethnically" in Israelite Galilee; (2) non-Israelite Jesus-followers, who are part of the movement constituted by "the renewing power of the kingdom of God manifested in Jesus . . ." and who, though ethnically and culturally outsiders, "identify with Israel's history and cultural heritage." Horsley comments that her "identity, like the identities of many 'postcolonial' people today, is hybrid"; (3) "marginalized, desperate, poor, widowed or divorced women." Through a mixture of subordination (she does not question Jesus' racist and sexist slur in calling her a "dog," 7:27) and quick-witted assertion (the dogs eat crumbs, 7:28), she gains her daughter's exorcism. As a "paradigm of faith and leadership and service," she "secures the participation and position of non-Israelite peoples . . . in the movement of the fulfillment of Israel, in the kingdom of God . . . in contrast to Jerusalem leaders such as Peter . . . ."[39]

Two readings of this passage focus on both ancient imperial-colonial formations and issues of contemporary globalization. Musa Dube's discussion of the Matthew passage follows some 150 pages that outline an understanding of "postcolonial feminist interpretation" as "an overall analysis of the methods and effects of imperialism as a continuing reality in global relations."[40] She argues that Matthew is an imperializing text that presents Rome and its agents positively while presenting other colonized groups such as the Jerusalem "religious leaders" negatively.[41] In this context, the scene with the Canaanite woman is a text that needs depatriachalizing and decolonizing. The male, traveling, racially and class-wise superior Jesus, to whom is given "all authority in heaven and earth" (28:18), is a subjugating figure with power, privilege, and divine authority. As a Canaanite, the woman is inferior, a foreigner, representing land that Israel conquered and possessed, a character to be "invaded, conquered, annihilated" in the Gospel's Christian mission. The woman's demon-possessed daughter characterizes this foreigner as "evil and dangerous." The woman's needy and desperate beseeching of the disinterested Jesus who labels her, without contest, a dog, shows the mission to the nations to be one of subjugating the different rather than one of liberating interdependence. Dube finishes her book with a call to join the continuing global struggle against patriarchal and colonizing oppression.[42]

Laura Donaldson's reading focuses not on the woman but on her daughter.[43] Donaldson begins by siding with Spivak concerning postcolonial criticism's "refusal to acknowledge women except by subsuming them under the more general category of 'the colonized.'" She employs Spivak's notion of "ethical singularity," which requires "deep engagement with a singular figure to guard against facile appropriations of the oppressed by well-intentioned radicals." Donaldson's focus on the daughter means setting aside readings that privilege salvation history, pietistic individualism, or deviant demon-possession that is "coercively cured." Instead, Donaldson posits, the daughter's inability to speak might associate her with indigenous women who used "ecstatic states or altered forms of consciousness as especially powerful sites of knowledge" and may signify the beginning of "a vocation known to indigenous peoples for millennia as shamanism."[44] Donaldson sees the ancestor of this "emergent shaman" in the story of the witch of Endor (1 Sam 28:7). She positions her reading as a demonstration of the biblical narrator's underestimating of the ability of such indigenous characters to talk back to their subjugators (echoing Spivak's question whether the subaltern can speak) and a rejection of readings that silence the daughter and render her invisible.

These readings, largely exemplifying the first and third emphases of Segovia's threefold schema, seek in different ways, in Sugirtharajah's words, "to puncture the Christian Bible's Western protections and pretensions, and to help reposition it in relation to its oriental roots and Eastern heritage."[45]

Sugirtharajah provides an example of another dimension of postcolonial biblical criticism: namely, analysis of the interpretations of biblical texts in relation to the imperial-colonial formation of "western hegemony and expansion." Sugirtharajah examines, for example, the use of biblical texts in sermons preached by English preachers on September 25, 1857, a day of "humiliation" proclaimed by Queen Victoria because of insurrection in India: ". . . . These homilies became a vehicle for defining British national identity in terms of God's forces fighting against God's enemy. The sermons were a classic example of how colonial relationships were forged and how the dominant self defined the other and in turn defined itself by the exclusion of the other . . . . The sermons were a potent mixture of nationalism, xenophobia, and biblical evangelism."[46]

The interpretation of the Bible secured British superiority in terms of God's purposes and defined Indians as ungrateful, contemptible, idol-loving, barbarous natives rebelling against "a benevolent ruler."[47] The Collect for the day prayed that God would "[t]each the natives of British India to prize the benefits which Thy good Providence has given them through the supremacy of this Christian land . . . ."[48]

The Bible functioned to provide "commentary on the current situation" mainly through typological interpretation whereby biblical events and narratives anticipated and paralleled the British-Indian situation.[49] Old Testament texts dominated the biblical texts used for the homilies; here because of space we will note some of the NT passages.

- One of the lessons for the church services was Acts 12:1–17, concerning the unsuccessful efforts to imprison Peter and futile attempts to prevent

the preaching of the Gospel. The parallel presents Indian resistance to Christian Britain as equally futile.
- Acts 17:30–31 provided justification for the day of humiliation with its exhortation to repent before the day of judgment. The day of humiliation was "a chance once again to make Britain worthy of her call and an opportunity to preach repentance and prayer as a way of avoiding God's chastisement."[50]
- One preacher used the parable of the talents to portray India as a talent given to Britain, which, if Britain did not act prudently, would be taken away.
- Another preacher likened the rebellious action of the Indians to the enemy in the parable of the wheat and the tares who sowed tares or weeds among the wheat (Matt. 13:24–30). The parabolic—and colonial—enemies are identified as the devil.
- Another preacher found the rebellion's cause in the failure of the British to take seriously the great commission to preach the Gospel to every creature (Matt. 28:19–20).
- Another appealed to Romans 13:1–7 to justify using the sword—military action—as retributive justice for attacks on British citizens.
- Only four preachers out of the 193 sermons on which *The Times* newspaper reported made "love your enemies" (Matt. 5:44) their central text or concern.

Sugirtharajah's discussion shows these homilies and biblical texts to be representations of imperial-colonial power inequities and constructions of both colonizers and colonized to the advantage of the former.

CONCLUSION

Our discussion has presented postcolonial biblical criticism primarily as an "optic" or way of looking that shapes a particular praxis. At the center of its gaze is the geopolitical entity of empire and the diverse manifestations and representations of the inequitable power dynamics of imperial-colonial formations. In terms of Segovia's threefold schema, biblical texts emerge from worlds of imperial-colonial formations, which postcolonial criticism makes explicit. Likewise, it also analyzes interpretations of biblical texts that, in the contexts of empire, secure, though at times also resist, imperial-colonial formations. Biblical texts and interpreters inhabit a current world in which the practices and legacies of imperial-colonial formations remain and where the vision and tasks of reading, writing, and living justly throughout the whole of the human community remain unfinished. Postcolonial work turns its readers to these tasks.

KEY TERMS

binary. A simplistic view of the interaction between colonizer and colonized might see the former as having all the power and the latter as having no power. Postcolonial work, though, has troubled this simple presentation of each side. It has increasingly recognized the complexities of the interactions between colonizer and colonized in which numerous dynamics are operative.

colonialism. This term is frequently matched with the term "imperialism." Colonialism commonly refers to the settlements established by a dominant center in a distant territory whose structures, resources, and labor the center seeks to control. That is, colonialism focuses on the subordinated's reception or negotiation of the center's power.

hybridity. The term at heart refers to "mixing." The term recognizes that the interaction between colonizer and colonized is not "one-way traffic" from the powerful to the less powerful in which only the colonizer impacts the colonized. Rather, the interaction is marked by hybridity or ambiguities (colonizers become anxious; the colonized imitate their oppressors) in which the identities and cultures of both entities are impacted in multiple ways.

imperialism. This term (often matched with "colonialism") commonly denotes the practice, theory, and attitudes of the dominating center over a distant territory and its people and resources. This dominance may involve the center's physical presence in the colony, but the exertion of power need not involve physical presence. The term emphasizes the originating and dominating center.

optic. This term literally refers to a "way of looking." It is a useful way of thinking about postcolonial work not as a fixed method ("first you do this, then you do this . . . ,") but as ways of looking at imperial-colonial experiences and situations that focus on the dynamics of power, gender, class, race/ethnicity, and sexual orientations, and on the visions of societal interaction and humanity operative in these situations. This way of looking decenters Western interests and privileges.

subaltern. The term refers to colonized people subjugated by imperial power. The term first came into postcolonial discourse in reference to colonized people in South Asia. But its usage has expanded to denote a perspective "from below" that attends more to the circumstances and experiences of colonized peoples than to the self-serving and normalizing depictions of the colonizers.

NOTES

1. Useful introductions include Patrick Williams and Laura Chrisman, eds., *Colonial Discourse and Post-Colonial Theory: A Reader* (New York: Columbia University Press, 1994); Bill Ashcroft, Gareth Griffiths, and Helen Tiffin, eds.,

The Post-Colonial Studies Reader (New York: Routledge, 1995); Leela Gandhi, *Postcolonial Theory: A Critical Introduction* (Edinburgh: Edinburgh University Press, 1998); Robert Young, *Postcolonialism: An Historical Introduction* (Oxford: Blackwell, 2001); Robert Young, *Postcolonialism: A Very Short Introduction* (Oxford: Oxford University Press, 2003).
2. Fernando Segovia, "Mapping the Postcolonial Optic in Biblical Criticism: Meaning and Scope," in Stephen Moore and Fernando Segovia, eds., *Postcolonial Biblical Criticism: Interdisciplinary Intersections* (London: T. & T. Clark, 2005), 23–78, esp. 65.
3. R. S. Sugirtharajah, "Postcolonial Theory and Biblical Studies," in Ismo Dunderberg, Christopher Tuckett, and Kari Syreeni, eds., *Fair Play: Diversity and Conflicts in Early Christianity* (Leiden: Brill, 2001), 541–52, esp. 541.
4. Ibid., 547, 552.
5. http://fajardo-acosta.com/worldlit/glossary.htm.
6. http://www.answers.com/topic/postcolonial.
7. Homi Bhabha, *The Location of Culture* (New York: Routledge, 1994).
8. A longer version appears in Gayatri Chakravorty Spivak, *A Critique of Postcolonial Reason: Toward a History of the Vanishing Present* (Cambridge, MA: Harvard University Press, 1999), 266–311.
9. http://www.answers.com/topic/postcolonialism.
10. http://en.wikipedia.org/wiki/Postcolonialism.
11. Ibid.
12. Bhabha, *Location of Culture*.
13. Ibid., 36–39.
14. Frantz Fanon, *The Wretched of the Earth* (New York: Grove Press, 1963), 15, 40, 42–52.
15. http://www.eurozine.com/articles/2008-01-09-mbembe-en.html. See also Achille Mbembe, *On the Postcolony* (Berkeley: University of California Press, 2001).
16. Segovia, "Mapping," 64–76.
17. Ibid., 64–65.
18. Ibid., 66–67.
19. Edward Said, *Culture and Imperialism* (New York: Vintage Books, 1994), 9.
20. Segovia, "Mapping," 67–68.
21. Ibid., 68–69.
22. Ibid., 70.
23. Ibid., 70–74, esp. 71.
24. Ibid., 74–75.
25. Mark Allan Powell, *What Is Narrative Criticism?* (Minneapolis: Fortress, 1990), 6–10.
26. For gaps, see Wolfgang Iser, *The Act of Reading: A Theory of Aesthetic Response* (Baltimore: Johns Hopkins, 1978).
27. For this development, see Fernando Segovia, "Postcolonial Criticism and the Gospel of Matthew," in Mark Allan Powell, ed., *Methods for Matthew* (Cambridge, MA: Cambridge University Press, 2009), 194–237.
28. For examples, see Fernando Segovia and R. S. Sugirtharajah, eds., *A Postcolonial Commentary on the New Testament Writings* (New York: T. & T. Clark, 2007).
29. Segovia, "Postcolonial Criticism," 215–16.
30. Sugirtharajah, "Postcolonial Theory," 546–47.
31. For example, Richard Horsley, ed., *Paul and Empire: Religion and Power in Roman Imperial Society* (Harrisburg, PA; Trinity Press International, 1997); Wes Howard-Brooks and Anthony Gwyther, *Unveiling Empire: Reading Revelation Then and Now* (Maryknoll, NY: Orbis Books, 1999); Warren Carter, *Matthew*

and Empire: Initial Explorations (Harrisburg, PA; Trinity Press International, 2001); Richard Horsley, *Jesus and Empire: The Kingdom of God and the New World Disorder* (Minneapolis: Fortress, 2002); Brian Walsh and Sylvia Keesmat, *Colossians Remixed: Subverting the Empire* (Downers Grove, IL: Intervarsity, 2004); Warren Carter, *John and Empire: Initial Explorations* (New York: T. & T. Clark, 2008); Davina Lopez, *Apostle to the Conquered: Reimaging Paul's Mission* (Minneapolis: Fortress, 2010); Neil Elliott, *The Arrogance of Nations: Reading Romans in the Shadow of Empire* (Minneapolis: Fortress, 2010).

32. Stephen Moore and Fernando Segovia, "Postcolonial Biblical Criticism: Beginnings, Trajectories, Intersections," in Moore and Segovia, eds., *Postcolonial Biblical Criticism*, 7–8.
33. Fernando F. Segovia, *Decolonizing Biblical Studies: A View from the Margins* (Maryknoll, NY: Orbis Books, 2000), 125
34. Sugirtharajah, "Postcolonial Theory," 551–52.
35. Warren Carter, *Matthew and the Margins: A Sociopolitical and Religious Reading* (Maryknoll, NY: Orbis Books, 1999), 66–89; Carter, "The Gospel of Matthew," in Segovia and Sugirtharajah, *Postcolonial Commentary*, 69–104.
36. Carter, *Matthew and the Margins*, 112–16.
37. K. C. Hanson and Douglas Oakman, *Palestine in the Time of Jesus: Social Structure and Social Conflict* (Minneapolis: Fortress, 1998), 106–10.
38. Juvenal, *Satire* 4.37–55, in *Juvenal and Persius*, trans. G. G. Ramsay (Cambridge, MA: Harvard University Press; London: William Heinemann, 1979).
39. Richard A. Horsley, *Hearing the Whole Story: The Politics of Plot in Mark's Gospel* (Louisville, KY: Westminster John Knox, 2001), 212–15.
40. Musa Dube, *Postcolonial Feminist Interpretation of the Bible* (St. Louis: Chalice, 2000), 48.
41. Ibid., 127–84.
42. Ibid., 146–53, 197–201.
43. Laura Donaldson, "Gospel Hauntings: The Postcolonial Demons of New Testament Criticism," in Moore and Segovia, eds., *Postcolonial Biblical Criticism*, 97–113.
44. Ibid., 104–5.
45. Sugirtharajah, "Postcolonial Theory," 545–46.
46. R. S. Sugirtharajah, "Salvos from the Victorian Pulpit: Conscription of Texts by Victorian Preachers during the Indian Rebellion of 1857," in Sugirtharajah, *The Bible and Empire: Postcolonial Explorations* (Cambridge, MA: Cambridge University Press, 2005), 60–97, esp. 66–67.
47. Ibid., 83.
48. Ibid., 65.
49. Ibid., 91–94.
50. Ibid., 67.

FOR FURTHER READING

Dube, Musa. *Postcolonial Feminist Interpretation of the Bible* (St. Louis: Chalice, 2000).
Moore, Stephen, and Fernando Segovia, eds. *Postcolonial Biblical Criticism: Interdisciplinary Intersections* (London : T. & T. Clark, 2005).
Segovia, Fernando, and R. S. Sugirtharajah, eds. *A Postcolonial Commentary on the New Testament Writings* (New York: T. & T. Clark, 2007).
Young, Robert. *Postcolonialism: A Very Short Introduction* (Oxford: Oxford University Press, 2003).

Chapter 7

Postmodernism

HUGH S. PYPER

Postmodernism is not a technique but an attitude, a way of approaching things. It might be called a worldview, except that one of its central tenets is that any claim to an overarching theory or model that accounts for the way things are is, in principle, unsustainable. It takes leave to question every so-called grand narrative of history and every development that makes universal claims. Many biblical scholars have rejected that attitude, which is their prerogative, although some of the rejection has been on the inaccurate grounds that postmodernism is simply relativism or irresponsible play with the text. Others have attempted in various ways to co-opt its methods as part of the repertoire of techniques of biblical criticism, another tool to employ in the service of textual analysis, higher criticism, and historical inquiry.

This is perhaps inevitable, but it mistakes the nature of postmodern reading. While there may be methodological insights to be gleaned from postmodern readings, postmodernism can set a question mark against the whole enterprise of reading: why we read, how we read, and who we as readers are. For those who have a term paper or an article on a biblical text to produce, such questions may be a luxury, but to shy away from them or leave them unexamined may leave us trapped in a series of unconscious assumptions and cultural practices. Postmodernism provides few answers, but it can lead us to realize that the answers we think we have are less secure than we imagine.

At its best, postmodernism discovers the points of undecidability in the text. In that process, it makes a distinction between levels of undecidablity. Our usual understanding when we are trying to make a decision is that we should gather all the facts and then decide. Postmodernists have a number of problems with that process. Can we ever gather all the facts? How do we know what counts as a relevant fact? Does that not imply that we have to make prior decisions about the decision we are going to make? More fundamentally, if we ever were in possession of all the facts, then would we need to make a decision at all? The course of action would presumably be logically deducible from the facts. Decisions are only necessary where we cannot deduce things. This does not mean that we can just make arbitrary decisions in the face of what we know. It is only by hard work that we can find the exact point at which facts and deductions fail us and so have an idea of what decision we are faced with.

A BRIEF HISTORY OF POSTMODERNISM

Postmodernism is characterized by a rejection of what is called "the genetic fallacy," or the idea that by describing how something began, you have explained it. In the light of this, to give an account of the origin of postmodernism is contradictory, but its rejection of "grand narrative" must be seen against the background of twentieth century history, although its roots go back earlier. Notoriously, the disaster of the First World War put an end to the Enlightenment "grand narrative" of inevitable progress, intellectual and social, and its faith in the power of rationality to lead to harmonious living. Dark and irrational aspects of human culture came to the fore. The power of the rational and objective human intelligence to unravel the secrets of nature and of the human mind came under question. After all, the same rational man who masters the universe (and the gendered language is appropriate) spends a third of his life asleep, prey to the terror and unreasonableness of the dream world. The twentieth century has been called the century of dreams because of the renewed cultural interest in this aspect of human experience, but by rights it has a good claim to the label "century of nightmares."

The Second World War and its aftermath only confirmed that the rival grand narratives of Marxism and fascism were themselves illusory. It revealed the shocking persistence of prejudice and irrational hatred and the power of propaganda rather than argument to sway human behavior, not to mention the new reality of the human capacity to destroy the planet with nuclear weapons. We should not underestimate, however, the importance for the main proponents of postmodernism in France of the impact of the internecine horror of the Algerian struggle for independence. Jacques Derrida (d. 2004), the most prominent figure in the debates over postmodernism, was a French Jew from Algeria. An outsider wherever he found himself, he concluded that the attempt to secure any identity was riven with fatal contradictions. In the appropriation of postmodernism in the United States, the different but equally traumatic experience of the Vietnam War was also crucial.

These political disruptions went along with key developments in a number of fields of intellectual inquiry. One important contribution is that of Ferdinand de Saussure (Switzerland; d. 1913) who proposed a theory of linguistics where meaning depended on difference, a word that becomes key to postmodern interpretation. To oversimplify drastically, his theory broke with the idea that a word or a sound unit somehow had an intrinsic identity to which meaning could be assigned. On the contrary, it is not the sound itself that carries meaning, but the fact that it is different from another sound. Language then becomes a system of relations between sounds, and what our ears are attuned to is not the sound itself but its difference from another sound.

This is a challenge to the view that somehow there is a primordial meaning in words and that they carry an intrinsic power. One reading of the story of the naming of the animals in Genesis 2, the Bible's account of the origin of language, would see Adam as pronouncing *the* name for each animal brought before him: "whatever the man called every living thing, that was its name" (Gen. 2:19). This is not simply a biblical idea. The idea that there was a true name of each thing has prevailed in many cultures. Whatever the myriad of names in the multiplicity of human languages, for each thing and person there is a true name and the one who found that would have power over whatever was named.

Saussure suggests another view, which has roots back to the nominalist philosophers of the medieval period. The name Adam gives is just that: the pragmatic invention of a human being, serving to differentiate cat from dog. Which is labeled does not matter in the least as long as those who share a language simply concur in applying the distinction consistently. We find meaning not by looking behind the word to the object it matches, but by negotiating with our fellow speakers.

Saussure's idea of difference that arose in the field of linguistics was given much wider significance through the work of Claude Lévi-Strauss (France; d. 2009) and the movement that became known as structuralism. Lévi-Strauss took the principle of difference as constitutive of all human thought and thus of all human culture. Human understanding is structured around a series of binary oppositions, and individual human cultures are the results of the attempts to deal with the inevitable contradictions and inconsistencies that arose. In particular, myths arose as an attempt to deal with perceived contradiction. Structuralism, as this movement was dubbed, accounts for all human culture on this structure and so as a "grand narrative" was open to question by postmodernism, and its particular manifestation as "post-structuralism."

While Saussure and Lévi-Strauss described language and culture in terms of a system of differences, seemingly unrelated developments in science and mathematics took place that led to a new view of the human understanding of the world. Somewhere in the ancestry of postmodernism is Einstein's theory of relativity and the development of quantum theories, in particular Heisenberg's so-called uncertainty principle. This goes together with the insight the mathematician Gödel put forward in his incompleteness theorems, which declare that no system that describes the arithmetic of natural numbers can account for all its axioms. There is always some axiom that is both true and unprovable. This is not to say that these scientists would recognize or endorse the more popular appropriation of their ideas, but they confirm the turn against grand narrative by suggesting that, as a matter of principle, not even the "grand narratives" of physics or mathematics could be all-encompassing.

Another important source is the work of Sigmund Freud and his analysis of the unconscious. Freud, after all, for all his obsession with being taken seriously as an objective scientist, was a man who worked with texts and whose patients became represented as texts through their own dream reports and in Freud's case-studies and the vast literature they have spawned. What he made more explicit than any of his predecessors, although it was no new discovery, is the way in which what texts do not say is at least as significant as what they do say. Furthermore, what is included or excluded depends on decisions that their authors may well be unaware that they have made, let alone why. Indeed, the author may be the least reliable person to explain the text as he or she is the last one to be able to articulate what the text has suppressed.

Put Freud together with Saussure, and you end up with the work of Jacques Lacan (France; d. 1981). The strengths and weaknesses of postmodernism as it developed into a critical movement largely stem from Lacan. He was an astute reader, but he was also an inveterate tease. Nothing pleased him more than to produce a deliberately outrageous and mystifying text and then to watch as his devoted readers proceeded to find profound insights in it and to turn it into a new methodology.

He is rather a King Canute figure. The popular understanding of King Canute's attempt to turn back the sea is that he is an example of the self-delusion of the power-mad. What is often forgotten is that the original story is one of a king who goes through with the charade in order to shame his courtiers who were flattering him by ascribing miraculous powers to him. Like Canute, Lacan is in the business of tempting his followers into betraying their own folly, but has been taken by many as the source of that folly. His fundamental insight, that the unconscious is itself structured like a language, underlies much postmodern thought.

So too do the ideas of the philosophers Gilles Deleuze (France; d. 1995) and Pierre-Félix Guattari (France; d. 1992), whose writings defy easy summary. Their writings embody their attempt to subvert the metaphor of the "tree of knowledge," a hierarchical and ordered structure. This is a biblical reference, of course, although not confined to the Bible. Their alternative is the "rhizome," the lateral, underground spreading network. Their attempt to write in a way that reflects this new paradigm rather than propagating the hierarchical and logical systems in which most readers have been trained is inevitably baffling. Is this a con-trick, where disciplined thought is replaced by a license to incoherent rambling, or is this a necessary radical displacement of a tradition of thinking that has led to the current social and ecological disasters of the modern world? Of course, it could, in some measure, be both.

Important as these writers are, the key figure in any discussion of postmodernism is the philosopher Jacques Derrida, who was mentioned earlier. A controversial figure (many philosophers have refused to recognize what he did as philosophy), it is Derrida's prolific writings that provide much of the characteristic vocabulary that has come to be associated with postmodernism and his individual approach, which has been labeled "deconstructionist."

DECONSTRUCTION

Deconstruction is a difficult term to come to grips with. It is not at all the same as "dismantling" a text in the sense of taking it to pieces to see how it works, or to prevent it from working, although some biblical scholars seem to take it in that sense. This is again an assimilation of postmodernism to the kind of dissection of the text that, for instance, source criticism entails. Deconstruction is concerned with the way in which the text in question reveals the inevitable gap between content and expression and the inevitable failure of the text as a system to account for itself. This is what Derrida, in a characteristic neologism, referred to as "*différance*." This word combines elements of the French terms for "difference" and "deferral" and as such is untranslatable. It also accounts for the sometimes annoying habit among postmodern writers to use brackets, slashes, and even crossings out to talk about what cannot be talked about. A word will be quoted but crossed out as a sign that it is the instance of *différance* that is at issue.

Part of the problem that deconstruction demonstrates is the incoherence of what Derrida labels "logocentrism." By this he means what he diagnoses as the fundamental assumption that underlies Western thought: that knowledge is to be equated with presence. There is a biblical aspect to this discussion, of course, although it also depends on Greek Stoic philosophy. The word "logocentrism" recalls the beginning of John's gospel where everything stems from the Word (*logos*), which is with God and is God. In the end, meaning is to be found not in the physical text of the Gospel, but in the person that the Gospel is about who exists in the presence of God. If we as readers could be in the presence of God, the need for speech and writing about God, including John's Gospel, would be gone. Writing, in this traditional account, is a faulty record of speech, and speech is a faulty transmission of the thought of the speaker. The ideal would be to be fused with the understanding of the author, or even, in Schleiermacher's well-known slogan, to understand the author better than he understands himself.

The need to rely on language is a sort of fall. Writing then becomes a further fall. It may allow communication at a distance in space and time, but at the price of losing the nuance of tone of voice or facial expression and the immediate context of the writing. There is a hierarchy that valorizes presence over speech and speech over writing.

Derrida turns this hierarchy on its head. Presence is not the presupposition of writing. Writing is all that we have; it is the notion of presence that is a derived one, a kind of illusion that a particular approach to text needs to assume. This means that, contrary to some caricatures, postmodern and poststructuralist approaches insist on the most detailed and careful attention to the details of a text. It is not at all a matter of frivolous and careless misreading justified by personal whim and fantasy.

Indeed, the ancestry of postmodern reading in rabbinic midrash, although that can be overstated, comes through here. Derrida is well aware of this connection. The rabbis may come up with interpretations that seem fanciful to a secular biblical scholar, but what they are doing comes out of an obsessive attention to every letter of the text. So too in postmodernism. Casual critics of the Bible find it easy to pick holes in texts they have lazily glanced at. Only the most detailed attention will show, however, where there are grammatical and lexical oddities that may betray the tensions and suppressions that the text bears witness to.

One element of postmodern reading is its attention to the literal structure of the words and the texts often manifested in arguments based on associations between words through puns and assonance. In the right hands this can be creative and suggestive; in the wrong hands it can lead to a kind of sterile word play that its detractors rightly deplore. One example is the way in which the relationship between the word "text" and its etymology is exploited. "Text" is related to "textile" and "texture" through the Latin root *texere*, "to weave." One way to understand the postmodern approach to texts is to see it in terms of this metaphor. We may look at a piece of clothing, for instance a shirt, as an object in its own right or, in Platonic terms, as an instantiation of some perfect "shirtness." Looked at another way, however, the substance of any shirt is a certain length of cotton thread, and the shirt comes from the particular way in which the thread is woven round itself. The shirt may look self-sufficient, but any textile will have a point where the thread begins and ends. Find that point, and the textile can be unraveled. The thread can then be rewoven into any other textile that might be desired.

This may seem banal in the extreme, but it is a necessary counter to any claim that the shirt has some kind of metaphysical essence and the thread is merely the accident that embodies it. In the same way, the argument goes, any text will have points where the ends show, so to speak, a point where the inevitable mismatch between the text's claim to authority as an embodiment of some prior Word and the reality of the undecidabilities of language will surface. Find that point, and the text can be unraveled, deconstructed.

THE HUMAN CONDITION

A postmodern approach to reading is thus not just difficult to encapsulate in a set of propositions and formulae; to do so goes against the spirit of the approach. The difficult works of Deleuze, Guattari, Lacan, and Derrida actively resist summary and reduction to sound bites. The difficulty of reading them is an important aspect of what they are trying to impart.

Many postmodern insights, however, are encapsulated in a remarkable painting by the Belgian artist René Magritte (d. 1967), which he titled *The Human Condition*. The title might seem inappropriate at first. The picture at first glance is a pleasant but not particularly striking depiction of a curtained window that looks out on to a green landscape with a prominent tree in the foreground.[1] On closer inspection, however, it turns out that standing in front of the window is a canvas on an easel. The picture on the canvas exactly matches the part of the scene outside the window that it covers. It is only because of a few lines of white that mark the edge of the canvas that the viewer can see where the demarcation line is. The tree we see is painted on the canvas and is not outside the room.

On further thought, however, things become even more complicated. Is there a tree outside at all? We cannot tell, because the canvas that seems to be reproducing the scene through the window is, inevitably, between us and whatever is to be seen through that part of the window. For all we know, the real scene through the window could be of a derelict building or a parking lot. Short of removing the canvas, we cannot tell. We have no way of knowing whether the tree in the painting is out there or is a product of the artistic imagination of whoever painted the picture.

This in turn may remind us that there is actually no "out there" in the painting. If we could delete the painting of the painting, all we would see is the bare canvas Magritte used. We cannot see out of this window. Indeed, for all we know what appears to be a window giving us a view of the outside could itself be a *trompe-l'oeil* painting on the wall of the room in front of which the canvas has been placed.

Is there a real tree out there? That becomes a very complex question. This then reminds us that the whole scene is in fact a painting. There is no outside, no window, no room and no easel, simply a pattern of color on a canvas put there by Magritte (or so we are led to believe).

A postmodern perspective on the Bible, or any text, argues that questions about the historicity of the text and the intentions of its authors are often similar to asking the question, Is there a real tree in Magritte's painting? or its slightly more nuanced version, Is there a tree outside the window? How would we tell? This is the point behind Derrida's much derided statement that "*Il n'y a pas de hors texte* [There is nothing outside the text]."

This analysis of Magritte's painting does not deny that there are real trees and that they can be seen through windows. It simply shows that such questions directed to the painting are not answerable. We could imagine an assiduous art critic visiting Magritte's house and finding that there was a window exactly like the one in the painting, looking out on a similar idyllic view. If he then discovered that in that view there was a tree exactly like the one outside the window in the painting, what would that prove? Indeed, if there was a tree just like the one in the painting, it would be very strange. Surely the tree should have grown and changed since Magritte painted the scene. In fact, it might lead us to suspect that the owners of Magritte's house had made sure that the tree was kept in trim to match the painting. Which then is the more real, the tree in the painting or the tree outside?

Empirical investigation can tell us much, but it cannot answer the question of the tree in the painting. Who could answer it then? Surely the artist could? There we hit a number of other snags. In the first place, Magritte is dead and so we can only rely on written sources or others' memories for his testimony. Yet, suppose that we could meet him and ask him whether there is a tree outside the window. Would he answer us? The whole point of the painting is to leave us guessing and thus to make us reflect on the way in which we make sense (and the emphasis is on the word *make*) of patterns of color on canvas.

Even if we pressed him to say yes or no, would we believe his answer? We have no way of checking that he is telling the truth. After all, unless we catch him at the moment of creating the painting (and how do we pinpoint that?), the Magritte we ask has to remember what a younger Magritte did. Are we even sure that he would ever have known the answer to the question? When he was painting it, did the reality of the tree matter to him? Did he have to decide? In this case, even if we could get back to the author and even if we could reliably discover his intentions, his answers could not settle what is in fact an unanswerable conundrum. The existence of the tree is undecidable. We will never have enough information to be sure which alternative is correct.

Undecidability is at the heart of the postmodern analysis. It is where things are truly undecidable that decisions have to be made. In contrast to a modernist view, which would say that we can only decide between alternatives once we have the full picture and all the information necessary, a postmodern approach points out that the full picture is never full enough and that, in the end, decisions are, to use a phrase often associated with the philosopher Kierkegaard, a "leap of faith." That, in this kind of analysis, is the "human condition" that Magritte refers to in the title of his painting.

If, after all, there is nothing outside the text, and each text is defined by its relationships to other texts, then studying the most widely disseminated of texts seems a good place to start tracing the shape of that extraordinary sphere of human culture. As we have seen, we will get furthest with this approach if we look in our text for the places where the processes of its own construction and interpretation are nearest the surface; passages where the acts of reading, writing, and interpretation are foregrounded are the ones to home in on.

JESUS READS THE SCRIPTURES

One passage that deals quite overtly with the issues of reading the text is the episode in Luke 4:14–30 in which Jesus begins his ministry in the synagogue in Nazareth.[2] Actually, this is the only passage in the whole of the New Testament where Jesus specifically reads a scroll of the Scriptures. Elsewhere he quotes them, but only here does he read them. The programmatic importance of this passage for Luke's Gospel as a whole is widely recognized.[3] According to Marguerat and Bourquin, the episode in Luke 4 acts as an "overture'" to Jesus' ministry in the Gospel.[4] It quite specifically offers a model for reading the Hebrew Scriptures—and not just anyone's reading. The figure put in place of the reader in this text is Jesus itself.

The twist that the current reading will explore could be summed up in the claim that this passage could equally well, and maybe more accurately, be titled "Jesus does *not* read the Scriptures." It is in such seeming contradictions that the story's interest lies. Careful attention to the detail of this narrative shows that it can be read as a story not of reading but of being read. On this account, it is not about words, but about silence. A key word, the verb "read," is absent and unspoken at a crucial point in the story. The text of Luke, I suggest, shows us that far from providing readers with certainty, the Hebrew Scriptures face them with undecidable questions. Luke's text deconstructs the act of reading the Scriptures, but inevitably in the process exposes itself to the reader's deconstruction.

The passage begins in Luke 4:14 with the return of Jesus "in the power of the Spirit" to Galilee. In the context of this reading, it is significant that the narrator explicitly foregrounds the flow of information in the story. Jesus has been teaching in other synagogues and the favorable reaction to this teaching is reported. News (*phēmē*) has been spreading through the neighborhood, almost as if it radiated from the figure of Jesus. What he has been teaching is not reported, however. The important fact is that stories are being told, not what they are telling. Stories about Jesus are already at work in Luke's story and the Jesus of story arrives in Nazareth before Jesus himself. These stories reflect other people's readings of Jesus.

The narration then turns to the specific incident of Jesus' arrival in Nazareth, which is explicitly described as where he was brought up, or nurtured—and, presumably, learned to read. He follows "his custom" and attends the synagogue. This is an intriguing way of putting it. It is "his" custom, not the custom of the community. Jesus' autonomy and authority are subtly underlined here. Is Jesus unusual in this regular synagogue attendance?

When Jesus "stands up to read," he is presented as taking the initiative. As modern readers, we lack knowledge of the context in which this action occurs. Who normally decided who would read in the synagogue, and on what basis? Is this an unusual honor accorded to a celebrated son of the city returned home, or part of the usual courtesies afforded to a guest, or something that would be expected of any visitor? The problem may not simply be one for modern readers, however. How much did Luke's Greek-speaking readers know of the conventions of a Galilean synagogue? Indeed, if there is one thing that Luke does make clear, it is that this is no ordinary day in the synagogue, but one where expectations had grown that a unique event might take place.

However that may be, the next portion of the narrative slows down quite significantly as verbs of action begin to pile up. Jesus *is given* a scroll of the prophet Isaiah, he *unrolls* it and he *finds* the place where a passage that Luke quotes for us is written. Again, the details are hard to pin down. We do not know how free or how radical his choice of this text was. Was it the appointed reading for the day, or chosen for him by someone else, or Jesus' own choice?

What the text does tell us is that, whatever the context, it is Jesus who unrolls the scroll and finds the specific passage, which is then quoted. This list of verbs turns our reading gaze onto what Jesus is doing, not what he is thinking. But why this painstaking focus on Jesus' actions?

The actions conceal a mystery. How did Jesus find the passage that Luke goes on to cite? What Luke quotes is a conflated passage, basically drawn from Isaiah 61:1–2 with insertions from Isaiah 58:6. Unless the synagogue at Nazareth had its own unique and otherwise unattested version of Isaiah, Jesus could not literally have found "the place where it was written." Note, too, that Luke could not be more specific that what he is quoting to us are the words written in the scroll, not the words that Jesus spoke.[5] We are reading over Jesus' shoulder, in effect. The fact is that the only place the exact words recorded in Luke 4:18–19 as Isaiah's are written in that form is in Luke 4:18–19, a circularity that can do odd things to the mind if one thinks too long about it. Let us quote this passage in the RSV version:

> The Spirit of the Lord is upon me, because he has anointed me to preach good news to the poor. He has sent me to proclaim release to the captives and recovering of sight to the blind, to set at liberty those who are oppressed, to proclaim the acceptable year of the Lord.

Puzzling though this text and its provenance are, the key point is what happens next. Once again a sequence of verbs turns our attention to Jesus' actions, recorded in suspenseful detail: he *closes* the scroll, *returns* it to the attendant, and *sits* down: verb after verb. Quite explicitly, we are told that all eyes in the synagogue are fixed on him. The reader, too, has been led to concentrate on this detailed explanation of relatively routine actions, which again serve to increase narrative suspense. But one key verb is missing. We are never told that Jesus actually reads the words aloud to the people.

Commentators universally assume that he did read. Presumably, it is so obvious that he did so as to go without saying. Yet the text makes such play of the mechanical handling of the scroll, which surely could also be taken for granted. If he reads aloud at all, we can assume that Jesus must at least open the scroll and find the passage.

So often, questioning what is too obvious to question is the crucial move in the deconstruction of a text. Why can we not read this as a story, not of reading, but of silence? From the textual evidence, we could legitimately construct a scene where Jesus unrolled the scroll and, as the congregation waited breathlessly, silently scrutinized the passage. Holding that silence, he rolled up the scroll, handed it to the attendant, and sat down with the gaze of all upon him, leaving the audience dumbfounded by his actions but now in an even more impatient fever to hear what he might be about to say.

What a powerful dramatic gesture! What a focus, too, on the gaze of the congregation, on the eye rather than the ear. They are watching, not listening. As a result, moreover, what a weight of expectation is thrown onto the words that Jesus eventually utters, the first direct expression in the text of Luke's Gospel of Jesus' teaching, so highly praised and eagerly awaited.

Before the chorus of objections that this drama is an impossible scenario in the synagogue of this period breaks out, there are four points to be made. The first is that, although common sense may insist that Jesus must read the scroll, common sense in this case has no direct textual support. Second, the only direct evidence we have for the practice of scriptural reading in synagogues in Galilee in the first century CE is to be found only in this passage.[6] Quite bluntly, we have no sure way of knowing what the norm for such an occasion might have been. Third, whatever is happening here, it is not a normal event. It is set apart to begin with by the heightened expectations of the congregation based on the exceptional reputation of the reader, but whatever happens goes further and confounds even those exceptional expectations. Fourth, the clue of the "impossible" text in Luke 4:18–19 gives us leave to question whether a realistic record of a possible event is the point at issue in this text.

Here is a strange gap in the text, a reticence about what seemed to be the key moment in the story, the act of reading. Here too is an undecidability. Did Jesus read? If we assume he did, are we doing anything very different from assuming the tree in Magritte's painting is outside the window? The text that is supposed to be revealing this to us is in fact concealing it from us.

However he has done it, Jesus has created an expectant silence in which he "begins to speak," and the narrator prolongs the tension by introducing the speech with this slightly ponderous circumlocution that may also reinforce the point that these words are Jesus' first direct words of preaching. As a result of all these techniques, these opening words invite particularly close reading. "Today," says Jesus, " today this scripture has been fulfilled in your hearing."[7]

The first word he speaks is "Today." This is a prime example of deixis, that is, of the phenomenon of a word that only has meaning with reference to a particular set of concrete circumstances. Within any written text, these words have a particular effect of at once uniting and separating a range of potential readers and audiences. In the present case, there is the "today" of the day Jesus was in Nazareth (a date in the fourth decade of the first century CE), there is the "today" of the writing of the text (at least a few decades later, and itself as multiple as the number of recensions the text has been through), and there is the "today" of the reader. The same word can point to at least these three sorts of date, and to an infinite variety of actual dates. The same ambiguity affects the phrase "this scripture."

Importantly for the present discussion, Jesus' actions and words provoke the congregation to its own act of reading, as Stephen Moore explains:

> by an act of reading he [Jesus] gestures to that immaterial *eidos* that "is not and never will be perceivable with physical eyes"—his own identity as the near-illegible sign . . . said to effect release from blindness, misery and oppression. The congregation's initial response is to "gaze" at him. . . . Now Jesus' ideal reading of scripture consists in letting scripture read *him*. But his pre-scribed role is precisely what his audience cannot, or will not, read. And in refusing the ideal reading it assumes its own part in the script.[8]

Though we can contest details of Moore's interpretation, he draws attention to another failed act of reading. The gaze of the congregation, fixed on Jesus, fails to see him for what he is. They misread him, or at least that is Luke's opinion.

Who he is, what he has done, and what his words mean are all questions raised for these readers of Jesus in the Nazareth synagogue. What would fulfillment *today*, this very day, mean to them? Jesus does not say that the Scripture "will be" fulfilled or "is being" fulfilled, but that it "has been" fulfilled. Is the congregation justifiably expecting the captives to be released and the blind to see, right here and now? Jesus' message includes his listeners by direct address—"your hearing." Yet fulfillment is in the "ears," not in the sight. Fulfillment is not to occur before the eyes, which have been fixed on Jesus' actions, but through some unexplained emancipation of the ear. "Your" of course, is also a deictic term that leaves open the crucial question of just who is being addressed by this word—the congregation as reader or some other group of later readers of the text?

Luke then presents us with the congregation's reaction. They "bear witness" and "marvel" at Jesus' "words of grace," or so the RSV puts it. The conjunction of the two verbs is commonly taken by commentators and translators as an expression of enthusiasm so that *marturein* is translated as "speaking well" of Jesus.[9] This interpretation adds to the anomaly that so enthusiastic a crowd turns against Jesus at the end of the story. It may not be the only possibility, however. The only other use of the verb *marturein* in the Gospel is in Luke 11:48, where the lawyers are accused of "witnessing" to the deeds of their forefathers by building tombs of the prophets whom their ancestors killed. This is hardly a virtue, nor is it their conscious intention. Both in chapter 11 and in the present context it seems to me that the verb could carry something closer to its meaning that they "made themselves visible" or showed themselves in their true colors. *Thaumazein* (marvel, wonder) is also an ambiguous verb—it may imply confusion rather than admiration. However these words are translated, the important point is that the focus is again on the congregation, on the readers of Jesus and not on Jesus himself. Jesus' words provoke the congregation into speech that opens them to judgment that gives away the inadequacy of their reading of him.

Their response is summed up by Luke in the single ambiguous question "Is not this Joseph's son?" Of course, it is a highly artificial narrative convention to make the whole congregation speak one question with one voice; only the narrator can be the source of this question. This is not unimportant, however, and in the discussion that follows I shall continue to treat the congregation as a single character in the narrative.

The important point is that the question is directed not at what Jesus read or what he has done, but at who he is. There is no discussion of the textual problems of the passage from Isaiah, or the implications of this claim of the fulfillment of the Scriptures. Indeed, we cannot tell from this reaction what the audience has heard of the Isaiah passage. Its reaction is not to the text but to Jesus' first explicit speech, the first speech of his ministry in this Gospel. As far as the congregation is concerned, the Isaiah text might as well not have been read aloud.

The question that is raised is about Jesus' origins, and it is established through paternity and the community's recognition of that familial context. Opinions vary as to whether this is the scornful recollection of Jesus' humble beginnings or the pride of a parochial crowd identifying itself with the local boy made good. Either reading is possible, but the question makes central an assumption that explaining this unprecedented event and person involves determining his origins. In this process, the community is checking out *its* story of who Jesus is.

Clearly, the question is not directed to Jesus, expecting his answer, but is directed internally among the congregation. It is not a request for information, but something designed either to establish or to maintain a common narrative context for Jesus. In this process, the congregation has been provoked into giving voice to its own reading, not of the Scripture, but of Jesus. By categorizing him as Joseph's son, it can reestablish him as someone over whom the community has a claim.

The point may be to counter Jesus' hubris in aligning himself with the Scripture and thereby illegitimately setting himself against the community, or alternatively it may be to establish the community's right to be identified with Jesus' own assertions of his authority and his relationship to the fulfillment of the Scripture. The question as to his paternity has a note both of reassurance and anxiety, of recognition and estrangement, of, in a root sense, the familiar and unfamiliar: is Jesus one of the "family" or not. But above all it is a question: the one "fact" that the congregation thinks it knows about Jesus, his paternity, is now thrown into doubt. Neither the Scripture nor Jesus' words have given them certainty. It has demanded a decision. Is Jesus Joseph's son?

Jesus' next utterance is intriguing in this context. He performs a reciprocal act of reading when he reads the congregation's next speech into its mouth, if we may put it this way: "Doubtless you will quote to me this proverb . . . ," he begins. What they will say is not original, however, but the recitation of a proverb, even a cliché: "Physician, heal yourself."[10] They have heard what happened in Capernaum, now they want to see it done here and now. What was done away from home ought to be done all the more at home, in Jesus' "fatherland," and the reiteration of the centrality of paternity to identity is no accident. Again the ambiguity of the word "fatherland" as applied to Jesus from the point of view of Luke's reader ironically brings to the fore the inappropriateness of any community claiming its territory as Jesus' home in some particular sense. More pertinently, stories about Jesus are not enough: what they want is direct evidence.

Whatever is the case, Jesus continues with what will become his characteristic emphatic "Amen." "No prophet is honored in his fatherland," he tells them, in a phrase which also has a proverbial ring. The community's reliance on stock phrases and received wisdom handed down from the "fathers" may be under satirical attack here. Yet if we follow the usual assumption that the crowd's initial reaction is favorable, something odd is happening. Jesus, in that reading, has just received a favorable reception in his fatherland. Does that mean he is not a prophet—or not a prophet as the congregation understands that term? Or is the reference to the unrecognized prophet to Isaiah? Either way, if this proverb is true, the congregation is presented with a paradox. Any native-born prophet it recognizes and acclaims, any prophet it wants to include in its own sense of the "fatherland," is *ipso facto* not a prophet. If they recognize one of their own as a prophet, then there are two options: either that person is not a prophet or he is not truly "at home" in the synagogue in Nazareth.

In the context of our concentration on reading, what is striking is that Jesus goes on to flesh out the implications of this with an explicit example of reading and interpreting scriptural texts that deal with prophets. This time he gives the congregation a reading of two episodes from the books of Kings: Elijah's rescue of the woman of Sarepta in the famine, and Naaman's cure by Elisha.

What interesting readings these are, because what Jesus points to is an absence, or a silence, in the two narratives. "Many widows were in Israel . . . and to not one of them was Elisha sent . . . many lepers were there in Israel, and none of them was cleaned" (Luke 4:25–27). The sufferings of the people of Israel, Jesus points out, do not figure at all in these stories. They concentrate on the survival and healing of obscure or even hostile foreigners. Who then are the "poor," the "captives," the "blind," and the "oppressed" in the passage from Isaiah that has just been quoted? The assumption that this is Israel, and more specifically, those in the synagogue in Nazareth, is thrown into question.[11]

The implication is clear. The fulfillment of the Scripture will not, as the congregation understandably assumes, be manifested in the healing of the blind and leprous of Nazareth. Far from the city being able to bask in the reflected glory of its greatest son, *nothing* will happen. The fulfilled Scripture is silent on the subject of Nazarenes; it is the healing of others that will be the fulfillment. As Israelites, they are read out of what they have always read as their own story in their own synagogue.[12]

They will see nothing happen. Fulfillment, in Jesus' words, is for the ear, the ear of those who "today" hear Luke's story read, not for the Nazarenes in their synagogue on the day of the narrative. The new community is formed of those who hear the story, those who inhabit it in a "today" directed toward the reader, not to those gathered to see Jesus in the synagogue at Nazareth. Those present with Jesus are not privileged by their proximity. It is those who hear and read about him in distant times and places who will experience fulfillment.

This accounts in part for the congregation's rage and for its futile attempt at the end of the story to preempt unwittingly the silencing of Jesus that occurs in the crucifixion. Jesus' reading of Scripture excludes the very people who thought that they inhabited it, whose "fatherland" it was and whose sense of identity and location depends on it. They are in the story to be read out of it.

Furthermore, this reading of Scripture occurs in a highly significant textual context. The book is *closed* before Jesus speaks, closed and returned to its place and therefore, in one strict but undeniable sense, unreadable. Luke's text shows these categories reversed and rethought. It shows us how to read a closed book, and how the transition between the two forms of community both sustained by texts needs an atextual mediation in the figure of Jesus. Of course, Luke is caught in the impossibility of representing the absence of text through a text. The category that can operate across this boundary is silence, the silences bounded and shaped by text and speech. Jesus closes the book and provides the silence in which his audience is induced to "bear witness" to their own readings.

What is both inside and outside the text and the reader is silence. In a perhaps too poetical phrase, we could say that Jesus slips away into the silences of the text, evading the textual categories of insider and outsider in the impossible category of the "in the midst." It is this impossible middle that Jesus occupies, enabling the feat of reading the closed book of the Old Testament and the writing of a New Testament.

In this context, the following quotation from John Caputo may be helpful: "God's address to us is always accompanied by silence, that the trace of God is invariably marked by undecidability. We are unsure of the difference between the work and the silence, between what is God's saying and what is God's silence, what is God's word and what is ours, what is God's silence and what is ours, that is the way undecidability hovers over sacred texts."[13]

It is this undecidability that is the characteristic of the deictic words of the story. This is obvious in a word like "today," or in the expression "this scripture." It is less obvious, but present, in words like "father" and "fatherland." It is true, too, of "inside" and "outside." The undecidabilities encapsulated in Luke's text—Did Jesus read or not read the Scripture? Who are the poor and oppressed? When is "today"? Insider or outsider?—deepen the silence in the synagogue at Nazareth, which in its turn invites the reader to bear witness to his or her telling of the story of whose son Jesus may be, even as he slips away into the silences between the words.

THE FUTURE OF POSTMODERNISM

The main accusation against postmodernism is its irresponsibility, in a literal as well as derived sense. The postmodern reading, so the accusation goes, does not admit that it is answerable to anyone and refuses the responsibility of being faithful to the text, its historical context, and the intentions of its authors.

Even Magritte, however, can be challenged. All of this analysis relies on the fact that we have, as viewers, learned ways of looking at paintings and interpreting them. How much of this is a culturally determined skill? We could at least imagine showing this painting to someone from another culture where realistic painting was not practiced. Would they raise the same questions? Would they see the same problems? Would they be able to interpret the subtle clues Magritte includes of the easel and the edge of the canvas as implying that there was a painting in front of the window?

What does it mean to people of different educational or cultural backgrounds? If they were simply to tell us that it looked to them like a pattern of color on canvas, would they be wrong? In another slogan that is often misinterpreted, postmodern writers such as Foucault have taken leave to question the usefulness of the term "human" in a phrase like "the human condition." Is there any one such identifiable thing? Do women and men share the same condition, or are there differences? Once we begin to ask that question, gender, race, age, economic circumstances, language, and innumerable other differentials begin to crowd in. What is it that humans share as humans? What, if anything, then, distinguishes human beings from animals?

At one extreme, this sort of questioning can lead to complete relativism, where each individual's experience is unique. If that is the case, then there is no way of accounting for any communication between people. Clearly, then, there is little point in you reading my writing. In particular, the chance for oppressed or neglected groups to make their voice heard seems to be undercut, with the effect, whether deliberate or not, that the political and economic status quo becomes entrenched with no possibility of effective opposition. Postmodernism becomes a sort of effete fiddling while Rome burns that has silenced the most vulnerable and rendered argument pointless.

A more positive view is possible, however. Postmodernism reminds us that the act of communicating depends on faith, on taking a chance on the undecidable question of whether we share enough that I can learn from your experience and vice versa. What is important, from this point of view, is not to deny any sort of human solidarity, but to question the definitions that are used. Famously, the charge is that what European philosophy and science have promoted as an objective view, which can be shared by anyone with the requisite level of rational thought, is in fact the view of a particular cultural subgroup of "dead white European males" whose claim to dispassionate objectivity masks assumption about who has power and who has the right to define the human.

Magritte's painting serves again to show the problem and the possibilities. It depends on a shared vocabulary of painting, and his work was done in Belgium around a century ago. Biblical studies involves working with artifacts that are much more ancient from a cultural context that we no longer share. We can be fairly confident that we know who the painter of this painting is, even if that knowledge is necessarily limited and even if it does not in the end help to resolve the question. In the case of biblical texts, their authorship is disputed and the possibility of multiple editing and of errors in transmission means that we cannot be sure that we have what any author we might identify originally wrote. Almost all the evidence we have comes from the texts themselves, or from other texts with complex and dubious relationships to the ones we have.

This is what can make postmodern approaches a life-line for biblical studies rather than a threat. If postmodernism reveals that the search for the original meaning and intention of an original author in the most contemporary of texts is both impossible and in the end may be beside the point, biblical scholars should rejoice. If determining the meaning that the author intended is what interpretation entails, then biblical scholars are almost impossibly handicapped compared to scholars of contemporary literature. However, if what we do with any text is about negotiating with undecidable questions of textuality and the identity of the community of readers, then biblical scholars are in no worse shape than any other readers and indeed may have something to teach them.

Yet, once you have made the point that undecidability is at the heart of all texts, including biblical texts, what is the way forward? Is there a future for postmodern and deconstructive approaches to texts that is more than simply proving the same point on a different passage? My own prediction is that a whole range of questions and methods will continue to be applied to the Bible; linguistic, text-critical, and historical, as well as the various insights from reception criticism, theological reflection, and ideological and political criticisms. Postmodern approaches have no interest in providing some definitive alternative reading of the biblical text. In this range, however, deconstructive readings will persist as a constant reminder, rather like the slave hired to whisper in the ear of a triumphant Roman general the sobering statement, "This too will pass." What they can do is to keep all forms of reading humble and open, and to remind each reader that every reading decision they make says as much about the reader as it does about the text. They remind us of the joy and the responsibility of reading.

KEY TERMS

deconstruction. Deconstruction is the process by which the inevitable contradictions between the content and the rhetoric of a text, especially where it alludes to the acts of reading and writing, lead to a point where the reader is left with an unsolvable problem that demands what seems an entirely arbitrary decision.

différance. A word coined by Derrida that combines elements of the French words for "difference" and "deferral" and that expresses his insight that meaning is always elusive because it depends on an endless deferral of the perception and resolution of differences in a text rather than being something that an author possesses and then gives to a reader.

genetic fallacy. The mistaken idea that a complex system can be explained by recounting the story of its origins. The corollary is that the origins of a complex artifact like a text cannot be unambiguously deduced from its present state.

grand narrative. An account of the way things are that claims to have a validity for any observer regardless of his or her point of view. While allowing for different perspectives, a grand narrative claims to transcend these. Postmodernism denies that such a claim of transcendence is sustainable, and furthermore suspects any such claim of hiding what is in fact a claim to power by a sectional interest.

logocentrism. Narrowly, the assumption underlying the Western tradition that the spoken word has more authority and authenticity than the written word. More broadly, logocentrism hankers after a perfect transparency of communication between two persons. Speech, in this view, is a poor substitute for this and writing is a further remove from the ideal situation of full presence.

undecidability. The point at which reason and analysis arrive at an impasse or aporia where no amount of further evidence can help the reader to decide on meaning. Rigorous attention to the text and cogent thought are necessary to pinpoint undecidability in a text.

NOTES

1. "*The Human Condition* (painting)," *Wikipedia,* last modified March 1, 2013, http://en.wikipedia.org/wiki/The_Human_Condition_(painting).
2. A fuller version of this discussion was published as Hugh S. Pyper, "Jesus Reads the Scriptures," in George Aichele and Richard Walsh, eds., *Those Outside: Noncanonical Readings of the Canonical Gospels* (London: T. & T. Clark, 2005), 1–16.
3. For the most convenient and thorough summary of the current state of research on this text, see Michael Prior, CM, *Jesus the Liberator: Nazareth Liberation Theology I (Luke 4.16–30)* (Sheffield: Sheffield Academic Press, 1995). Prior devotes a book to these verses because, as he puts it, "Virtually all scholars agree that this is a key passage in Luke's gospel" (p.15).
4. Daniel Marguerat and Yves Bourquin, *How to Read Bible Stories* (London: SCM, 2011), 168.
5. In this regard the complex history of scholarship that seeks to reconstruct Jesus' sermon and regards the present passage as some kind of summary of a sermon based around putative lectionaries and the use of Targumim, however historically plausible, is strictly beside the point. See, for instance, the discussion in Charles A. Kimball, *Jesus' Exposition of the Old Testament in Luke's Gospel* (Sheffield: Sheffield Academic Press, 1994), 101–14.
6. Prior (*Jesus the Liberator*, ch. 4 "The Historicity of the Nazareth Synagogue Scene"; 101–25) sets out and assesses the evidence from Philo, Josephus, Qumran, and rabbinic texts. He has more interest in the question of historicity than

the present writer, but makes no more firm a statement than the following: "Luke's details of the scene in the synagogue in Nazareth do not appear out of place in the pre-70 AD period" (115).
7. Readers may now protest that surely this must mean that Jesus read aloud to those who are spoken to. The congregation must know what "this scripture" refers to. But we have already seen that, in the narrow sense, this phrase can only refer to a passage in Luke, not in any Isaiah scroll in Nazareth. Nor does this rule out the possibility that Jesus has remained silent, as in that case "this writing" could refer to the entire written scroll.
8. Stephen D. Moore, *Mark and Luke in Poststructuralist Perspectives: Jesus Begins to Write* (New Haven, CT: Yale University Press, 1992), 126.
9. This reading could be defended by pointing out the positive implication of Jesus' speech being described as "words of grace." It is a moot point, however, whether this reflects the congregation's judgment or the narrator's.
10. Joel Green (*The Gospel of Luke,* New International Commentary on the New Testament [Grand Rapids: Eerdmans, 1997], 216) calls it "a well known maxim in antiquity."
11. For a further exploration of the ambiguous status of Elijah and Elisha as "insiders" and "outsiders" in Israel and how this relates to the narratological models that they provide for Luke in his account of Jesus, see my "The Secret of Succession: Elijah, Elisha, Jesus and Derrida" in A. K. M. Adam, ed., *Postmodern Interpretations of the Bible—A Reader* (St Louis: Chalice, 2001), 55–66.
12. Here it is worth mentioning Prior's concern to counter the common conception that this is a repudiation of any mission to the Jews (*Jesus the Liberator,* 58–60). I agree that this is not the implication of the text. On the contrary, what is offered is an alternative conception of "Israel" that can include both Jew and Gentile. The argument in this paper is that what is being reconfigured in a remarkable manner is the relationship between community and text, so that the newly understood Israel, which is in continuity with, not separated from, the old can be configured around the new text of the gospel. The synagogue in Nazareth is not simply a synecdoche for first-century Judaism—its particularity and locality are not accidental to the story.
13. John D. Caputo, *More Radical Hermeneutics: On Not Knowing Who We Are* (Bloomington, IN: Indiana University Press, 2000), 220.

FOR FURTHER READING

Adam, A. K. M., ed. *Handbook of Postmodern Biblical Interpretation.* St. Louis: Chalice, 2000.

———, ed. *Postmodern Interpretations of the Bible: A Reader.* St. Louis: Chalice, 2001.

———. *Faithful Interpretation: Reading the Bible in a Postmodern World.* Minneapolis: Fortress, 2006.

The Bible and Culture Collective. *The Postmodern Bible.* New Haven, CT: Yale University Press, 1995.

Collins, John J. *The Bible after Babel: Historical Criticism in a Postmodern Age.* Grand Rapids: Eerdmans, 2006.

Hart, K. *Postmodernism: A Beginner's Guide.* Oxford: Oneworld, 2004.

Jobling, David, Tina Pippin, and Ronald Schleifer, eds. *The Postmodern Bible Reader.* Oxford: Blackwell, 2001.

Marguerat, Daniel, and Yves Bourquin. *How to Read Bible Stories.* London: SCM, 2011.

Moore, Stephen D. *The Bible in Theory: Critical and Postcritical Essays.* Atlanta: Society of Biblical Literature, 2010.

———. *Mark and Luke in Poststructuralist Perspectives: Jesus Begins to Write.* New Haven, CT / London: Yale University Press, 1992.

Nutu, Ela. *Incarnate Word, Inscribed Flesh: John's Prologue and the Postmodern.* Sheffield: Sheffield Phoenix Press, 2007.

Sherwood, Yvonne, ed. *Derrida's Bible (Reading a Page of Scripture with a Little Help from Derrida).* New York: Palgrave Macmillan, 2004.

Sherwood, Yvonne, and Kevin Hart, eds. *Derrida and Religion: Other Testaments.* New York: Routledge, 2005.

Chapter 8

Psychological Biblical Criticism

D. Andrew Kille

Human beings have left their traces all over the Bible. Wherever the biblical traditions have been developed, retold, edited, taught, preached, read, and interpreted, they have been filtered through and shaped by the human mind. Sometimes the evidence is strong, and we can easily follow the traces, while other times require a careful analysis to examine the subtle and elusive effects of the psyche on the text.

Simply stated, psychological biblical criticism uses the tools and models of psychology—ways of understanding human behavior and mental processes such as perception, intuition, cognition, memory, personality, motivation, emotion, and so on—to examine all phases of biblical texts from their authors to their interpreters. Psychological approaches may include studying the origins, authorship, and structures of texts—both conscious and unconscious; their transmission, interpretation, and alteration across time, geography, and culture; their expression in other forms, such as art and music; their impact on readers; and the history of how they have shaped both individual and communal values, attitudes, and behavior.

Psychological biblical criticism cannot be identified with any single methodology. No step-by-step instructions exist for doing psychological criticism, and any given approach will depend on the dimensions of the text the interpreter desires to address and the psychological theory employed to those purposes. What characterizes psychological criticism is a *way of reading* that is critically sensitive to psychological factors, structures, dynamics, relationships, and interactions in and beyond the biblical text.

HISTORY AND DEVELOPMENT

The roots of psychological criticism go far back into the history of biblical interpretation. Indeed, the modern discipline of psychology itself emerged from Christian study of the nature of the human soul, or psyche (Greek *psychē*). Clearly, early theologically motivated investigations into the nature and activity of the soul cannot be equated with the concerns and methods of the modern science. Psychological analysis has developed through three phases. Folk wisdom offers the earliest manifestation of an awareness of human behavior. From observing people around them, everybody "knew" what made people behave the way they do. Those observations of one's neighbors were distilled into folk sayings and became a part of the received wisdom in a community.

The next step of development led to systematic but prescientific exploration of behavior. In the church, it took the form of philosophical studies of the soul—the *psychē*—and its attributes. Key figures in the development of proto-psychology included Tertullian (ca. 150–220), Augustine (354–430), and Aquinas (1225–1274). Luther's colleague Philipp Melanchthon became, in the sixteenth century, the first scholar to use the term "psychology" in the academy to describe investigations into the nature and operation of the soul.

The birth of modern psychology is most often dated to the work of Wilhelm Wundt, who founded a school for experimental psychology in Leipzig in 1879. For the first time, psychology moved from the realm of the philosophers into the world of science and began to develop into the discipline we recognize today. However, also in Germany, biblical psychology had already taken significant steps forward. In 1855, twenty-four years before Wundt established his laboratory, Franz Julius Delitzsch, a highly regarded professor of Hebrew and Old Testament and author of numerous commentaries on both Old and New Testaments, wrote *A System of Biblical Psychology* (*System der biblischen Psychologie*), in which he combined theological investigation with insights from emerging psychological experiments. Among the questions he considered was how biblical studies and scientific investigations might appropriately inform each other.[1]

During this transitional period, before psychology became a household word, M. Scott Fletcher published *The Psychology of the New Testament* in 1912. Fletcher was even more oriented toward the new discipline of psychology than Delitzsch had been and devoted the latter portion of his book to correlating psychological terminology with biblical concepts.[2]

Although there was a significant body of work employing psychological approaches to the Bible, for many years it remained mostly unknown. One reason for this was the dominance of the historical-critical method in biblical studies, which left little room for psychological perspectives. Another was the somewhat "hit-and-run" nature of studies within the psychology of religion that dealt with the Bible. Essayists of varying backgrounds—biblical scholars, psychologists, anthropologists, theologians, pastoral counselors, and religious educators—might find an interesting insight or psychological phenomenon, write a single paper, and then move on. Often they either brought little depth of understanding to biblical criticism or else were not fully grounded in psychology. There was no systematic approach or effort to collaborate and build on each other's efforts.

Three significant conceptual shifts opened a space for the renewal of psychological approaches, which began roughly in the 1970s and 80s. The first was the progressive "psychologization" of Western culture. Terms and concepts like "ego," "transference," "neurosis," "complex," or "Freudian slip" that had once been the language of professionals in the field of psychology crept into daily usage, and the figure on the therapist's couch became an immediately recognizable theme in cartoons, on TV, and in movies. Contemporary culture had become far more sensitive to psychological motivations and patterns of interaction that affect human experience.

A second shift took place within biblical studies, breaking the hegemony of the historical-critical approach that had dominated the field for over a century and allowing for the rise of new critical methods, including interdisciplinary approaches that drew on the tools and perspectives of the social sciences. Some approaches, such as reader-response criticism, incorporated (often implicitly) psychological assumptions about social interaction or cognitive processes of reading, learning, and interpretation.

The third shift was in the field of psychology itself. In the early years of the twentieth century, psychological work had been dominated by two schools of thought: (1) depth psychology, such as that of Freud and Jung, which focused on unconscious motivations and pathologies; and (2) behaviorism, which turned its attention only to observable behavior, to stimulus and response. More recently, other psychological theories have emerged that study object relations, cognitive learning, psychosocial development, family systems, or the effects of trauma.

Several notable publications that marked the revival of interest in psychological approaches appeared at the same time. The *Journal of Psychology and Theology* was established in 1973, followed by the *Journal of Psychology and Christianity* in 1982, and *Biblical Interpretation: A Journal of Contemporary Approaches* in 1994. Walter Wink issued *The Bible in Human Transformation*, his challenge to historical-critical scholarship and call for a psychoanalytical approach in 1973, and demonstrated this new approach in *Naming the Powers* (1984) and *Transforming Bible Study* (1980).[3] Wayne G. Rollins's *Jung and the Bible* (1983) not only described how important the Bible had been to C. G. Jung, and how

Jungian concepts might contribute to the study of the Bible, but perceptively went on to suggest that "psychological criticism will emerge in the years ahead as another of the critical tools biblical interpreters can employ."[4] Wilhelm Wuellner, professor of New Testament, and Robert Leslie, emeritus professor of psychology and counseling, collaborated to produce *The Surprising Gospel*, bringing together tales from the New Testament with psychological insights from several theorists.[5] At the same time in Germany, New Testament scholar Gerd Theissen published *Psychological Aspects of Pauline Theology* (1983), and priest, theologian, and psychotherapist Eugen Drewermann produced a two-volume work, *Tiefenpsychologie und Exegese* (*Depth-psychology and Exegesis*), using analytical psychology to approach the symbols and themes of the Bible.[6] Since that time, the number and variety of psychological biblical studies has multiplied greatly. Since 1991, "Psychology and Biblical Studies" has been an active division within the Society of Biblical Literature.

Such great diversity both in methods of biblical criticism and in psychological theory makes attempting a comprehensive description of psychological biblical criticism a formidable challenge. Psychological phenomena are not the result of a single cause or source, and thus different researchers, depending on their theoretical orientation, intentions, and even their personalities, will highlight different aspects, organize information in different ways, and identify different dimensions of human behavior. No fewer than fifty-four specialized divisions currently make up the American Psychological Association, often with sharply differing opinions about what counts as psychological data and how that information should be arranged and interpreted.

Biblical studies today also present a dazzling array of methods and approaches, each with particular assumptions about what matters in the text, and what tools are best to help tease out the necessary details for understanding it. Roughly speaking, different exegetical and hermeneutical approaches might be said to address three levels of the text. It is not possible to separate the levels entirely from each other, but naming them can offer a useful heuristic framework.[7]

The first dimension can be called the world *behind* the text. At this level are all the factors that go into the origin, authorship, editing, and historical context of the text. The second dimension is the world *of* the text, which involves the structures evident in the language and structures of the text itself—narration, description, ordering, characterization, and rhetoric—that tell the story, offer an argument, or express an emotion. The third dimension is the world *in front of* the text, where a reader, hearer, or interpreter encounters the text, bringing their own expectations and understandings. It is in this world that the interaction of reader and text works to change the reader's perceptions, attitudes, and insight into the world around.

Historical-critical study focused primarily on the world *behind* the text, doing careful and extensive historical investigation, seeking to uncover the original form of the text and understand the historical context in which it emerged. Some early efforts at psychological interpretation attempted to do much the same, doing "psychoanalysis" of biblical figures like Moses, Jesus, or Paul. However, psychology is not a particularly good tool for such investigations; psychoanalysis requires extensive information about a patient and the opportunity to check insights or hunches with the person. Not only is there only limited information about personalities in the Bible, but that information has been sifted through long processes of composition, editing, and transmission, which have obscured whatever living figure may lie behind the text. Nor is there access to the person in order to confirm any hypothesis. Efforts of this kind were doomed to failure, especially when those attempting them were ignorant of, or simply refused to engage, the history of composition and transmission.

It is in relation to the world *of* the text and especially the world *in front of* the text that psychological approaches have more to offer. The Bible does not use psychological language, but nevertheless it speaks of human emotions and behavior—will, joy, grief, rage—in ways that ring true. It uses structures of narration and argument that seek to affect our ways of thinking and presents us with symbols and images that connect with our deepest experience. When examined with care for cultural and historical context, such symbols can point us toward archetypal commonalities and psychic resonances.

The world *in front of the text* is the world of actual readers and interpreters, and here we actually can have access to readers and their imaginative interaction with the text. We are able to explore how the Bible works on cognitive structures and processes, how a reader's personality affects his or her reading, and how the Bible affects those who read or hear it for good or ill.

MAPPING THE FIELD

It is not possible to offer an exhaustive description of how psychological biblical criticism operates or of the methods, terms, and working premises that are involved. It is perhaps more productive to map out the basic areas of interest that the field comprises.

In his exhaustive and seminal introduction to psychological biblical criticism, *Soul and Psyche*, Wayne G. Rollins describes the fundamental aspects of a psychological critical approach to the Bible and its readers in terms of a revisioning of the biblical text in five areas: biblical origins, the text itself, biblical interpretation, "biblical history," and the fundamental purpose of the Bible.[8]

Such a revisioning of biblical origins involves a move from historical context and events to consideration of the psychological dynamics and experiences manifested in readers and interpreters of the text that give rise to the religious impulse. It examines the text for archetypal and mythical themes and symbols and considers how they may have shaped the consciousness of individuals and communities that have encountered the Bible. And it may seek to discern traces of psychic factors that may have led authors and editors to choose and shape the ideas, images, and expressions within the text.

Approaching the text itself, psychological criticism considers how texts "work" at all: by what mechanisms or processes does a text affect behaviors, attitudes, and relationships in those who hear or read them? It asks what unconscious factors might be active in the language and genre of the biblical writings alongside more conscious dimensions. It seeks to illuminate the psychodynamics of religious phenomena encountered in the text, such as glossolalia, conversion, dreaming, demon possession, and prophecy. Further, it attends to the psychological dynamics of plots and interactions between characters in the text, including how such defense mechanisms as repression, sublimation, projection, or transference may be at work. It identifies the psychodynamics of personality, the religious impulse, and how the Bible describes and elaborates its own psychology. Finally, it remains sensitive to how the Bible may have therapeutic or pathogenic effects on its readers.

A psychological critical approach understands reading, hearing, and interpretation as psychic events that are shaped by factors of cognition, personality, and social relationships that lead readers to bring certain expectations to the text and attends to how those dimensions change in the encounter. Interpretation does not remain simply a verbal process, but includes other modes of response that amplify the text and enable an active, imaginative approach, which itself holds clues to psychic structures and habits. Dance, music, liturgy, art, and ritual all hold potential for uncovering more unconscious dimensions of meaning.

The fourth area is to re-approach biblical history, taking into account not only the prehistory of the Bible's development but also the post-history of its impact on individuals and communities. Attention is paid to how the Bible has served as a catalyst for human perception and action and how it has served as text or pre-text for undergirding or challenging attitudes and relationships—prejudices, animosities and violence, or openness, compassion, and peacemaking.

Finally, such criticism considers the fundamental purposes of the Bible in a new light. It views the Bible as a transformative book, one that seeks to have an effect on its readers and to bring them to new levels of understanding and insight. Seeing the purpose of the text as dedicated to the "cure of souls," psychological criticism will note how its symbols and motifs, language and story serve to activate processes of individuation and greater consciousness.

Psychological biblical criticism can yield both exegetical and hermeneutic insights. Exegesis can be described as involved in examining the world *of* the text, while hermeneutics turns its attention to what happens *in front of* the text with readers and interpreters.

While "exegesis" has sometimes been limited to the investigation of historical and cultural setting of the text and to the original intentions of the writers, psychological exegesis reminds us to attend to the human patterns of behavior that are an essential component of any human endeavor. Conscious *and unconscious* factors are at work in every individual who is involved with the production, transmission, or interpretation of the text. It is not always easy to tease out these unconscious dimensions, and some critics may question whether it is possible at all. But with care and attention, the approach can offer new insights and deeper understandings.

Psychological exegesis may involve exploration and explanation of the symbols and motifs found in the Bible. Symbols by their very nature are polyvalent and serve multiple functions in a text. They operate at the level of consciousness to communicate meaning, but bring with them an unconscious dimension as well, working at levels other than thought and rationality. Symbols may also be, as C. G. Jung believed, a way of bringing balance to the psyche, of compensating for one-sidedness within the personality. Symbols may also be archetypal—appearing in consistent patterns and interactions that transcend time, space, and culture. Analyzing these symbols can trace similarities and commonalities that point to archetypes within the human psyche, characteristic modes of patterning and comprehending one's self and experiences.

The psychodynamics evidenced in the texts also offer a challenge for exegetical work. While the Bible does not use contemporary psychological terms, its pages are full of descriptions of human behavior, attitudes, intentions, interactions, and transformations. The characters of biblical stories strike us as believable because we recognize that their words and actions reflect our shared humanity. Psychological models of the human psyche that describe the psyche's development, modes of expression, and interrelations can illuminate these psychodynamics of the texts, both the conscious and unconscious. They can identify characteristic psychic defense strategies of repression, denial, projection, and transference. Further, they can follow the process of individuation that may unfold within a story or map the family dynamics at play.

All this must be done with care, since texts are not only psychological phenomena but are also multiply determined. Failing to acknowledge historical contexts or literary conventions within the text can lead to misidentifying what is present in the text and forcing the evidence to fit the exegete's pet theory.

We have mentioned how early attempts to psychoanalyze biblical personalities often failed to take into account other determinants of the text, such as literary conventions and the history of transmission. This, however, is not to say that such investigations are entirely without merit. David Halperin's study of the psychology of the prophet Ezekiel, Barbara Leung Lai's recent work on Daniel and Isaiah, and Terrance Callan's exploration of Paul all demonstrate what can be accomplished with care and a multidisciplinary approach that carefully considers the multiple factors that shape the tradition.[9]

Despite the limitations that are inherent in the text, it is certainly possible to consider biblical personalities as *literary characters*. As such, they have a life of their own, and all literature depends on our recognizing a kinship with the characters. Psychological criticism can illuminate the dimensions of personality, characteristic interactions, and affiliations or conflicts among individuals in families, tribes, and communities.

Exegetical work may also concern itself with unpacking descriptions of religious experience in the text. A variety of personal and communal religious practices and rituals are described—and prescribed—in the Bible. Research into brain functioning, cognitive processing, and the role of the unconscious can give insight into such extraordinary phenomena as speaking in tongues and demon possession or the functions and results of everyday activities of prayer and ritual. It can illuminate accounts of visions, prophetic ecstasy, mystical experience, and especially dreaming, which Freud described as "the royal road to the unconscious." Rituals such as baptism or communion also carry symbolic and archetypal dimensions that touch and transform participants inwardly. All forms of psycho-spiritual experience described in the Bible are potentially ripe areas for investigation.

Psychology becomes an even more useful tool in relation to hermeneutics, dealing with interpreters and the tasks of interpretation. In some cases, it is possible to observe the interaction of a reader and the text directly and to describe how personality types, cognitive styles, and psychic processes affect the process of reading. In other cases, it is possible to track the history of the impact that the biblical text has had over time and to identify psychological structures and dynamics. Texts contain objectifications of human experiences and serve to communicate by engaging not only the mind but also the heart, soul, and will of those who hear or read them. Psychological criticism considers all these dimensions.

Reader-response criticism attends closely to how readers actually read and describes the process of moving through a text, anticipating the next step and revising their understanding as their reading unfolds. Such processes can be conscious, but they also involve unconscious factors and processes in which the reader connects the present experience with previous emotional associations going beyond conscious thought.

Different readers bring different lenses to their reading; critics have come to acknowledge the impact that their social location and cultural background have in the process of interpretation. Along with those outer dimensions, readers also bring inner dynamics, including their personalities, experiences, family relationships and emotional responses, which all affect the process of reading.

Hermeneutics has long acknowledged the important role that a reader's presuppositions play in the process of interpretation. Along with those presuppositions, individuals also bring characteristic ways of taking in and processing information. Knowing those predispositions can help to explain why people come up with greatly differing understandings of the same text as demonstrated in H. Edward Everding's work on cognitive styles, or Leslie Francis and Andrew Village's study in hermeneutics and personality type.[10]

Unconscious factors in the interplay of reader and text can be pursued using methods developed in the practice of psychotherapy, such as free association or Jungian amplification and active imagination. Centuries of just such activities—known in such forms as midrash, preaching, art, music, and drama—give witness to the ways that the symbols, themes, characters, and movements of the Bible have continued to change and inspire readers and communities.

Another concept that can inform hermeneutics is the psychological dynamic of *transference*. In the therapeutic relationship, the patient unconsciously redirects his or her emotions from some previous relationship to the therapist. Transference can lead the person to idealize the therapist, to be erotically attracted to him or her, or to respond with untoward rage or dependency. Texts as well can stir up profound emotional responses, and a psychologically-informed hermeneutics may help to identify the dynamics of transference.

A final question with regard to hermeneutics concerns why and how the Bible actually catalyzes a response from the reader. Different psychological models offer suggestions as to what goes on in the apprehension of the text. Insights from cognitive learning theory can help us understand how texts help to create mental images that can serve as models and motivations for an individual to change his or her behavior. Cognitive mapping processes might inform us as to how the biblical worldview is incorporated into a person's ways of perceiving and organizing reality.

Depth psychological approaches can highlight unconscious aspects of the interaction. For example, object relations theory looks to the ways in which the developing mind internalizes important individuals and things in the surrounding world as structures within the mind, and subsequently filters later experiences and encounters through those "objects." Jungian psychology would affirm the role of archetypes in reading. Stories, symbols, and movements within the text are not only expressions of the psyches of the authors or compilers, but also continue to resonate deeply within the psyche of the reader. Symbols may serve a compensatory function, balancing the wholeness of the psyche within the reader or his or her community, or may unfold into further possibilities for consciousness.

The methods and perspectives of psychological biblical criticism are astonishingly varied. The findings of psycholinguistics and studies of memory have been used to examine oral processes and their development into written language. "Split-brain" studies of how the two hemispheres of the brain function differently—the left brain dealing with language, time, logic and analysis, and the right brain with art, imagination, and spatial and nonverbal activities—inform how the Bible is experienced and integrated. Behavioral concepts of positive and negative reinforcement have been used to analyze the dynamics of reward and punishment in examples like the Deuteronomic Code.

Freudian approaches seek to examine unconscious dynamics in the minds of authors, characters in the text, and readers. Convinced that myths and legends are a form of unconscious expression akin to dreams, Freudian critics have used the tools of dream analysis to uncover unconscious psychodynamics hidden beneath the surface meanings of the texts. Freudian analysis has been applied not only to the characters in the Bible, identifying their motivations and flaws, but also to the reader's interaction with those characters.

Jung's analytical psychology has proved particularly sympathetic to religious expression, and its concepts of archetypes and the ways they are expressed in symbols, myth, and dreams have served to explore biblical texts. The images, symbols, personalities, and stories of the Bible can be seen and developed as archetypal expressions that invite investigation. The cycle of individuation, that characteristic path by which a person moves into psychological maturity and wholeness, appears again and again.

Jung's theory of personality, which identifies characteristic ways by which people perceive the world around them and then process and evaluate their information and experience, has not only helped to explain why people read particular texts differently, but has also anticipated the kinds of readings that might result. Techniques of amplification and active imagination, which allow symbols and stories to develop and live onward as they find expression in new forms, offer additional tools for getting at deeper dimensions of the text.

Other psychological theories trace the development of personality, cognitive ability, and relational abilities, or examine how people relate psychologically to one another in particular contexts such as families or communities. They explore how human beings set goals and exercise will, find meaning or grieve its loss, deal with disaster or trauma, and experience anger or compassion. Wherever these attitudes, actions, or reactions cross paths with the Bible, psychological criticism can help to identify, describe, and illuminate the psychic processes at work.

RELATION TO OTHER METHODS

We have already noted that psychological biblical criticism is not a method per se, but a particular sensitivity to psychological dynamics at work in the text. In this respect, it can be compared to feminist criticism. Feminist criticism is not defined by a single methodology, but by a concern for the political, social, cultural, and economic forces that impact the lives of women. Feminist criticism might focus on individual figures in the Bible, the dynamics of interaction within stories, implicit social structures and ideologies that frame women's roles, and the ways that the interpretation of the Bible has affected women for good or ill across the centuries.

Psychological criticism likewise has resonances with social-scientific criticism, which employs the tools of sociology and anthropology to explore the texts. Social-scientific criticism uses models of social interaction developed in the contemporary world to analyze social phenomena that appear in the Bible or shape its traditions. Like psychology, sociology deals with human behavior. However, it deals with group behavior, which is often more visible and accessible than the inner worlds of individuals. There are areas where the two fields overlap—there are branches of social psychology that focus on group interactions, and some sociological theories address issues of conceptual worlds, identity development, and deviant behavior that are closely connected to individuals. Both approaches share concerns about the reliability of the text as a resource for their particular field, competence with the models used for analysis, and validity of those models in dealing with the Bible.

Many critical approaches include implicit psychological models of thinking, learning, and relating within their systems. Rhetorical and structuralist criticism deal with the structures of communication and language, considering how language actually works to persuade an audience or how the elements within a language system work together to convey meaning. All these involve psychological processes of perception, cognition, and decision making. Reader-response methods seek to describe how readers construct meaning as they move through a text. Practitioners of this method often trace their own cognitive processes in reading a text by way of illustration. Psychological criticism seeks to make explicit and systematic what these other approaches only hint at.

EXAMPLE: GENESIS 2 AND 3

The story of the creation of human beings and the events in the garden of Eden found in Genesis 2:4b–3:24 has attracted much attention from biblical scholars of all kinds over the years. Something about the way it has been, and continues to be, an elemental story in Western culture and imagination suggests that unconscious depths are at work. It deals with fundamental issues of human existence: obedience and disobedience, sexuality and vulnerability, a sense of loss. It touches on relationships—between God and humanity, between man and woman, and between human beings and the created world. The symbols of forbidden fruit, the tempting serpent, the first man and woman reappear often in literature and in art ranging from the Sistine Chapel to the daily comic strip. The story has made a profound connection with readers through the centuries.

Critics of many different theoretical orientations have sought to illuminate the psychological dimensions of Genesis 2–3.[11] For the purposes of illustration, we will focus primarily on the insights into the tale offered from a developmental perspective.[12]

Developmental psychology as elaborated by Erik Erikson argues that there are distinctive stages of psychosocial development that are typical of human beings as they move from infancy through childhood and adolescence into adulthood. They seem to be essentially universal across cultures, as they are based in the child's growing cognitive, social, and psychological capacities. The garden narrative of Genesis 2 and 3 offers some notable parallels to those stages, marked off by transitional passages. In developmental terms, the story is about moving from infancy into adulthood.

After creating the human being, God places him into a garden whose name means "pleasant." It is full of trees, pleasant to look at and good to eat. Two trees are singled out: the tree of life, representing the lushness of infancy, and the tree of knowing. "Knowing" in Hebrew tradition carries intellectual, experiential, and sexual overtones that have yet to unfold. This infancy section is marked with the description of the four rivers flowing out of the garden, an image of unrestrained life watering the world.

Movement into childhood begins with hearing the prohibition against eating (too soon?) from the tree of knowing. The result will be "death," though the full meaning of that death is yet to be seen.

It is not good for this new creation to be alone; developing a capacity for relationship is one of the key tasks of maturation. God brings various animals to the man so that he can name them. Naming involves the essential task of speech and developing language, an important step in making relationship possible. Naming further requires the man to make distinctions between the animals and between animals and himself. These are important abilities for childhood cognitive development and forming a capacity for reasoning. The man is beginning to develop his identity by differentiation from others, and with that new identity he can and must find new ways to relate to others.

The creation of the woman represents the growing awareness of gender differentiation, as well. Original unconscious feelings of oneness are now being challenged by new-found separation and personal identity. This section ends with a comment on marriage, a rite of passage that foreshadows a future entry into adulthood. However, the man and woman are not yet ready for such a step; they are still unashamed of their nakedness, still living in a childlike world.

Up to this point growth has been initiated only by God, but now another figure enters the scene. The serpent has a dual role of representing life and renewal (the serpent sheds its skin and becomes a new creature) and the threat of death. The serpent serves now as an emblem of wisdom, which can be life-affirming or life-threatening. The woman is the one first challenged by the serpent to take another step toward independence. This may be because girls generally develop more quickly than boys. The serpent's question ("Did God say . . . ?") challenges her to sort through her grasp of the situation and to make decisions about what to do next.

In ancient Israel, the capacity to know good and evil is essential for moral agency. Discernment is the first requirement for doing good. When the couple eats the fruit, what dies is not their physical bodies, but their immature perceptions of the world. They have entered adolescence, with all its promise and terrors. Childish ways of being have now passed away to make room for more adequate understanding. As their eyes are opened, they become aware of their nakedness—their psychological vulnerability, defenselessness, and shame. Ego identity in adolescence is fragile, and in their heightened new self-awareness they hurry to cover their nakedness with whatever may serve the purpose.

God reenters the picture and draws the man and woman out of hiding with questions that again require them to consider their actions and the consequences. Neither is yet ready to accept responsibility; the man is defensive, and attempts to deflect blame onto God for creating the woman. The woman, in turn, seeks to deflect the blame onto the serpent. This is evidence that their newly gained consciousness is still not fully developed; they cannot yet stand on their own.

Identity formation in adolescence involves a growing awareness of the options in life and the realities that must be encountered as a person moves toward adulthood. In the section that follows, God lays out the closely intertwined potentials and limitations on adult life. The stage of adulthood involves the tasks of generativity, work to care for and multiply life. The woman's potential for sexuality, pregnancy, and childbearing, linked to her sexual desire for her husband, will of necessity bring with it the prospect of pain and suffering. The man's potential links him again to the earth, and involves the work of cultivation, producing food to sustain life. This prospect, too, brings with it the inherent requirement for hard labor and a recognition that no matter how hard he may work, his efforts may not accomplish what he desires. The earth itself can produce not only food, but also useless vegetation. When at last he dies, the man will return to the ground again.

To one who has previously known only the carefree world of childhood, these realities may well appear as "curses." The many cares and concerns of adult life are inseparable from the new potentials that adulthood offers. New possibilities bring new responsibilities; what the child could blissfully ignore, the adult must now weigh and tend to.

It is at this point that the man names his wife Eve. Naming in the Bible often marks significant changes of personality or identity, and Eve's new name, interpreted as meaning "living," is closely linked to her sexual maturity and potential for motherhood. She has gained her own identity as an individual.

God, like a wise parent, equips Adam and Eve for their inevitable departure from their childhood home by clothing them with animal skins. God acknowledges that humanity has developed a capacity for discernment, for recognizing right and wrong and for making choices. They also now have the ability to produce and care for life—both children and crops. They have become "like one of us" (3:22). It is only when the man and the woman have achieved this level of development that it becomes impossible for them to eat from the tree of life. Returning to that tree, which represents a childish, unconscious union with the world, would be a retreat from reality, a return to now inadequate ways of thinking and perceiving. So God drives them out of the pleasant garden and blocks the path to the regressive tree of life. Once a person has moved into consciousness, there is no going back.

LIMITATIONS OF THE APPROACH

Psychological perspectives offer powerful tools for dealing with the Bible in all its manifestations. Yet they must be employed with care and informed by other methods of biblical interpretation so as to separate psychological aspects of the texts from those that arise from literary convention or theological constructs. They must also be used with sensitivity to the changes in human behavior over time and culture.

The most common charge leveled against the approach is that of "psychologizing," that is, attempting to force a text to fit the Procrustean bed of the interpreter's pet theory. As noted above, every human action has multiple factors that shape it, and even within psychological perspectives there are a number of ways to explain human behaviors. No attempt to reduce the text to a single dimension—whether psychological, historical, or ideological—can be considered adequate for interpretation.

A second common objection is that psychology is a project only of recent times, and attempts to apply contemporary categories to ancient phenomena are inappropriate and misleading. Critics point out that much of modern psychology focuses on the consciousness and experience of the individual, while the world of the Bible was organized socially and communally. A person in that world was not concerned about their own needs or problems but found their identity and sense of self in the group.

While this objection may alert the critic to the dangers of applying a psychological viewpoint without due reflection, changes in the cultural or historical valences of symbols, stories, and activities can be taken into account so that the object of study is placed firmly within its proper context. In addition, more recent developments in psychology have focused on systems of social interaction, construction of identity through relationship, and other group-based ways of looking at human experience.

Basic to all forms of biblical criticism is a belief that there is continuity between ancient writers and modern interpreters. Without some commonality of language, experience, and modes of expression, we would be unable to make any sense out of ancient writings at all. The well-established practice of looking to the symbols, myths, and legends of the ancient world as aids to understanding the Bible witnesses to our belief that modern readers, with modern sensibilities, can nonetheless bridge the distance between our time and theirs.

The key to appropriate use of psychological criticism lies in finding a good fit between the chosen psychological theory and the aspect of the Bible under study. It is essential that critics understand that the Bible is a written text, not a person, and cannot simply be psychoanalyzed as if it were a patient on the couch. They should be aware of exactly what it is they are studying—whether it lies behind, within, or in front of the text—and be willing to use additional tools of historical, literary, and cultural analysis to set the context. They need to work at an appropriate level of generalization, acknowledging that the material at hand is limited in its extent and detail.

Ultimately, it is clear that a reading of the Bible that ignores the psychological dynamics that are unavoidably involved in any human activity is no more complete than one that disregards the historical, literary, or ideological dimensions of the text. Psychological biblical criticism continues to prove its value in the field.

KEY TERMS

active imagination/amplification. Methods developed in Jungian psychology in relation to working with dreams. In active imagination, the dreamer recalls the setting and movement of the dream and then imaginatively allows it to unfold further than its original form. Amplification involves expanding the symbols of a dream or myth by directed associations with other symbols or stories.

archetype/archetypal image. An inherited pattern of structuring experience within the unconscious psyche. Archetypes are the source of archetypal images and symbols that manifest themselves in dreams and myths. Archetypes are preexisting patterns within the unconscious psyche that serve to structure and interpret experience. Jung believed they were both inherited and universal. Archetypes cannot be directly known but express themselves through the images and symbols often found in dreams and myths, such as the Hero, the Wise Old Man, or the Mother.

behavioral psychology. A psychological approach that limits itself to studies of observable behavior, focusing on mechanisms of stimulus and response.

cognitive psychology. A psychological approach that studies thinking. It explores the workings of such mental processes as memory, learning, decision making, and problem solving.

conscious/consciousness. Awareness of one's own thoughts, mind, or motivations.

depth psychology. A psychological approach that understands personality and behavior in relation to unconscious dynamics. Freudian psychoanalysis, Jung's analytical psychology, and object relations theories are all examples of depth psychologies.

developmental psychology. A psychological approach that deals with the psychological development of the individual from childhood through adulthood.

individuation. In Jungian psychology, the process of psychological development into a unique individual and movement toward psychic wholeness.

object relations theory. A psychological approach that focuses on how individuals develop by internalizing representations of important people and objects. These internalizations are the "objects" through which the individual relates to the world.

personality. The mental, emotional, and social attributes of an individual that form an organized mode of behavior. Several theorists have proposed systems for identifying and classifying particular patterns or *personality types*.

psychē. Greek word for "life," "breath," or "soul," used to refer to the human mind or inner spirit. In *depth psychology* it is used to refer to the whole of an individual's inner being, both conscious and unconscious.

psychoanalysis/psychoanalytic psychology. The field of psychology developed by Sigmund Freud, also known as Freudian psychology. It centers on analyzing unconscious dynamics in individuals and treating them by bringing them to consciousness.

psychodynamics. Characteristic modes of interaction among psychological factors, often unconscious, which result in outwardly observable behavior.

psychologizing. Interpreting texts in terms of psychological issues only, imposing a chosen psychological framework onto the text, or reducing the elements of the text to an illustration of a psychological theory.

transference. A process in which a person's emotional response to one person is unconsciously shifted to different person. The object of transference is often the therapist.

unconscious. Those aspects of the psyche of which an individual is not aware, but which nonetheless affect behavior.

NOTES

1. Franz J. Delitzsch, *A System of Biblical Psychology*, trans. R. E. Wallis (Grand Rapids: Baker Book House, 1966).
2. M. Scott Fletcher, *The Psychology of the New Testament* (New York: Hodder and Stoughton, 1912).
3. Walter Wink, *The Bible in Human Transformation: Toward a New Paradigm for Biblical Study* (Philadelphia: Fortress, 1973); *Transforming Bible Study: A Leader's Guide* (Nashville: Abingdon, 1980); *Naming the Powers: The Language of Power in the New Testament* (Philadelphia: Fortress, 1984).
4. Wayne G. Rollins, *Jung and the Bible* (Atlanta: John Knox, 1983), 128.
5. Wilhelm Wuellner and Robert Leslie, *The Surprising Gospel: Intriguing Psychological Insights from the New Testament* (Nashville: Abingdon, 1984).
6. Gerd Theissen, *Psychologische Aspekte paulinischer Theologie* (Göttingen: Vandenhoeck und Ruprecht, 1983); ET: *Psychological Aspects of Pauline Theology* (Philadelphia: Fortress, 1987). Eugen Drewermann, *Die Wahrheit der Formen: Traum, Mythos, Märchen, Sage, und Legende* (vol. 1 of *Tiefenpsychologie und Exegese*; Olten: Walter-Verlag, 1984); *Die Wahrheit der Werke und der Worte: Wunder, Vision, Weissagung, Apokalypse, Geschichte, Gleichnis* (vol. 2 of *Tiefenpsychologie und Exegese*; Olten: Walter-Verlag, 1984).
7. This tripartite division of the text is based on the work of Paul Ricoeur and Sandra Schneiders.
8. Wayne G. Rollins, *Soul and Psyche: The Bible in Psychological Perspective* (Minneapolis: Augsburg Fortress, 1999).
9. David Halperin, *Seeking Ezekiel: Text and Psychology* (University Park, PA: Penn State Press, 1993). Barbara Leung Lai, *Through the "I" Window: The Inner Life of Characters in the Hebrew Bible* (Sheffield: Sheffield Phoenix Press, 2011). Terrance Callan, *Psychological Perspectives on the Life of Paul: An Application of the Methodology of Gerd Theissen* (Lewiston/Queenston/Lampeter: Edwin Mellen, 1990).
10. H. Edward Everding, et al., *Viewpoints: Perspectives of Faith and Christian Nurture* (Harrisburg, PA: Trinity Press International, 1998). Leslie Francis and Andrew Village, *Preaching with All Our Souls: A Study in Hermeneutics and Psychological Type* (New York/London: Continuum, 2008).
11. For a more detailed study, see D. Andrew Kille, *Psychological Biblical Criticism* (Minneapolis: Fortress, 2001).
12. This section is based primarily on Lyn Bechtel, "Developmental Psychology in Biblical Studies," in J. H. Ellens and W. G. Rollins, eds., *Psychology and the Bible: A New Way to Read the Scriptures*, vol. 1, *From Freud to Kohut* (Westport, CT: Greenwood-Praeger, 2004), 119–38.

FOR FURTHER READING

Blessing, Kamila. *Families of the Bible: A New Perspective.* Psychology, Religion, and Spirituality. Santa Barbara, CA: Praeger, 2010.
Bufford, Rodger K. *The Human Reflex: Behavioral Psychology in Biblical Perspective.* San Francisco: Harper & Row, 1981.
Carroll, Robert P. *When Prophecy Failed: Cognitive Dissonance in the Prophetic Traditions of the Old Testament.* New York: Seabury, 1979.
Edinger, Edward F. *The Bible and the Psyche: Individuation Symbolism in the Old Testament.* Studies in Jungian Psychology by Jungian Analysts. Toronto: Inner City Books, 1986.
Ellens, J. Harold, and Wayne G. Rollins, eds. *Psychology and the Bible: A New Way to Read the Scriptures.* 4 vols. Westport, CT: Greenwood-Praeger, 2004.
Francis, Leslie J. *Personality Type and Scripture: Exploring Mark's Gospel.* London: Mowbray, 1997.
Johnson, Cedric B. *The Psychology of Biblical Interpretation.* Grand Rapids: Zondervan, 1983.
Kille, D. Andrew. *Psychological Biblical Criticism.* Guides to Biblical Scholarship, Old Testament Series. Minneapolis: Fortress, 2001.
Kunkel, Fritz. *Creation Continues: A Psychological Interpretation of the Gospel of Matthew.* New York: Paulist, 1987.
McGann, Diarmuid. *The Journeying Self: The Gospel of Mark through a Jungian Perspective.* New York: Paulist, 1985.
Miller, David L., ed. *Jung and the Interpretation of the Bible.* New York: Continuum, 1995.
Newheart, Michael Willett. *"My Name Is Legion": The Story and Soul of the Gerasene Demoniac.* Collegeville, MN: The Liturgical Press, 2004.
Os, Bas van. *Psychological Analyses and the Historical Jesus: New Ways to Explore Christian Origins.* London: T. & T. Clark, 2011.
Rashkow, Ilona N. *Taboo or Not Taboo: Sexuality and Family in the Hebrew Bible.* Minneapolis, MN: Fortress, 2000.
Rollins, Wayne G. *Jung and the Bible.* Atlanta: John Knox, 1983.
———. *Soul and Psyche: The Bible in Psychological Perspective.* Minneapolis: Fortress, 1999.
Rollins, Wayne G., and D. Andrew Kille, eds. *Psychological Insight into the Bible: Texts and Readings.* Grand Rapids: Eerdmans, 2007.
Sanford, John A. *The Man Who Wrestled with God: Light from the Old Testament on the Psychology of Individuation.* Revised and updated ed. New York: Paulist, 1987.
———. *Mystical Christianity: A Psychological Commentary on the Gospel of John.* New York: Crossroad, 1993.
Schwartz, Matthew B., and Kalman J. Kaplan. *Biblical Stories for Psychotherapy and Counseling: A Sourcebook.* New York: Haworth Pastoral Press, 2004.
Scroggs, Robin. *Paul for a New Day.* Philadelphia: Fortress, 1977.
Theissen, Gerd. *Psychological Aspects of Pauline Theology.* Philadelphia: Fortress, 1987.
Zeligs, Dorothy. *Psychoanalysis and the Bible: A Study in Depth of Seven Leaders.* New York: Bloch, 1974.

Chapter 9

Queer Criticism

KEN STONE

In 1995, two professors of English, Lauren Berlant and Michael Warner, contributed a queer little essay in a journal published by the Modern Language Association of America. Though their article is titled "What Does Queer Theory Teach Us about X?" Berlant and Warner avoid giving definitions of "queer theory." Instead, they propose the phrase "queer commentary" as an alternative to "queer theory," partly to indicate that queer criticism (a term they also use) involves more than academic theorizing. Even then, they explicitly refuse "to define, purify, puncture, sanitize, or otherwise entail the emerging queer commentary." Rather, Berlant and Warner emphasize the experimental nature, the "mongrelized genres" and "varied shapes," of queer criticism.[1] By using an alternative phrase, "queer commentary," to unsettle what had already become in their field the more common term, "queer theory," Berlant and Warner attempt to keep alive queer criticism's challenge to habit and convention, not only in the realms of sex and politics, but also in the academy.

The phrase "queer commentary" certainly did not supplant "queer theory" in the field of English literature. Nevertheless, it has an obvious appeal for any reflection on the role of queer criticism in biblical studies, where "commentary" has a long history as a term for conventional scholarship. By modifying the respectable term "commentary" with the less reputable term "queer," "queer commentary" evokes a mode of biblical criticism that partners established scholarly questions and assumptions with new, and potentially controversial, ones.[2] It would not be quite right to call the resulting queer criticism a method, if by method one means a set of agreed upon steps that reliably lead disciplined readers to shared conclusions. However, queer criticism can be understood as a kind of interpretive sensibility or style of reading, which shapes particular interpretations of texts to varying degrees.

Although it will be important to keep in mind the heterogeneity of queer commentary that Berlant and Warner emphasize, in this chapter the most significant characteristics of queer criticism include the following:

1. Queer criticism calls attention to sexual practice and gender, often in relation to one another, as key sites for the interpretation of cultural, social, and textual meanings and practices.
2. Queer criticism emphasizes the fact that meanings and practices associated with sex, gender, and kinship vary significantly across cultures and histories, or even within a single culture. This emphasis contrasts with all attempts to stabilize the meanings and practices associated with sex, gender, or kinship by grounding them in a supposedly unchanging nature, assumed cultural universals, or religious revelation.
3. Working under the influence of thinkers and ideas associated with "queer theory," queer criticism tends to be suspicious of organizing sexual and gender meanings too rigidly around stable binary oppositions such as male and female, masculine and feminine, or heterosexual and homosexual. Instead, queer criticism emphasizes the fluidity and unpredictability of gender, sexual desire, and sexual practice, as well as the instability of the binary oppositions that are thought to structure them.
4. The tendency for readers (including scholars) to universalize a particular set of modern, Western norms for sexual practice, gender roles, and family structures is analyzed critically by queer criticism as "heteronormative." At its most basic, "heteronormativity" is the institutionalized preference for opposite-sex sexual relationships over same-sex sexual relationships. However, a number of other assumptions and practices are also associated with heteronormativity, including the beliefs that binary gender roles follow naturally from biological sex; that sexual desire and sexual practice follow from gender roles and/or biological sex; that an individual's biological sex, gender roles, sexual desires, or sexual practices are consistent over time; that kinship units ideally form around a monogamous, opposite-sex couple; and that sexual activity is most appropriately aimed at romantic love, reproduction, and childbirth. Although heteronormativity may appear to be self-evidently good to its supporters, queer criticism notes that heteronormativity often leads to

the marginalization or persecution of individuals and populations who fall short of its ideals.
5. As part of its attempt to analyze and undermine heteronormativity, queer criticism focuses on examples of cultural phenomena, practices, and individuals that do not conform to heteronormative ideals. While many such examples may be marginal, queer criticism assumes that even dominant or canonical figures and texts will sometimes exhibit characteristics that do not align completely with heteronormative presuppositions. In other words, heteronormativity is never as coherent as its supporters claim. Attention to incoherence in sexual or gender matters is important because such incoherence may point toward possibilities for resisting or transforming heteronormativity in the present or the future.
6. Queer criticism increasingly explores the ways in which norms and practices for gender, sex, and kinship are intertwined with other sorts of norms and practices, including those pertaining to nation, ethnicity, race, and religion. Moreover, queer criticism may extend its resistance to norms for sex, gender, and kinship to other types of norms, such as norms for reading and scholarship.

These characteristics of queer criticism are by no means exclusive to it. Indeed, the boundaries between queer criticism and other types of criticism are porous. Queer criticism of biblical texts, for example, can overlap with several other types of biblical criticism, including not only historical and literary criticism but also feminist criticism, sociological and anthropological criticism, ideological criticism, and poststructuralist or deconstructive criticism. Moreover, not every example of queer criticism will include all the features listed above. Just as queer criticism rejects monolithic and normalizing definitions of sex, gender, and kinship in favor of heterogeneous ones, it may avoid monolithic definitions of queer criticism and emphasize the diversity of queer approaches that do or could exist. Nevertheless, readings of biblical texts that are shaped by several of the features listed above can usefully be referred to as queer criticism.

In the remainder of this chapter, I will elaborate on the sketch I have just given of queer criticism. After summarizing several trends from outside of biblical scholarship that have shaped contemporary queer studies, I will turn to a reading of Genesis 18 and 19 to consider questions that might interest queer commentary.

INFLUENCES ON QUEER BIBLICAL CRITICISM

Queer biblical criticism is influenced by several academic approaches that developed outside of religious studies, including lesbian and gay studies and queer theory. Although these approaches first emerged in a significant way in the North American academy during the 1990s, a number of earlier academic developments paved the way for them. One of the most important of these developments was the rise of feminist studies, which has produced a large body of sophisticated analyses of gender and kinship across a range of academic disciplines. Questions about sexuality and its relation to gender have been at the center of much feminist research. However, this research has not led to a single feminist approach to sexuality, but rather to multiple feminist perspectives. Several of these feminist approaches to sexuality have been crucial for the subsequent development of queer studies.[3]

One analytical tool that has been influential within feminism and important for some queer studies is the distinction between sex and gender. According to the conventional terms of this distinction, "sex" refers to biological differences between male and female while "gender" refers to social or cultural differences between "masculine" and "feminine" behaviors, roles, or identifications. The distinction was first proposed by psychiatrists as a way of accounting for individuals of one biological sex who identified with a different gender. However, many feminists use the sex/gender distinction to analyze women's oppression while rejecting the attempt to ground such oppression in supposed biological facts. The mechanisms for the subordination of women do not lie simply at the level of individual prejudice, but rather are social and structural. As anthropologist Gayle Rubin argued, the "'sex/gender system' is the set of arrangements by which a society transforms biological sexuality into products of human activity, and in which these transformed sexual needs are satisfied." Rubin also noted that these arrangements represent "the part of social life that is the locus of the oppression of women, of sexual minorities, and of certain aspects of human personality within individuals."[4] Rubin herself later insisted that many sexual matters were inadequately understood if they were reduced to gender questions and that it was sometimes important to "separate gender and sexuality analytically" in order to "think" some sexual questions.[5] This separation allowed queer studies to examine a wider range of sexual practices, including controversial practices such as sadomasochism, from a number of diverse perspectives and not only through feminist lenses.[6] However, the original sex/gender distinction has also been crucial for gender-related analyses within queer studies. For example, the distinction between biological sex and social gender makes it possible to analyze situations in which biological sex and social gender are combined in unconventional ways, as in Judith Halberstam's study of "female masculinity" or "masculinity without men."[7]

Equally important for the development of queer studies were the movements for gay and lesbian liberation and the growth of openly gay populations in urban areas, particularly in the United States and Western Europe. Such movements both nourished and served as objects of analysis for scholars who pioneered the historical and social-scientific study of homosexuality.[8] These historical and sociological analyses also laid the groundwork for a rethinking of gay "identity" that became important for queer studies. While scholars were able to find a wealth of information pertaining to homosexual practice and gender nonconformity, their research made it apparent that modern Western gay and lesbian identities were significantly shaped, and even in some ways made possible, by developments and conditions that were specific to the societies in which they appeared.[9] Even if same-sex desires and practices were found nearly everywhere, gay and lesbian identities as they currently exist in the West were not.

This conclusion was underscored by the work of anthropologists and historians who investigated the practices and meanings associated with same-sex sexual contact, both in contemporary non-Western societies and in the distant past. For example, ethnographic studies of Papua New Guinea revealed that young males in some societies became men through a rite of passage that required them to ingest the semen of older males in practices of oral intercourse.[10] Anthropologists working in Latin America noted that no shame or identity classification accrued automatically to men who consistently played the active role in same-sex intercourse.[11] Classics scholars drew attention to the fact that, in ancient Greek societies, particular types of sexual contact between males were tolerated so long as they followed certain protocols of gender, status, and penetration. Specifically, adult male citizens were expected to be the active, penetrating partner in sexual intercourse while the role of passive partner could be played by women, male adolescents, male slaves, or other males of subordinate status.[12] These sorts of studies showed that, while same-sex sexual contact was more widespread than has often been realized, such contact has frequently taken forms that are different from the forms associated with modern gay and lesbian identities.

A related argument was made by the French philosopher Michel Foucault. Foucault called attention to the increasing concern with sexuality in modern medical, psychiatric, educational, and legal discourses. In Foucault's view, these discourses shape what we understand as "sexuality" through productive mechanisms of power and knowledge such as observation, classification, diagnosis, and the state management of populations. Partly as an effect of these power/knowledge mechanisms, sexuality came to be conceptualized in the West as that area of life in which the "truth" of one's self can most reliably be deciphered. This development had particularly significant consequences for conceptualizing homosexuality. In Foucault's words, homosexuality came to be understood "less as a habitual sin than as a singular nature. . . . The sodomite had been a temporary aberration; the homosexual was now a species."[13] Like the anthropological and historical research noted above, but with emphases peculiar to his philosophical project, Foucault's work had the effect of making distinctions between assumptions about homosexuality that are characteristic of modern Western societies and assumptions about same-sex relations found in other times and places.

Cumulatively, these developments made it possible to speak of the "social construction" of homosexuality by the early 1990s.[14] They also contributed to the birth of the new interdisciplinary field of lesbian and gay studies.[15] However, the conclusions being reached within that field had paradoxical results. Although the historical and sociological specification of conditions for the emergence of modern lesbian and gay identities appeared initially to have consequences primarily for our understanding of homosexuality, the study of this problem had an impact on the understanding of opposite sex relations as well. After all, dominant notions of "heterosexuality" require for their existence notions of a coherent "homosexuality," in relation to which notions of "heterosexuality" are differentially defined. Thus, the critical reexamination of homosexuality had the effect of undermining binary distinctions between homosexuality and heterosexuality. As a consequence of the study of lesbian and gay communities and identities, it even became possible to speak about "the invention of heterosexuality."[16] The point behind this phrase is not that opposite-sex relations did not exist prior to such an "invention." Rather, the point is that "heterosexuality" as it exists in the modern West is associated with a range of specific meanings and practices that are not identical to the meanings and practices associated with opposite sex relations in other times and places. For example, while heterosexuality today is often understood to preclude the likelihood that a male who has sexual relations with a woman will also enjoy sexual relations with other males, such an understanding would be quite foreign to ancient Greece, where it seems to have been assumed that some men enjoyed sexual relations with both adult females and male youths. Such men could not be classified either as homosexual or heterosexual, according to conventional uses of those terms.

This sort of deconstruction of the opposition between homosexual and heterosexual came to be associated during the 1990s with queer theory. Although the phrase "queer theory," coined by feminist theorist Teresa de Lauretis, resists easy definition, queer theory often takes its starting point from a critical interrogation of the conceptual categories that shape much thinking about sexuality and gender.[17] This interrogation is generally not understood to be neutral, but rather as engaged in resistance to heteronormative assumptions and practices. For example David Halperin, in a book about Foucault and queer politics, argues that "queer . . . acquires its meaning from its oppositional relation to the norm. Queer is by definition whatever is at odds with the normal, the legitimate, the dominant."[18] For Halperin, as for some other queer theorists, queer subjectivity and agency are not necessarily coterminous with homosexual object-choice; and they cannot be assumed to exist simply because an individual self-identifies as lesbian, gay, or bisexual (though Halperin himself, like many queer theorists, does identify as gay). Such self-identification may offer an opportunity for queer subjectivity, but a movement or analysis is in Halperin's view "genuinely *queer* insofar as it is broadly oppositional."[19] Thus, for Halperin, a queer politics or analysis does not acquire its shape from an assumed homosexual identity, but rather from the process of resisting structures of knowledge and power associated with heteronormativity.

Eve Kosofsky Sedgwick, one of the thinkers most associated with queer theory, has pointed out that the semantic background of the word "queer" includes such meanings as "across" or "athwart." Sedgwick therefore uses the word to indicate movement "across genders, across sexualities, across genres, across 'perversions.'"[20] Although Sedgwick refrains from any narrow definition of the word, she suggests "that 'queer' can refer to: the open mesh of possibilities, gaps, overlaps, dissonances and resonances, lapses and excesses of meaning when the constituent elements of anyone's gender, of anyone's sexuality aren't made (or *can't be* made) to signify monolithically."[21] Thus queer studies do not simply emphasize the fact that the meanings and practices associated with sex and gender are culture- or society-specific. They also note that, even within a particular culture or society, the meanings and practices associated with gender and sexual practice are heterogeneous. As Sedgwick points out, social constructions of sexuality do not always follow one another in an orderly progression, as some historical studies of homosexuality have implied. Careful attention shows rather that "unexpectedly plural, varied, and contradictory" meanings and practices can coexist.[22] Indeed, queer theory assumes that multiplicity and contradiction are found, not only within the same society, but often within the same person.

This emphasis on variation, multiplicity, and movement across binary oppositions is also characteristic of the work of Judith Butler, another thinker often associated with queer theory. In her influential book *Gender Trouble*, Butler notes that analytical distinctions between sex and gender, though allowing for recognition of the social interpretation of sexed bodies, still rely on underlying assumptions about binary distinctions between male and female bodies and gender identities that need to be reexamined critically, or "troubled." Butler therefore queries the self-evident nature of both gendered *and* sexed bodies, suggesting that "gender ought not to be conceived merely as the cultural inscription of meaning on a pregiven sex ... gender must also designate the very apparatus of production whereby the sexes themselves are established."[23] Although such claims are counterintuitive, Butler is led to them partly because assumptions about the two sexes often have the effect of privileging heterosexual relations. As Butler points out:

> "Intelligible" genders are those which in some sense institute and maintain relations of coherence and continuity among sex, gender, sexual practice, and desire. . . . The heterosexualization of desire requires and institutes the production of discrete and asymmetrical oppositions between "feminine" and "masculine," where these are understood as expressive attributes of "male" and "female." The cultural matrix through which gender identity has become intelligible requires that certain kinds of "identities" cannot "exist"—that is, those in which gender does not follow from sex and those in which the practices of desire do not "follow" from either sex or gender.[24]

In order to think about gender in an alternative way, Butler develops her influential "performative" theory of gender. Instead of understanding gender as a social interpretation of a supposedly substantive biological sex, Butler's theory of gender performativity argues that the illusory stability of gender and sex results from repeated and ritualized practices. These practices do not express stable truths of sex and gender. Rather, the impression of stability is produced by what Butler calls the "stylized repetition of acts." In Butler's words,

> ... the substantive effect of gender is performatively produced and compelled by the regulatory practices of gender performance. Hence ... gender

> proves to be performative—that is, constituting the identity it is purported to be. In this sense, gender is always a doing. . . . There is no gender identity behind the expressions of gender; that identity is performatively constituted by the very "expressions" that are said to be its results.[25]

Butler thus understands gender performativity as a temporal process in which gender norms are cited or repeated. One cannot simply get away from gender norms into a utopian, gender-free space. Rather, through ongoing citations and repetitions of gender norms, one "does" gender as what Butler calls "a practice of improvisation within a scene of constraint."[26]

At the same time, the ongoing repetition or citation of gender norms frequently results in occasions where sex, gender, sexual desire, and sexual practice are not aligned neatly in accordance with such norms. That is to say, "male" and "female" actors and speakers may act or speak in ways that stand in tension with, or contradict, the norms of "manhood" and "womanhood" to which, in a given context, "males" and "females" are supposed to conform. As Butler observes, gender "is an assignment which is never quite carried out according to expectation, whose addressee never quite inhabits the ideal s/he is compelled to approximate."[27] One task for queer criticism, then, is to call attention to the gaps that open up between, on the one hand, ideals and norms for sex, gender, and sexual practice; and, on the other hand, actual instances of gender performance and sexual activity. Much work in "transgender" queer criticism has grown out of such attention.

Theorists have also increasingly recognized that norms and meanings for sex and gender cannot be understood adequately without taking into account the ways in which they are structured by assumptions about race, ethnicity, nation, and class. Beliefs about "manly" or "womanly" behavior, including appropriate sexual behavior and kinship norms, vary according to the racial, ethnic, and class backgrounds of both the individuals who are being evaluated and the individuals who are making evaluations. Moreover, racism and classism are often structured through sexual stereotypes. The need to understand the articulation of sexuality and gender "in relation to race and . . . attendant differences of class or ethnic culture, generational, geographical, and socio-political differences" was noted already by de Lauretis in her foundational article on "queer theory."[28] While detailed analyses along these lines have only slowly become more common, it is now widely recognized that queer studies must move "across," or "queer," the lines that in the past artificially separated the study of gender and sexuality from the study of race, class, ethnicity, and nation.[29]

Although queer studies became an important component of cross-disciplinary work in the academy by the beginning of the twenty-first century, the role of queer studies within biblical studies has been far more limited. Nevertheless, a number of essays and volumes written by biblical scholars have now appeared that either use the word "queer" or build on queer theories. Perhaps not surprisingly, these queer readings of biblical texts exhibit both continuity and discontinuity with the wider realm of queer studies.

As I have noted elsewhere, interpreters of the Bible tend to use the word "queer" in at least two, partly overlapping, ways.[30] In some cases, "queer" is used to refer to a kind of social or communal location out of which certain readers interpret the Bible. Thus, Mona West argues that it is important "to add the voice of the gay/lesbian/bisexual and transgendered community (Queers) to those marginalized groups who are reading the Bible from particular social locations . . . ."[31] West goes on to suggest that new light is shed on biblical texts when they are subjected to "a Queer reading of the Bible."[32] A "queer reading of the Bible," according to this common use of the term, is an interpretation of the Bible produced by a reader from the "community" of "Queers."[33]

On the other hand, some interpretations of biblical texts are more explicitly concerned to reread biblical texts in the light of emphases and ideas found in nonbiblical academic queer studies. Consistent with the emphasis on the social construction of sexuality, such interpretations usually acknowledge that the biblical texts were written in a historical context containing ideas about gender, sexual practice, and kinship that are very different from the assumptions held by most readers of the Bible today. This point, of course, is also made by historical, feminist, and social-scientific interpretations of the Bible and its ancient contexts.[34] Going beyond such interpretations, however, queer criticism will look more intentionally for ways to use the insights of queer studies to "trouble" the use of the Bible as a buttress for heteronormativity. Although the resulting "Bible Trouble" can be accomplished in many different ways,[35] the emphasis in this style of queer criticism falls less on the "queer" community of particular readers of the Bible and more on the fact that certain parts of the Bible itself can be read as "queer." After all, coming as it does from that time prior to the emergence of modern systems of sex, gender, sexuality, and kinship, the Bible does not always cohere with heteronormative assumptions. By using queer theory to, in the words of Stuart Macwilliam, "subject" biblical texts and biblical interpretation "to queer scrutiny," queer criticism calls attention to unexpected configurations of sex, gender, and kinship in the Bible and its history of reception.[36]

For example, queer criticism might call attention to texts in which the opposition between male and female is less stable than readers generally acknowledge.[37] Recognizing that the Bible was written prior to the creation of the binary opposition between heterosexuality and homosexuality, queer criticism calls attention to texts with surprising possibilities for a homoerotic reading.[38] Adopting Rubin's concept of "benign sexual variation" and putting aside heteronormative notions of "proper" sexual behavior, queer criticism exposes biblical texts in which sexual activity exhibits characteristics that parallel practices that today are widely stigmatized, such as pornography, sadomasochism, or public sex.[39] Drawing on queer explorations of the interrelations among sexuality, gender, ethnicity, and race, queer criticism can show the ways in which ethnic boundaries in the Bible are both established and destabilized in relation to gender and sexual practice.[40] Or, drawing on recent interest in reception histories of the Bible, queer criticism can illustrate some of the unexpectedly queer ways in which biblical texts have been read in the past, juxtaposing traditional heteronormative readings with queer possibilities.[41] This list of possible directions for queer criticism by no means exhausts the types of projects that might result from queer biblical interpretation. Like queer studies more broadly, queer commentary on the Bible is heterogeneous and open-ended.

A QUEER READING OF GENESIS 18–19

In order to consider further what queer biblical criticism might look like, I want to turn at this point to a reading of Genesis 18 and 19. Although Genesis 19, and more specifically the story of Sodom, has become notorious as a kind of proof text for the condemnation of homosexuality, my focus here will not primarily be a reexamination of the Bible's attitude toward same-sex relations. The question of "what the Bible says about homosexuality," though interesting and important in itself, is arguably not the best starting point for a queer reading, since that question is often shaped by a set of social and religious debates that are premised on heteronormative assumptions. While the threat of male same-sex rape does play a role in Genesis 19, that role is best understood within a more complicated set of dynamics of sex, gender, kinship, and ethnicity.

In the book of Genesis, Abraham is, first and foremost, a father. His role as father is underscored in the text by the meaning given to his name (Gen. 17:5) and by the God who names him. It is underscored as well by the divine promise, made several times, that he will father many nations; and by the narration of his fathering of sons born to several women. It has been emphasized by generations of readers, including scholars, who single out fatherhood as a dominant theme of these stories by referring to them as "the patriarchal narratives." And it continues to permeate our culture today, whether through the singing of popular songs about "Father Abraham" or through more solemn but increasingly routine references to Judaism, Christianity, and Islam as "Abrahamic religions."

If Abraham is a father, however, he is also a man. Although biblical scholars paid little attention to biblical constructions of manhood and masculinity until recently, that seems to be changing.[42] While masculinity studies and queer studies are not identical, queer criticism shares with masculinity studies an interest in constructions of manhood found in particular texts even as it goes on to note that such constructions are not fixed or stable.[43] Thus an initial focus for a queer reading of Genesis 18 and 19 is the construction of manhood, including Abraham's manhood, in those chapters.

The link between Abraham's role as father and his characterization as a man is already clear in chapter 17. Because this chapter comes from a different Pentateuchal source than Genesis 18 and 19, the stories are not always read together. However, a reader of Genesis 18 who reads the book sequentially will just have read an extended account of God's covenant promise to Abraham in chapter 17.

This priestly version of the covenant emphasizes Abraham's role as a father of many nations. However, it also associates Abraham's fatherhood with his physical maleness by emphasizing his circumcision, referring explicitly to his foreskin several times; and by describing Abraham's descendants as "seed," a word with specifically masculine connotations.[44] Although such language is not rare in the Bible, here it has the effect of calling attention to Abraham's manhood immediately prior to Genesis 18.

But what type of man will Abraham turn out to be? In asking that question, queer criticism recognizes that there is no automatic link between Abraham's physical maleness and his behavior as a character. Manhood is something that Abraham must perform. This attention to Abraham's performance of manhood is consistent with Butler's theory of gender performativity noted above. While Butler's concept of performativity is more complex than the mere use of the word "performance" indicates, the word can focus our reading of biblical texts in specific ways, as it does for example in Cynthia Chapman's examination of "masculinity as a cultural performance" in Assyrian and biblical prophetic texts.[45] There is also room for dialogue here between queer criticism and anthropological criticism; for the performance of masculinities is emphasized in anthropological studies of manhood that predate Butler's work. Indeed, Butler's *Gender Trouble* was influenced by anthropological research on "drag queens," men impersonating women for a living.[46] The importance of "performing" manhood is also underscored by anthropological research on honor and shame in Mediterranean and Middle Eastern contexts, which has proven useful for biblical scholars.[47] For example, Michael Herzfeld notes that, in certain Mediterranean villages, "there is less focus on 'being a good man' than on 'being *good at* being a man'—a stance that stresses *performative excellence* . . . ."[48] Herzfeld argues that men are evaluated not simply in terms of "*what* men do" but also "*how* the act is performed." "Performative excellence" for Herzfeld involves an ability to act in a manner that exceeds the performances of other men. By acting in exceptional ways and performing manhood with what Herzfeld calls "flair," men establish and distinguish themselves as men. Similarly, David Gilmore argues that "true manhood is a precious and elusive status beyond mere maleness, a hortatory image that men and boys aspire to . . . ." It "needs dramatic proof," and "there are always men who fail the test. These are the negative examples, . . . the men-who-are-no-men, held up scornfully to inspire conformity to the glorious ideal."[49] According to Gilmore, the successful man "acts on center stage."[50]

Gilmore's reference to "men-who-are-no-men" indicates that the successful performance of masculinity, the successful demonstration that one is, in Herzfeld's phrase, "good at being a man," often involves comparisons with other men who have not performed as well. These less successful performances are important for queer criticism, which is not content to sketch the cultural assumptions about gender that are presupposed by the text. Rather, starting from the cases of less successful gender performances, queer criticism emphasizes the instability of gender dynamics in the text. Characters do not straightforwardly embody male and female behavior, but are more or less successful at embodying norms that are, themselves, constantly in flux.

In Genesis 18 and 19, these unstable norms shape an implicit comparison between Abraham's more successful performance of manhood in Genesis 18 and Lot's less successful performance in Genesis 19. This comparison is made in several ways.

First, in comparison with Lot, Abraham is characterized more positively as a man who excels in hospitality. When Abraham sees travelers near his tent at the beginning of Genesis 18, he persuades them to stay with him by offering water to drink, the washing of feet, rest under a tree, and food to eat. He secures the assistance of both Sarah and a servant in the preparation of food for his guests, providing cakes, veal, curds, and milk. The description of Abraham's hospitality is surprisingly detailed, given the relatively spare use of descriptive detail found in most biblical narrative. The extent of the detail may signal the importance, for the story, of the matter being described. As Westermann notes, "The introduction is so detailed and carries such weight in itself as to be determinative of the narrative . . . ."[51] Abraham is here characterized as embodying in an exceptional way what Victor Matthews calls a "protocol of hospitality."[52]

Lot also greets two of Abraham's visitors in Genesis 19 when they arrive in Sodom. Because Lot offers food and lodging to these travelers while the other men of Sodom threaten to rape them, readers are understandably inclined to speak about Lot's hospitality as well and to compare his actions favorably to the inhospitality of the Sodomites.[53] Indeed, the story is surely constructed in such a way as to cast the men of Sodom in a more negative light than Lot.

However, if Lot's actions as host are compared with those of his uncle in the previous chapter, and not simply against the men of Sodom, his characterization as a man of hospitality seems diminished. Lot does offer food and a chance to wash feet; and he prepares a *mishteh*, which certainly implies the provision of drink and can be understood as a feast. However, the only food that is referred to explicitly in the description of Lot's hospitality is unleavened bread. This seems a rather meager meal in comparison with the food provided by Abraham. Perhaps more importantly, one of the items that is specifically described as being prepared, offered, and eaten in Genesis 18, which is missing in Genesis 19, is meat. Although it may be tempting to see this absence of meat in Genesis 19 simply as an accident of description, we should remember that, cross-culturally, meat often has specifically masculine connotations. Herzfeld, for example, notes that among his informants, "the consumption of meat [is] an essential component of male self-definition."[54] Discussing the competitive nature of serving food to guests, he observes that "[a] host who serves only a small amount of meat feels embarrassed since a meal without meat is not considered a meal at all."[55] Other anthropologists note that an association between masculinity and meat is derived from the traditional provisioning roles of men manifest in such gender-coded activities as hunting, fishing, and herding.[56] In the light of such associations, we may suspect that the absence of meat from Lot's table functions to diminish his manly hospitality, while simultaneously boosting by way of contrast the "performative excellence" of Abraham, who explicitly has meat prepared for his guests. The point here is not that Abraham is hospitable while Lot is inhospitable, but rather that Abraham's hospitality exceeds that of Lot, and is practiced with greater, and more masculine, "flair."

If the initial comparison between Abraham's hospitality and Lot's suggests that Abraham is "better at being a man" than Lot, the diminution of Lot's manhood that follows grows worse. The men of Sodom demand access to Lot's guests in order to rape them. Although this demand contributes to the negative characterization of the city of Sodom as an evil place, any application of this characterization to contemporary forms of homosexuality ignores the connotations of same-sex sexual violence in the ancient world. Within that context, sexual penetration is understood not in terms of sexual orientation but rather in terms of social submission, coded in gender terms.[57] The demand of the men of Sodom to "know" Lot's guests sexually would thus have had the effect of unmanning those guests. To the extent that hospitality and masculinity are intertwined, however, Lot's own manhood is threatened as well by the attack on his guests.

Thus Lot attempts to bargain with the men of Sodom, making the notorious offer of his own daughters as substitute objects of rape. Lot's offer is often, and rightly, criticized as a symptom of the patriarchal society that gave us the text, for it assumes that the rape of daughters might be preferable to the rape of male guests. By offering his daughters, Lot is no doubt trying to fulfill the male imperative in honor-intensive cultures to "protect his guest or the honour of his guest."[58] Yet even if we conclude that an ancient male audience would have shared this goal, we have little reason to believe that the offer of daughters would have been viewed positively in itself, or considered a credit to Lot. We know from other biblical texts, particularly Deuteronomy 22, that the sexual purity of a daughter was of great concern to fathers in the biblical world. And although fathers had significant authority to give their daughters to other men, Lot's actions obviously fall short of desired scenarios for such a giving of daughters. The anthropologist Nancy Lindisfarne, writing on the dynamics of honor and shame, notes that "a man may be labeled as 'dishonourable', or feminized as 'soft' or 'weak', when . . . he is forced to arrange a marriage for his daughter against his wishes."[59] Herzfeld, too, observes that a man who is "good at being a man . . . must protect his family from sexual and verbal threats . . . ."[60] Lot, by contrast, actually makes his daughters vulnerable to such threats when he is compelled to offer them, not as objects of marriage, but rather as objects of rape.

Lot's actions look even more questionable when his attempt to bargain with the men of Sodom in Genesis 19 is evaluated against Abraham's bargaining power in Genesis 18. Abraham, after all, spends a considerable amount of time persuading God to lower the number of righteous people who will have to be found in the city in order for God to spare it. As in the description of Abraham's hospitality, so also in the description of Abraham's bargaining, the text contains an unusual level of detail as Abraham works through the negotiation, with much deference but also determination. Ultimately, Abraham is successful: God agrees to spare the city if only ten righteous people are found in it. Lot, on the other hand, makes an attempt in a single verse to use his own daughters to bargain with the men of Sodom; and even this "desperate offer,"[61] to borrow Westermann's phrase, is rejected. The contrast between Abraham's negotiation and Lot's negotiation again functions to raise doubts about Lot's manhood, while underscoring Abraham's performative excellence.

Of course, Lot's manhood is challenged in a more serious way in the conclusion to Genesis 19, where Lot's daughters make their father drink wine and have sexual intercourse with him. Although scholars evaluate this scene in remarkably contradictory ways, Susanne Scholz notes that Lot here "is an unambiguous rape victim." Scholz is cautious about assuming a negative posture toward Lot's daughters, noting suggestions made by other feminist readers that the story of Lot and his daughters is a kind of male incest fantasy. Ultimately, however, Scholz does interpret the story as a rape scene, and possibly one that has connotations of, in her words, "homosexual rape."[62]

That last characterization interests me here, for it points toward a crucial component of the symbolic dynamics of manhood and sex in this scene. Lot's daughters assume the role of active sexual subject and make of their father a passive sexual object. Indeed, Lot's passivity is stressed in the text by the improbable representation of an unconscious man twice having sexual relations that result in conception. As mentioned above, sexual intercourse was widely understood in the ancient world as the penetration of a passive social subordinate by an active, social superior, normally male. Thus the passive position in male-male intercourse was considered shameful because it placed a man in the subordinate object position associated with women and, in some ancient societies, slaves and adolescents. If we read the assertive actions of Lot's daughters against this background, rather than that of incest fantasies, we recognize that here they adopt the more manly position. The two women are therefore masculinized. Indeed, they put their father in the position in which he had threatened to place them when he offered them to the men of Sodom. The effect of this gender reversal on Lot's manhood is similar to the effect that would be achieved if Lot were made the object of male rape: Lot is made a passive object. Thus a chapter that progressively emphasizes Lot's doubtful status as a man, at least in comparison with Abraham, climaxes, as it were, with the sexual symbolic emasculation of Lot. Although the incestuous nature of the union may increase the negative connotations, incest is probably secondary to the fact that Lot is unmanned, at least as far as the dynamics of gender are concerned. The effect on Lot's characterization is heightened by the fact that Lot is made a sexual object, not by other men (who usually adopt the active position in this sexual equation), but rather by women, who take on the subject position normally coded male.

If we want to think through the implications of this characterization within the context of ancient Israel, we have to note that the "punch line" of this story consists of the genealogical information at the end of chapter 19, which tells us that the sons born to Lot's gender-transgressive daughters were eponymous ancestors of the Moabites and Ammonites. Randall Bailey has argued that this story is one of several biblical stories that use depictions of negative sexual practice polemically to discredit members of other ethnic groups.[63] While Bailey focuses more on incest than Lot's symbolic unmanning, his argument underscores the importance of analyzing masculinities in such a way as to recognize the "co-constitutive" relationship of gender, ethnicity, and sexual practice.[64] Once the narrator states that these events served as the origin of Israel's traditional enemies, the Moabites and the Ammonites, it becomes possible to imagine that, as George Coats observes, Lot "[i]n his passivity, . . . represents an ethnological foil for the righteous Abraham."[65] Thus it is not only Abraham's manhood that is constructed through a contrast with the diminished manhood of Lot. So also the manhood of Israel, represented here by Abraham, is constructed through a contrast with the diminished manhood of Moab and Ammon. The Moabites and the Ammonites become, in Gilmore's terminology quoted earlier, "the men-who-are-no-men."

It is also important to note, however, that this negative effect on the reputation of the Moabites and Ammonites assumes both a negative judgment of Lot's passivity and a negative judgment of the sexual subjectivity of Lot's daughters. While such judgments make sense in the context of ancient Israel, a queer reading may want to pause before adopting them uncritically. With respect to Lot's passivity, for example, we may want to recall with Scholz those readings of Genesis 19 that find here a "fantasy" of incest. It is unlikely that most biblical scholars will be persuaded to read in terms of "fantasy;" and Scholz herself ultimately moves away from such a reading, as noted above. To the extent that one is willing to entertain a reading by way of fantasy, however, Scholz's invocation of "homosexual rape" may lead us to wonder whether a different kind of fantasy is at work here. Granted that the prospect of being emasculated was threatening to many of the Bible's ancient, and probably also modern, male readers, could we not entertain the possibility that a male fantasy of being unmanned by a woman underlies this text? Must we imagine that no male readers would have found Lot's passive position appealing? A queer reading will at least want to ask such questions.

Perhaps more significantly, to the extent that Lot's phallic daughters effect a gender reversal that unmans a patriarch, it is tempting to make them textual rallying points for a queer reading. These daughters might, for example, be seen as ancient examples of the "female masculinities" that Halberstam has argued need more attention. Although Halberstam recognizes that female masculinities have usually been seen negatively, she calls for an alternative queer approach that would not only analyze such masculinities but "affirm [female] masculinity despite the multiple sites in which that masculinity is challenged, denied, threatened, and violated."[66] Consistent with such an approach, a queer reading of Genesis might attempt to read against the grain by casting the adoption of the active, masculine role by Lot's daughters as a queer attempt to generate the Moabite and Ammonite nations. Such a reading would be in some ways consistent with certain feminist and historical-literary readings that already interpret Lot's daughters positively.[67]

But what about Abraham? Even if we grant that Genesis 18 and 19 construct Abraham's masculinity by emphasizing his "performative excellence" in comparison with Lot, we have to wonder how secure the manhood that results really is. Butler's work would encourage us to be attentive to the ways in which performances of gender appeal to norms while simultaneously failing to inhabit those norms completely. The slips and gaps that appear from performance to performance, or that open up between performance and ideal, are for Butler opportunities to call into question the inevitability and stability of hegemonic genders.

Thus we do well to recall one element of Genesis 18 that raises questions about Abraham's fatherly manhood. Although Sarah's famous laugh has attracted some attention from feminist scholars, I am interested here in the implications for manhood of the content of Sarah's remark, which follows her laugh (18:12). The text is clear about the fact that Sarah is too old to have children, and both the narrator and Sarah refer to Abraham's age as well. Sarah, however, also refers to pleasure, a pleasure that she apparently does not have and does not expect to have. While Abraham also laughs in 17:17, and refers to Sarah's age as well as his own, the reference to Sarah's pleasure is missing in Abraham's comment to himself in that chapter, as it is from the speech of God when God asks Abraham why Sarah has laughed in chapter 18. It is only Sarah who, in the words of Susan Haddox, "questions Abraham's potency and ability to give her sexual pleasure in his old age."[68] And this questioning has the effect of reducing Abraham's conformity with the ideals of manhood. Much like David in 1 Kings 1:1–4, who needs a woman in his bed to keep him warm but who no longer has sexual intercourse, Abraham has become impotent. He is too old to be "good at being a man" in that most "manly" of ways.

While Haddox connects what she calls Abraham's "mixed" manly features to a larger tendency in Genesis to prefer subordinate sons over hegemonic masculinities, my own inclination is to understand this complexity as an example of the inevitable instability of gender performance, which is emphasized by queer theory. Hegemonic masculinities, ancient and modern, attempt to establish themselves through comparisons between their own performative excellence and the feeble attempts at manhood by the "men-who-are-no-men." However, hegemonic performances always have points of vulnerability. If even Father Abraham struggles with an erectile dysfunction that can only be overcome with assistance from another male character (God), we have little reason to grant to Abraham's many sons, ancient or modern, a potency that never fails.

The point of a queer reading is not to choose among these possible interpretations, to say that "the text means *x* and not *y*," or to draw boundaries between proper and improper readings. Boundary troubling is, after all, constitutive of queer criticism. The point, rather, is to note the dynamics of gender and sexuality at work in both the text and its reception; and, instead of trying to control those dynamics, to let them loose through interpretation. For, ultimately, queer criticism insists that textual meaning is as complicated as sex and gender. The conclusions that we draw about the Bible are as varied as the identities, practices, and desires that we bring to it as gendered and sexual readers. Not only sex and gender, but also biblical meanings, have as much to do with our performance as they do with substantive facts.[69]

KEY TERMS

binary. A "binary" approach attempts to organize a field of meaning and practice in terms of two opposing, dualistic categories. Influential binary oppositions include those between male and female, heterosexuality and homosexuality, mind and body, reason and emotion, culture and nature, and human and animal. Like other forms of poststructuralist thought, queer theory tends to argue that binary oppositions are less absolute or stable than is often believed; but it focuses in particular on the instability of the oppositions between male and female and heterosexuality and homosexuality.

gender, gender construction. The term "gender" most often refers to cultural interpretations of sexed bodies, or to social roles and psychological experiences associated with sexed bodies. For example, even if bodies of the "same" biological sex are similar to one another (which is potentially a controversial claim), the understanding of what counts as "masculine" or "feminine" behavior or personality often differs radically from culture to culture or from one time period to another. The relationship between the body and its gendered behaviors is substantially shaped by social forces.

heteronormativity. "Heteronormativity" is the institutionalized preference for opposite-sex sexual relationships over same-sex sexual relationships. A number of other assumptions related to sex, gender, and kinship are also sometimes associated with heteronormativity. For example, heteronormativity may entail the beliefs that gender roles follow naturally from biological sex; that sexual desires follow naturally from gender roles; that an individual's sex, gender identity, sexual desires, or sexual practices are consistent over time; that kinship units ideally form around monogamous, opposite-sex couples; and that sexual activity most appropriately involves romantic love, marriage, and childbirth.

performative theory of gender. Although many people assume that stable genders result from biologically sexed bodies, a "performative" theory of gender argues that our impression of stable genders and coherently sexed bodies is actually an effect of the ongoing repetition of ritualized practices. As we attempt to conform our bodies, more or less adequately, to norms for gendered behavior, our belief that such norms are "natural" may increase. However, queer criticism pays close attention to the gaps and contradictions that inevitably emerge between stable norms for gender, on the one hand, and divergent performances of gender, on the other hand.

sex. The term "sex" most often refers either to biological distinctions between male and female bodies, or to various sexual activities (e.g., sexual intercourse) carried out by those bodies. However, some queer theorists question the extent to which "sex" is grounded in biology and argue that it is too simplistic to divide all humans into two "sexes."

NOTES

1. Lauren Berlant and Michael Warner, "What Does Queer Theory Teach Us about X?" *Publications of the Modern Language Association* 3 (May 1995): 344.
2. See, for further discussion, Ken Stone, "Queer Commentary and Biblical Interpretation: An Introduction," in Ken Stone, ed., *Queer Commentary and the Hebrew Bible* (Sheffield/Cleveland: Sheffield Academic Press/Pilgrim Press, 2001), 12–14. Cf. Stephen D. Moore, *God's Beauty Parlor: And Other Queer Spaces in and around the Bible* (Stanford: Stanford University Press, 2001), 12, 208n9.
3. See Annamarie Jagose, "Feminism's Queer Theory," *Feminism and Psychology* 19/2 (2009): 157–74, and sources cited there.
4. Gayle S. Rubin, "The Traffic in Women: Notes on the 'Political Economy' of Sex," in *Deviations: A Gayle Rubin Reader* (Durham and London: Duke University Press, 2011), 34.
5. Gayle S. Rubin, "Thinking Sex: Notes for a Radical Theory of the Politics of Sexuality," in *Deviations*, 179.
6. Cf. Gayle S. Rubin, "The Leather Menace: Comments on Politics and S/M," in *Deviations*, 109–36.
7. Judith Halberstam, *Female Masculinity* (Durham and London: Duke University Press, 1998).
8. For an influential example, see the early work of historian John D'Emilio, especially *Sexual Politics, Sexual Communities: The Making of a Homosexual Minority in the United States, 1940–1970* (Chicago: University of Chicago Press, 1983); and *Making Trouble: Essays on Gay History, Politics, and the University* (New York and London: Routledge, 1992).
9. See, e.g., Jeffrey Weeks, *Coming Out: Homosexual Politics in Britain from the Nineteenth Century to the Present* (London: Quartet, 1977); and *Sexuality and Its Discontents* (New York: Routledge and Kegan Paul, 1985).
10. See Gilbert Herdt, *The Sambia: Ritual, Sexuality, and Change in Papua New Guinea*, 2nd ed. (Belmont, CA: Wadsworth Publishing, 2005), which cites and discusses critically Herdt's earlier groundbreaking studies.
11. See, e.g., Roger Lancaster, "Subject Honor and Object Shame: The Construction of Male Homosexuality and Stigma in Nicaragua," *Ethnology* 27 (1988): 111–25.
12. See Kenneth Dover, *Greek Homosexuality*, 2nd ed. (Cambridge, MA: Harvard University Press, 1989); Eva Keuls, *The Reign of the Phallus: Sexual Politics in Ancient Athens* (Berkeley: University of California Press, 1985), 274–99; David M. Halperin, *One Hundred Years of Homosexuality and Other Essays on Greek*

Love (New York: Routledge, 1990), 15–71; and John J. Winkler, *The Constraints of Desire: The Anthropology of Sex and Gender in Ancient Greece* (New York: Routledge, 1990), 45–70.
13. Michel Foucault, *The History of Sexuality*, vol. 1, *An Introduction*, trans. Robert Hurley (New York: Random House, 1978), 43.
14. David F. Greenberg, *The Construction of Homosexuality* (Chicago: University of Chicago Press, 1990); and Carole S. Vance, "Social Construction Theory and Sexuality," in Maurice Berger, Brian Wallis, and Simon Watson, eds., *Constructing Masculinity* (New York: Routledge, 1995).
15. See Henry Abelove, Michèle Aina Barale, and David M. Halperin, eds., *The Lesbian and Gay Studies Reader* (New York: Routledge, 1993).
16. Jonathan Ned Katz, *The Invention of Heterosexuality* (New York: Penguin Books, 1995). See also Diana Fuss, "Inside/Out," in Diana Fuss, ed., *Inside/Out: Lesbian Theories, Gay Theories* (New York: Routledge, 1991), 1–10; David M. Halperin, *Saint Foucault: Toward a Gay Hagiography* (Oxford and New York: Oxford University Press, 1995), 43–48; and Annamarie Jagose, *Queer Theory: An Introduction* (New York: New York University Press, 1996), 16–19.
17. See, for discussion, Teresa de Lauretis, "Queer Theory: Lesbian and Gay Sexualities: An Introduction," in *differences: A Journal of Feminist Cultural Studies* 3/2 (1991): iii–xviii; Berlant and Warner, "What Does Queer Theory Teach Us about X?" Halperin, *Saint Foucault*; idem, "The Normalization of Queer Theory," *Journal of Homosexuality* 45/2–4 (2003): 339–43; Jagose, *Queer Theory*; and Nikki Sullivan, *A Critical Introduction to Queer Theory* (New York: New York University Press, 2003).
18. Halperin, *Saint Foucault*, 62.
19. Ibid., 63, emphasis his.
20. Eve Kosofsky Sedgwick, *Tendencies* (Durham and London: Duke University Press, 1993), xii.
21. Ibid., 8.
22. Eve Kosofsky Sedgwick, *Epistemology of the Closet* (Berkeley: University of California Press, 1990), 48.
23. Judith Butler, *Gender Trouble: Feminism and the Subversion of Identity* (New York: Routledge, 1990), 7.
24. Ibid., 17.
25. Ibid., 24–25.
26. Judith Butler, *Undoing Gender* (New York: Routledge, 2004), 1.
27. Judith Butler, *Bodies That Matter: On the Discursive Limits of "Sex"* (New York: Routledge, 1993), 231.
28. De Lauretis, "Queer Theory," viii.
29. See, e.g., Sullivan, *A Critical Introduction to Queer Theory*, 57–80; Siobhan B. Somerville, *Queering the Color Line: Race and the Invention of Homosexuality in American Culture* (Durham and London: Duke University Press, 2000); and Jasbir Puar, *Terrorist Assemblages: Homonationalism in Queer Times* (Durham and London: Duke University Press, 2007).
30. Stone, "Queer Commentary," 11–34.
31. Mona West, "Reading the Bible as Queer Americans: Social Location and the Hebrew Scriptures," *Theology and Sexuality* 10 (1999): 30.
32. Ibid., 36.
33. See, e.g., Robert Goss and Mona West, eds., *Take Back the Word: A Queer Reading of the Bible* (Cleveland: Pilgrim Press, 2000).
34. Cf. Bernadette Brooten, *Love between Women: Early Christian Perspectives on Female Homoeroticism* (Chicago: University of Chicago Press, 1996); Ken Stone,

Sex, Honor and Power in the Deuteronomistic History (Sheffield: Sheffield Academic Press, 1996); Athalya Brenner, *The Intercourse of Knowledge: On Gendering Desire and Sexuality in the Hebrew Bible* (Leiden: Brill, 1997); Martti Nissinen, *Homoeroticism in the Biblical World: A Historical Perspective*, trans. Kirsi Sterjna (Minneapolis: Fortress, 1998); Jon L. Berquist, *Controlling Corporality: The Body and the Household in Ancient Israel* (New Brunswick, NJ: Rutgers University Press, 2002); Susan Ackerman, *When Heroes Love: The Ambiguity of Eros in the Stories of Gilgamesh and David* (New York: Columbia University Press, 2005); Hilary Lipka, *Sexual Transgression in the Hebrew Bible* (Sheffield: Sheffield Phoenix Press, 2006); and Jennifer Wright Knust, *Unprotected Texts: The Bible's Surprising Contradictions about Sex and Desire* (New York: HarperCollins, 2011).

35. Cf. Teresa J. Hornsby and Ken Stone, eds., *Bible Trouble: Queer Reading at the Boundaries of Biblical Scholarship* (Atlanta: Society of Biblical Literature, 2011).
36. Stuart Macwilliam, *Queer Theory and the Prophetic Marriage Metaphor in the Hebrew Bible* (Sheffield: Equinox, 2011), 1.
37. See, e.g., Ken Stone, "The Garden of Eden and the Heterosexual Project," in Ellen T. Armour and Susan M. St. Ville, eds., *Bodily Citations: Religion and Judith Butler* (New York: Columbia University Press, 2006), 48–70; Ken Stone, *Practicing Safer Texts: Food, Sex and Bible in Queer Perspective* (London: T. & T. Clark, 2005), 111–28; Dale B. Martin, *Sex and the Single Savior: Gender and Sexuality in Biblical Interpretation* (Louisville, KY: Westminster John Knox, 2006), esp. 77–90; Moore, *God's Beauty Parlor*, 133–72; Deryn Guest, "From Gender Reversal to Genderfuck: Reading Jael through a Lesbian Lens," in Hornsby and Stone, eds., *Bible Trouble*, 9–43; and Deryn Guest, et al., eds., *The Queer Bible Commentary* (London: SCM, 2006).
38. See, e.g., Theodore W. Jennings Jr., *The Man Jesus Loved: Homoerotic Narratives from the New Testament* (Cleveland: Pilgrim Press, 2003); and idem, *Jacob's Wound: Homoerotic Narrative in the Literature of Ancient Israel* (New York and London: T. & T. Clark, 2005).
39. See, e.g., Virginia Burrus and Stephen D. Moore, "Unsafe Sex: Feminism, Pornography and the Song of Songs," *Biblical Interpretation* 11/1 (2003): 24–52; Ken Stone, "'You Seduced Me, You Overpowered Me, and You Prevailed': Religious Experience and Homoerotic Sadomasochism in Jeremiah," in Lisa Isherwood, ed., *Patriarchs, Prophets, and Other Villains* (London: Equinox, 2006); Stone, *Practicing Safer Texts*, 68–110; Lori Rowlett, "Violent Femmes and S/M: Queering Samson and Delilah," in Ken Stone, ed., *Queer Commentary and the Hebrew Bible*, 106–15; and Roland Boer, "Yahweh as Top: A Lost Targum," in Ken Stone, ed., *Queer Commentary and the Hebrew Bible*, 75–105.
40. See, e.g., Erin Runions, "From Disgust to Humor: Rahab's Queer Affect," in Hornsby and Stone, eds., *Bible Trouble*, 45–74; Manuel Villalobos, "Bodies Del Otro Lado Finding Life and Hope in the Borderland: Gloria Anzaldúa, the Ethiopian Eunuch of Acts 8:26–40, *y Yo*," in Hornsby and Stone, eds., *Bible Trouble*, 191–21; Ken Stone, "Queering the Canaanite," in Marcella Althaus-Reid and Lisa Isherwood, eds., *The Sexual Theologian: Essays on Sex, God, and Politics* (London: T. & T. Clark, 2004), 110–34; and Stone, *Practicing Safer Texts*, 46–67.
41. See, for example, Moore, *God's Beauty Parlor*, 21–89; Michael Carden, "Remembering Pelotit: A Queer Midrash on Calling Down Fire," in Stone, ed., *Queer Commentary and the Hebrew Bible*, 152–68; and Michael Carden, *Sodomy: A History of a Christian Biblical Myth* (London: Equinox, 2004).

42. See, e.g., Ovidiu Creanga, ed., *Men and Masculinity in the Hebrew Bible and Beyond* (Sheffield: Sheffield Phoenix Press, 2010), and sources cited by the authors. For an early attempt to take questions about manhood and masculinity seriously, see Harry A. Hoffner Jr., "Symbols for Masculinity and Femininity: Their Use in Ancient Near Eastern Sympathetic Magic Rituals," *Journal of Biblical Literature* 85 (1966): 329–32.
43. Cf. Ken Stone, "Gender Criticism: The Un-Manning of Abimelech," in Gale Yee, ed., *Judges and Method: New Approaches in Biblical Studies*, 2nd edition (Minneapolis: Fortress, 2007), 183–201.
44. Cf. Carol Delaney, *The Seed and the Soil: Gender and Cosmology in Turkish Village Society* (Berkeley: University of California Press, 1991); and idem, *Abraham on Trial: The Social Legacy of Biblical Myth* (Princeton, NJ: Princeton University Press, 1998).
45. Cynthia Chapman, *The Gendered Language of Warfare in the Israelite-Assyrian Encounter* (Winona Lake, IN: Eisenbrauns, 2004), 7. Chapman is explicitly indebted to Butler's work.
46. Esther Newton, *Mother Camp: Female Impersonators in America* (Chicago: University of Chicago Press, 1979).
47. See for discussion Stone, *Sex, Honor and Power in the Deuteronomistic History*, esp. 27–49.
48. Michael Herzfeld, *The Poetics of Manhood: Contest and Identity in a Cretan Mountain Village* (Princeton, NJ: Princeton University Press, 1985), 16, emphasis in original.
49. David D. Gilmore, *Manhood in the Making: Cultural Concepts of Masculinity* (New Haven, CT: Yale University Press, 1990), 17.
50. Ibid., 103.
51. Claus Westermann, *Genesis 12–36: A Commentary*, trans. John J. Scullion (Minneapolis: Augsburg, 1985), 274.
52. Victor Matthews, "Hospitality and Hostility in Genesis 19 and Judges 19," *Biblical Theology Bulletin* 22/1 (1992): 3–11. Cf. Victor Matthews and Don Benjamin, *Social World of Ancient Israel 1250–587 BCE* (Peabody: Hendrickson, 1993), 82–95.
53. Among many other examples, see Frank Anthony Spina, "Lot," in *Anchor Bible Dictionary*, vol. 4, ed. David Noel Freedman, et al. (Garden City, NY: Doubleday, 1992), 374; and Stuart Lasine, "Guest and Host in Judges 19: Lot's Hospitality in an Inverted World," *Journal for the Study of the Old Testament* 29 (1984): 37–59.
54. Herzfeld, *Poetics of Manhood*, 53.
55. Ibid., 130.
56. See Nick Fiddes, *Meat: A Natural Symbol* (New York: Routledge, 1991), 144–62.
57. See, for further discussion, Ken Stone, "Gender and Homosexuality in Judges 19: Subject-Honor, Object-Shame?" *Journal for the Study of the Old Testament* 67 (1995): 87–107; idem, *Sex, Honor and Power in the Deuteronomistic History*, 74–84; Nissinen, *Homoeroticism in the Biblical World*; and Ackerman, *When Heroes Love*.
58. Julian Pitt-Rivers, *The Fate of Shechem, or the Politics of Sex: Essays in the Anthropology of the Mediterranean* (Cambridge, MA: Cambridge University Press, 1977), 110.
59. Nancy Lindisfarne, "Variant Masculinities, Variant Virginities: Rethinking 'Honour and Shame,'" in Andrea Cornwall and Nancy Lindisfarne, eds., *Dislocating Masculinity: Comparative Ethnographies* (New York: Routledge, 1994), 85.

60. Herzfeld, *Poetics of Manhood*, 124.
61. Claus Westermann, *Genesis 12–36: A Commentary*, trans. John Scullion (Minneaplois: Augsburg, 1985), 302.
62. Susanne Scholz, *Sacred Witness: Rape in the Hebrew Bible* (Minneapolis: Fortress, 2010), 169, 173.
63. Randall Bailey, "They're Nothing but Incestuous Bastards: The Polemical Use of Sex and Sexuality in Hebrew Canon Narratives," in Fernando Segovia and Mary Ann Tolbert, eds., *Reading from This Place*, vol. 1, *Social Location and Biblical Interpretation in the United States* (Minneapolis: Fortress, 1995), 121–38.
64. On the "co-constitutive" nature of race and gender, see among others Laurel C. Schneider, "What Race Is Your Sex?" in Jennifer Harvey, Karin A. Case, and Robin Hawley Gorsline, eds., *Disrupting White Supremacy from Within* (Cleveland: Pilgrim, 2004), 142–64; and see the sources cited in note 29, above.
65. George Coats, *Genesis: With an Introduction to Narrative Literature* (Grand Rapids: Eerdmans, 1983), 147.
66. Halberstam, *Female Masculinity*, 19.
67. See, e.g., Tikva Frymer-Kensky, *Reading the Women of the Bible* (New York: Schocken Books, 2002), 257–63, 282; and Mark G. Brett, *Genesis: Procreation and the Politics of Identity* (New York: Routledge, 2000), 68–69.
68. Susan E. Haddox, "Favoured Sons and Subordinate Masculinities," in Ovidiu Creanga, ed., *Men and Masculinity in the Hebrew Bible and Beyond*, 7.
69. See for more discussion of this point Martin, *Sex and the Single Savior*; and Ken Stone, "Bibles That Matter: Biblical Theology and Queer Performativity," *Biblical Theology Bulletin* 38 (2008): 14–25.

FOR FURTHER READING

Butler, Judith. *The Judith Butler Reader*. Edited by Sara Salih. Oxford: Blackwell, 2004.
Guest, Deryn, et al., eds. *The Queer Bible Commentary*. London: SCM Press, 2006.
Hornsby, Teresa, and Ken Stone, eds. *Bible Trouble: Queer Reading at the Boundaries of Biblical Scholarship*. Atlanta: Scholars Press, 2011.
Jagose, Annamarie. *Queer Theory: An Introduction*. New York: New York University Press, 1996.
Macwilliam, Stuart. *Queer Theory and the Prophetic Marriage Metaphor in the Hebrew Bible*. Sheffield: Equinox, 2011.
Martin, Dale B. *Sex and the Single Savior: Gender and Sexuality in Biblical Interpretation*. Louisville, KY: Westminster John Knox Press, 2006.
Moore, Stephen D. *God's Beauty Parlor: And Other Queer Spaces in and around the Bible*. Stanford: Stanford University Press, 2001.
Stone, Ken. "Bibles That Matter: Biblical Theology and Queer Performativity." *Biblical Theology Bulletin* 38 (2008): 14–25.
———. "The Garden of Eden and the Heterosexual Project." In *Bodily Citations: Religion and Judith Butler,* edited by Ellen T. Armour and Susan M. St. Ville, 48–70. New York: Columbia University Press, 2006.
———. *Practicing Safer Texts: Food, Sex and Bible in Queer Perspective*. London and New York: T. & T. Clark, 2005.
———, ed. *Queer Commentary and the Hebrew Bible*. Sheffield/Cleveland: Sheffield Academic Press/Pilgrim Press, 2001.
Sullivan, Nikki. *A Critical Introduction to Queer Theory*. New York: New York University Press, 2003.

Index

Abelove, H., 173n15
Ackerman, S., 174n34, 175n57
active imagination, 144, 146, 150–51
Adam, A. K. M., 135, 135n11
Aichele, G., 95n17, 96, 134n2
Allaby, M., 43, 56
Althaus-Reid, M., 174n40
Althusser, L., 75n14
Ambrose, 36n9
anthropocentrism, 48–49
archaeology of knowledge, 3, 16
archetype, 141, 143, 144, 145, 151
Arjomand, S. A., 36n11
Armour, E. T., 174n37, 176
Ashcroft, B., 114n1
Augustine, 138
Avalos, H., 37

Baden, J. S., 36nn7–8; 37n18
Bailey, R., 169, 176n62
Barale, M. A., 173n15

Barthes, R., 81
Beal, T., 17nn3, 5; 18nn9, 15, 18, 19; 19, 19nn20, 27, 29; 20
Bechtel, L., 152n12
behavioral psychology, 139, 151
Bekkenkamp, J., 19n20
Benjamin, D., 175n52
Berger, A. A., 87, 92, 95nn40–41; 96n51
Berger, M., 173n14
Berlant, L., 155–56, 172n1, 173n17
Berquist, J. L., 174n34
Berry, R. J., 57
Berry, T., 42, 43–44, 56
Bhabha, H. K., 100, 102–3, 105, 115nn7, 12
Bielo, J. S., 6–7, 18nn10–11; 19
binary oppositions, 84, 93, 100, 103, 114, 119, 156, 171
Birch, C., 46, 56
Blessing, K., 153

Boer, R., 174n39
Bonnell, V. E., 17n2, 20
Bourchard, D. F., 17n6
Bourquin, Y., 125, 134n4, 135
Boyarin, D., 60, 64, 75nn11, 19; 76
Brenner, A., 36n12, 93, 95n17, 96nn56–57; 174n34
Brett, M. G., 176n66
Briggs, A. 77, 94n1
Brooten, B., 174n34
Brummett, B., 80, 95nn21–24; 96
Bufford, R. K., 153
Burke, P., 17n3, 20
Burrus, V., 174n39
Bussie, J., 76n24
Butler, J., 161–62, 165, 170, 173nn23–27; 174n37, 175n45, 176

Callan, T., 143, 152n9
Callaway, M. C., 81, 95n27
Caputo, J. D., 131, 135n13
Carden, M., 174n41
Carroll, R. P., 153
Carter, W., 116nn31, 35–36
Case, K. A., 176n63
Chandler, D., 96nn58–60, 62
Chapman, C., 165, 175n45
Chrisman, L., 114n1
Coats, G., 169, 176n64
cognitive psychology, 145, 151
Cohen-Eliya, M., 84, 95n36
Collins, J. J., 135
colonialism, 114
communication codes, 93–94
Conradie, E., 39, 42, 56
conscious, 142–43, 145, 149, 151
Copier, L., 92, 96n55
Cornwall, A., 175n59
Crawford, M., 91
Creanga, O., 175n42, 176n67
Culbertson, P., 92, 94n15, 96, 96nn54–55
cultural history, 1–4, 16
   of Bible, 3–6
   of Bible in practice, 6–14
culture, 16, 62

Daly, P. M., 95n39
Dault, D., 18n14, 20
Deal, W. E., 17nn3, 5; 18n9, 20
deconstruction, 121–22, 133
Delaney, C., 175n44

Deleuze, G., 120, 123
Delitzsch, F. J., 138, 152n1
D'Emilio, J., 172n8
depth psychology, 139, 145, 151
de Lauretis, T., 160, 162, 173nn17, 28
Derrida, J., 118, 121–23, 133, 135n11, 136
Descartes, 45
developmental psychology, 147–49, 151
différance, 121, 133
disability, 22, 32, 35
   in the ancient Near East, 26–28, 32
   cultural model of, 23, 25, 28, 31, 33, 35
   medical model of, 22, 24, 35
   social model of, 22, 24–25, 35
discourse/discursive practice, 3, 16, 61, 74
Donaldson, L., 111–12, 116nn43–44
Dorman, J., 37
Douglas, M., 2
Dover, K., 172n12
Drewermann, E., 140, 152n6
Dube, M., 111, 116nn40–42
Dunderberg, I., 115n3

Eagleton, T., 75n14
Earth Bible principles, 46
Earth Bible Team, 42, 45–47, 56
Eaton, H., 45, 56
ecojustice, 42, 55
ecojustice principles, 46–47
Edinger, E. F., 153
Edwards, D., 44, 56
Eley, G., 17n2
Ellens, J. H., 152n12, 153
Elliot, N., 116n31
Evans-Pritchard, E., 2
Everding, H. E., 144, 152n10

Fadness, G., 19n23
Fajardo-Acosta, F., 98
Fanon, F., 99–100, 103, 115n14
feminism, 44–45, 51, 62, 146, 158
Fewell, D. N., 7, 18n16
Fiddes, N., 175n56
Fineman, J., 60, 75n9
Fiorenza, E. S., 45, 58
Fletcher, M. S., 138, 152n2
Foucault, M., 2–4, 15–16, 17n6, 20, 61, 63, 75nn12–13; 132, 159–60, 173n13
Fox, M., 42, 56
Francis, L. J., 144, 152n10, 153
Freedman, D. N., 175n53

Fretheim, T., 52–53, 58
Freud, S., 120, 139, 144–45, 151–52
Frymer-Kensky, T., 176n66
Fuss, D., 173n16

Gadamer, H.-G., 5, 18n9
Gaiser, F., 57
Gallagher, C., 60, 75n10, 76
Gandhi, L., 115n1
Garber, M., 2, 17n1
Geertz, C., 2, 16, 19n30, 62, 74, 75n15
gender, 158, 161–62, 171
genetic fallacy, 118, 134
Gibson, M., 9, 18n19
Gilmore, D. D., 165, 169, 175n49
Gorsline, R. H., 176n63
Goss, R., 173n33
grand narrative, 118, 120, 134
Gray, P., 79, 96
gray texts, 55
Green, J., 135n10
Greenberg, D. F., 173n14
Greenblatt, S., 60, 74n4, 75nn5, 7
green texts, 55
Griffiths, G., 114n1
Guattari, P.-F., 120, 123
Guest, D., 174n37, 176
Gunn, D., 8, 18n16
Gwyther, A., 115n31

Habel, N. C., 40, 48, 55, 56n1, 57–58
Haddox, S. E., 170, 176n67
Halberstam, J., 158, 169, 172n7, 176n65
Hall, D., 42, 57,
Halperin, D. M., 143, 152n9, 160, 172n12, 173nn15–18
Hammer, Y., 84, 95n36
Hanson, K. C., 116n37
Hart, K., 135–36
Harvey, J., 176n63
Hearon, H., 75n20
Hens-Piazza, G., 74n1, 75nn18, 20; 76
Herdt, G., 172n10
Herzfeld, M., 165–67, 175nn48, 54; 176n60
Hess, M., 79, 94n15
heteronormativity, 156–57, 160, 171
Higgins, J., 17n4, 20
Hoffner, H. A., Jr., 175n42
Hornsby, T. J., 174nn35, 37, 40; 176
Horrell, D., 42, 56n1, 57–58

Horsley, R., 111, 115n31, 116n39
Hoskins, R. K., 11–14, 19nn20, 24–27
Howard-Brooks, W., 115n31
Hunt, C., 58
Hunt, L., 17n2, 20
hybridity, 103, 114

identification, 49–50, 53–54, 55
impairment, 22, 35
imperialism, 104–5, 111, 114
individuation, 143, 146, 151
intertextuality, 81, 84, 89, 91, 94
Iser, W., 115n26
Isherwood, L., 174nn39–40

Jagose, A., 172n3, 173nn16–17; 176
Jauss, H. R., 5, 17n8
Jennings, T. W., Jr., 174n38
Jobling, D., 135
Johnson, C. B., 153
Josephus, 134n6
Jung, C. G., 139, 143–46, 150–51, 152n4, 153
Juvenal, 116n38

Kamionkowski, T., 35n2
Kaplan, K. J., 153
Kaplan, S. L., 75n13
Katz, J. N., 173n16
Keesmat, S., 116n31
Kelly, C. G., 89, 92, 96nn44, 49–50
Kepnes, S., 75n11
Keuls, E., 172n12
Kille, D. A., 152n10, 153
Kim, W., 35
Kimball, C. A., 134n5
Knust, J. W., 174n34
Kooijman, J., 92
Kugel, J. L., 36n10
Kunkel, F., 153

Lacan, J., 120, 123
LaCapra, D., 75n13
Lai, B. L., 143, 152n9
Lancaster, R., 172n11
Lasine, S., 175n53
Lawes, R., 95n34
Lee, P.-L., 95n16
Lemish, D., 89, 91, 95n43, 96nn45, 47–48
Lemos, T. M., 36n6
Leslie, R., 140, 152n5

Lévi-Strauss, C., 119
Linafelt, T., 18n19
Lindisfarne, N., 167, 175n59
Lipka, H., 174n34
logocentrism, 121, 134
Lopez, D., 116n31
Lovelock, J., 42, 57
Luz, U., 18n9

Machery, P., 75n14
Macwilliam, S., 163, 174n36, 176
Magritte, R., 123–24, 127, 132
Malley, B., 18n12, 20
Mandolfo, C., 57
Marguerat, D., 125, 134n4, 135
Martin, D. B., 174n37, 176n68
masculinity, 164
Matthews, V., 166, 175n52
Mbembe, A., 103, 115n15
McCanles, M., 60, 74n3
McFague, S., 45, 57
McGann, D., 153
McIntosh, A. A., 76n23
McKay, H., 29–31, 36nn10, 12
McRuer, R., 37n15
McLuhan, M., 16, 19n31, 20
Meadowcroft, T., 42, 57
medium, 16–17
Melanchthon, M., 43, 57
Melanchthon, P., 138
Melcher, S., 37
Miller, D. L., 153
Milton, J., 86
Montrose, L., 60, 75nn8, 21
Moore, S. D., 76, 92, 95n28, 96n52, 108, 115n2, 116nn32, 43; 128, 135n8, 136, 172n2, 174nn37, 39, 41; 176
Morgan, R., 18n9
Moss, C. R., 36nn6, 8; 37
Mukerji, C., 78, 80, 94nn13–14, 95n20

Newheart, M. W., 153
Newton, E., 175n46
Niewert, D. A., 19nn21–22
Nissinen, M., 174n34, 175n57
Nutu, E., 136

Oakman, D., 116n37
O'Barr, W. M., 82, 95nn29–30
object relations theory, 145, 151
Olyan, S. M., 35n5, 37n16
optic, 97, 104–6, 108, 113, 114

Os, B. van, 153

Pardes, I., 51, 57
Parker, H., 78, 94nn8–12
Parmenter, D. M., 7, 18n13, 20
Pasolini, P. P., 9
Patterson, L., 60, 75n6
performance theory of gender, 161–62, 165, 171–72
personality, 143, 146, 151
Philo, 134n6
Pippin, T., 135
Pirson, R., 30–31, 37nn13–14
Pitt-Rivers, J., 175n58
Plumwood, V., 45, 58
Ponting, C., 45, 58
popular culture
    and feminist analysis, 80–81
    and rhetorical criticism, 80, 87
Poster, M., 75n13
Powell, M. A., 60, 74, 115nn25, 27
Prior, M., 79, 134nn3, 6; 135n12
$psych\bar{e}$, 138, 151
psychoanalysis, 140–41, 143, 151
psychodynamics, 142, 143, 145, 151
psychologizing, 149–50, 151–52
Puar, J., 173n29
Pyper, H. S., 134n2

Rakow, L., 80, 95n25
Randazzo, S., 82, 95n30
Raphael, R., 27, 35n3, 37n17
Rashkow, I. N., 153
reception history, 5, 17, 81, 85–87, 94
representation, 74
retrieval, 46, 50–51, 54, 55–56
Ricoeur, P., 152n7
Rollins, W. G., 139, 141, 152nn4, 8, 12; 153
Roncace, M., 79, 96
Rosenberg, B., 75n17
Rowland, C., 18n9
Rowlett, L., 174n39
Rubin, G. S., 158, 163, 172nn4–6
Runions, E., 174n40
Ryle, G., 74

Said, E., 36n11, 99–100, 102–3, 105, 115n19
Sandoval, T., 57
Sanford, J. A., 153
Sarna, N., 53, 58
Saussure, F. de, 81, 94, 119–20

Sawyer, J. F. A., 17n7, 96n60
Schipper, J., 35nn1–2, 36nn6, 8; 37, 76
Schleiermacher, F., 121
Schleifer, R., 135
Schneider, L. C., 176n63
Schneiders, S., 152n7
Scholz, S., 168–69, 176n61
Schudson, M. 78, 80, 94nn13–14; 95n20
Schwartz, M. B., 153
Scroggs, R., 153
Sedgwick, E. K., 160–61, 173nn20–22
Segovia, F., 104–8, 112–13, 115nn2, 16–18, 20–24, 27–29; 116nn32–33, 35, 43; 176n62
semiology, 81, 82–85, 94
Sewell, W. H., 17n2
sex, 158, 161–62, 172
Sheridan, A., 75n12
Sherwood, Y., 19n20, 76, 136
Shifman, L., 89, 91, 95n43, 96nn45, 47–48
Smith, W. C., 19n29
Somerville, S. B., 173n29
Southgate, C., 56–58
Speiser, E. A., 75n22
Spina, F. A., 175n53
Spivak, G. C., 101–3, 111–12, 115n8
Stavrakopoulou, F., 56–58
Stone, K., 172n2, 173n30, 174nn34–35, 37, 39–41; 175n43, 47, 57, 176n68
Storey, J., 78, 94nn2–7; 95nn25–26; 96
structure of feeling, 2, 4, 17
St. Ville, S. M., 174n37, 176
subaltern, 99, 101, 104, 114
Sugirtharajah, R. S., 107–8, 112–13, 115nn3–4, 28, 30; 116nn34–35, 45–50
Sullivan, N., 173nn17, 29; 176
suspicion, 45, 48–49, 52, 56
Syreeni, K., 115n3
Szönyi, G. E., 95n39

Tabari, al-, 36n11
Tertullian, 138

textuality, 74
Theissen, G., 140, 152nn6, 9; 153
thick description, 61–62, 74
Throntveit, M., 57
Tiffin, H., 114n1
Tolbert, M. A., 176n62
transference, 144–45, 152
Trudinger, P. L., 57–58
Tuckett, C. M., 18n9, 115n3

unconscious, 142–45, 147, 152
undecidability, 118, 124, 127, 131, 134

Vance, C. S., 173n14
Vander Stichle, C., 92, 96n55
Veeser, H. A., 75nn9–10
Village, A., 144, 152n10
Villalobos, M., 174n40
von Rad, G., 75n22

Wainwright, E. M., 80, 94n15, 95nn18–19; 96
Wallis, B., 173n14
Walsh, B., 116n31
Walsh, R., 134n1
Warner, M., 155–56, 172n1, 173n17
Watson, S., 173n14
Weber, M., 16, 78
Weeks, J., 172n9
West, M., 163, 173nn31–33
Westermann, C., 75n22, 166, 168, 175n51
White, L., 42, 58
Williams, P., 114n1
Williams, R., 2–4, 16, 17n4, 20
Wink, W., 139, 152n3
Winkler, J. J., 173n12
Wuellner, W., 140, 152n5
Wundt, W., 138
Wurst, S., 57

Young, R., 115n1, 116

Zeligs, D., 153

www.ingramcontent.com/pod-product-compliance
Lightning Source LLC
Chambersburg PA
CBHW032037290426
44110CB00012B/848